SCHOOL DESEGREGATION
IN THE CAROLINAS

SCHOOL DESEGREGATION IN THE CAROLINAS
Two Case Studies

William Bagwell

UNIVERSITY OF SOUTH CAROLINA PRESS
Columbia, S. C.

Dedicated to those brave students, parents, and school leaders whose valiant efforts as "pioneers" in the early years of school desegregation did much to prepare the way for better educations and better lives for untold thousands who have followed them.

CONTENTS

TABLES

ACKNOWLEDGMENTS

I am indebted to many persons and organizations for encouragement and support in carrying out this study. Special credit must be given to several sources of financial and related support, including the Quaker Leadership Grants Program of the Friends World Committee, the Mary E. Campbell Memorial Fund, the National Conference of Christians and Jews, and the American Friends Service Committee.

Dan W. Dodson, H. Harry Giles, and William Van Til, my special advisors at New York University, were most helpful through their wise counsel and guidance in planning, developing, and completing this study.

Without the skill, patience, co-operation, and encouragement of Mildred J. Hardy, Anya Lincoln, Susan Mountz, and Emma Head, who typed, provided editorial assistance, or otherwise aided in the preparation of this manuscript in its various drafts, this work might never have been completed.

I am indebted to numerous friends and associates, especially Gil Roland, Jean Fairfax, Tartt Bell, Charles Davis, Miriam W. Fountain, and the late Catherine Evans, for their moral support and encouragement.

Above all, I must express my gratitude to my wife, Maude, and the other members of our family. Their patience and consideration were invaluable to me during the several years that this study overshadowed and often displaced most aspects of a "normal" family life.

Cheyney, Pennsylvania
April, 1971

WILLIAM BAGWELL

xv

SCHOOL DESEGREGATION
IN THE CAROLINAS

INTRODUCTION

THE PROBLEM

With public education becoming a major sector of the nation's life and economy, and with racial segregation continuing to loom as one of education's biggest problems, it is needless to add that all possible aid from social science and other realms of knowledge is urgently needed.

The chief purpose of this study is to provide some assistance in understanding and perhaps in coping with this problem. The study was designed to be an exploratory one directed toward discovering and evaluating in the community setting the intergroup relations principles or factors involved in the social change connected with school desegregation.

Specifically, an effort has been made to validate in the actual ongoing process of school desegregation a number of selected theoretical or academic principles or factors which social scientists have claimed to be relevant to this social change. To do this, case studies were made of the overall school desegregation situation in two southern communities to determine whether the specific principles or factors existed, how important each was, and what their relationships were to each other and to the overall pattern of community interaction over school desegregation.

In pointing up the significance of the desegregation problem, Arnold Toynbee has suggested that when the history of the twentieth century is written the most important aspect of

1

that work will be the conflict between the white and colored races of mankind and how, or whether, this conflict is resolved. It will take precedence over even the East-West ideological conflicts, as important as they may be.[1]

Certainly the problem of racial conflict is a world-wide one. It occupies an increasing amount of time and effort in government circles, from the United Nations to the local city council; it is major news in the press; it invades and influences many aspects of society in almost every part of the world.

This problem as relating to the United States, was put into perspective several years ago by John Popham of the *New York Times*.[2] He called it a "social revolution with profound implications for domestic accord and world leadership." He described the problem as involving the "dramatic, legal and social adjustments facing the South as a result of the Supreme Court decision that public school racial segregation laws are unconstitutional." He added, however, that "the tensions that have arisen in the region underscore the fact that the problem has national dimensions" and concluded that "the problem must be resolved in terms of the action, attitudes and behavior of the entire country."

The significance of the Supreme Court's 1954 ruling on school desegregation and its implications for education as well as other aspects of life in America is indicated by the fact that every major religious body in the nation has been compelled to issue statements relating to the decision and its implementation; both national political parties in their 1960, 1964, and 1968 presidential platforms gave major attention to civil rights and school desegregation; the Civil Rights Bill of 1964 included a major section on school desegregation; the National Education Association and other education bodies have clarified their own racial stands and implemented desegregation policies within their own ranks; and hardly a local

---

[1] Arnold Toynbee, "War of the Races," *New York Times Magazine*, August 7, 1960.

[2] *New York Times*, March 13, 1956.

or national political campaign in the South since 1954 has been able to ignore the desegregation issue.[3]

Statistically, school desegregation has affected much of the nation, but especially the seventeen southern and border states and the District of Columbia. Before 1954 schools in these states were segregated almost without exception; however, by December, 1964, some public school desegregation had taken place in each state. Overall, one fifth of the nearly six thousand school districts in this area officially desegregated during this period, bringing slightly more than 10 percent of the region's black students into classrooms with white children.[4]

Nevitt Sanford, speaking as president of the Society for the Psychological Study of Social Issues in 1958, called the school desegregation issue "profoundly important, highly controversial and of great scientific significance. It challenges the social scientist in each of his major roles, that of researcher, consultant and social reformer."[5]

William Van Til, an educator who has been a participant in several cases regarding school desegregation, has written that "the great new frontier in intercultural education, as yet scarcely explored through research, is the problem of school desegregation and integration."[6] Thomas Pettigrew, social psychologist, presents the need for research in dramatic terms:

[3] For background on politics and voting and role of racial issue in southern politics, see V. O. Key, Jr., *Southern Politics in State and Nation.* For data on race and politics since 1954, almost every issue of *Southern School News,* and numerous publications of the Southern Regional Council, and the U. S. Commission on Civil Rights contain contemporary material on this subject. See also James W. Silver, *Mississippi: The Closed Society.*

[4] *Southern School News,* December 1964, pp. 1, 12. By the fall of 1964 there were 5,973 school districts in the region, 1,282 of them having some desegregation. Of the 3,521,482 black pupils in the region at the time, 379,321 of them were in school with whites.

[5] R. Nevitt Sanford, "Foreword," in *The Role of the Social Sciences in Desegregation: A Symposium.* New York: Anti-Defamation League of B'nai B'rith, August, 1958, p. 2.

[6] William Van Til, "Intercultural Education," *Encyclopedia of Educational Research,* p. 707.

1. Desegregation is a now-or-never phenomenon; we either start studying it immediately, or we lose our chance completely.

2. Our scientific insights and methods are needed to help in the solution of the many complex problems raised by such sweeping social changes.

3. The process offers us a rare opportunity to test many of our theoretical formulations in the field on an issue of maximum salience.[7]

The need for increased research in the field of school desegregation has been emphasized by many social scientists, among them such leaders as Ira A. Reid, Harry W. Roberts, Herbert Wey, Robin M. Williams, Jr., and H. Harry Giles.

Scope of Study

In planning the current study, it seemed wise to set certain limitations on its scope, both for clarity of purpose and to keep the research within workable bounds. First, the time limit was confined to the period from the date of the U. S. Supreme Court's ruling on the *Brown* case in May, 1954, to the end of the 1964–65 school year. Next, the study was limited specifically to desegregation in elementary and secondary schools.

Other limits governed the kinds of communities to be considered for study. Included were communities which could be designated as urban centers, those which were located geographically in the southeastern part of the nation, specifically in North and South Carolina, and those in which some degree of school desegregation existed *per se* for one or more school years during the 1954–65 time period of this study.

Basic Assumptions

At the same time, three basic assumptions regarding school desegregation as a phenomenon and regarding the role of the

[7] Thomas F. Pettigrew, Introduction to special issue on "Desegregation Research in the North and South," *Journal of Social Issues*, 15:1, No. 4, 1959.

social sciences in relation to it were made in setting up the study. First, it was assumed that the Supreme Court ruling on *Brown* v. *Board of Education of Topeka* and its implementation decisions of 1955 and afterward were legal and constitutional. It was assumed, secondly, that the issue of school desegregation would continue to be a major problem in the South and in the nation for at least another generation. Finally, it was assumed that social and behavioral scientists have a professional as well as a moral responsibility to share and to test any theory and experience which may be applicable to and which may facilitate social change in as positive and constructive a manner as possible.

In planning this study, it was anticipated that one or more identifiable hypotheses would develop from it. However, in an exploratory study such as this, any hypotheses or null hypotheses should grow out of the research findings, as indicated by several authorities on research methods. One group of scholars expressed it this way: "In many areas of social relations significant hypotheses do not exist. Much exploratory research therefore must be done before hypotheses can be formulated. Such exploratory work is an inevitable step in scientific progress."[8]

Definitions

Several terms as used in this study need to be defined or explained. These include:

Desegregation—the removal of segregation barriers, legal and physical, which prevent black children from attending white or desegregated schools. *Desegregation* is distinguished from integration in that the latter implies much more than the mere removal of segregation barriers. Integration implies a positive acceptance by whites of blacks as persons into the group.
Applicable—in this study, *applicable* refers to whether the selected intergroup relations principles or factors are pertinent or

[8] Claire Selltiz, et al., *Research Methods in Social Relations*, p. 39.

relevant, or whether they apply at all to a specific school desegregation situation.

Principle—a theoretical concept explaining or describing the operation of psychological or social forces. In this study, the term applies to principles which have been set forth by previous researchers as relevant or applicable to social changes such as school desegregation.

Factors—existing social phenomena. In this study, the term applies to phenomena such as community social attitudes, economic conditions, or other existing situations which may have had some influence on the accomplishment of school desegregation.

PROCEDURES

Three specific problems arose in the course of planning this study. The first, a procedural one, involved the compilation of a selected list of the outstanding principles and factors relevant to the school desegregation process. The next problem, also a procedural one, involved the selection of two communities which would be as representative as possible of a number of others in the South, so that any findings which should accrue from the study might have some applicability or relevance to the desegregation problem in other places. The last problem, the central one in the study, was to examine methodically the school desegregation process in the two communities so as to arrive at as much of a whole, nonfragmented view as possible. Involved in this examination was an effort to determine the presence, the importance, and the relationship, if any, of the selected principles and factors, and whether there was any relationship between them and the overall pattern of community interaction over desegregation.

Compilation of Principles and Factors

The first problem was to arrive at a list of the most outstanding intergroup relations principles or factors relevant to and significant in the process of school desegregation.

The data for this problem included the numerous intergroup

relations principles or factors which have been advanced or promoted by recognized social scientists and educators in articles in various scholarly journals, published and unpublished research monographs, and other articles and books in the fields of human relations, sociology, education, psychology, educational sociology, educational psychology, social psychology, social anthropology, political science, social history, law, and government.

A search of the above-mentioned literature resulted in the compilation of a list of more than one hundred such principles or factors. Several scholars and researchers had already compiled their own lists of principles or factors which they considered to be important to school desegregation.[9] A number of other theories, principles and factors were found in working manuals or handbooks by Dean and Rosen, Williams, Suchman, and Wey and Corey.[10]

[9] Kenneth Clark, "Some Principles Related to the Problem of Desegregation," *Journal of Negro Education*, 23:339–47, 1954; Robin Williams and Margaret Ryan, *Schools in Transition*, pp. 239–40; James Vander Zanden, "Turbulence Accompanying School Desegregation," *Journal of Educational Sociology*, 32:68–75, October 1958; Fred Reuter, "An Administrator's Guide to Successful Desegregation of the Public Schools" (unpublished doctoral thesis, New York University, 1961), pp. 149–52; Bonita Valien, "Racial Desegregation of the Public Schools in Southern Illinois," *Journal of Negro Education*, 23:303–309, 1954; Harold Turner, "A Study of Public School Integration in Two Illinois Communities" (unpublished doctoral thesis, George Peabody College, 1956), pp. 226–38; Dan W. Dodson and Margaret E. Linders, "School Desegregation and Action Programs in Intergroup Relations," *Review of Educational Research*, 29:378–87, October 1959; Dan W. Dodson, "Toward Integration," *Journal of Educational Sociology*, 28:49–58, October 1954; Robert Dwyer, "A Study of Desegregation and Integration in Selective School Districts of Central Missouri" (unpublished doctoral thesis, University of Missouri, 1957).

[10] John Dean and Alex Rosen, *A Manual of Intergroup Relations* (contains twenty-seven "propositions" related to intergroup relations); Robin Williams, *The Reduction of Intergroup Tensions*, pp. 36–77 (discusses 102 "propositions"; Dean, and Williams, Edward Suchman, et al. *Desegregation: Some Propositions and Research Suggestions*, pp. 9–77 (discusses a number of "propositions" related to social stratification, power in the community, public opinion and propaganda, interaction and

There was considerable duplication and overlap among the many principles and factors in these various sources, however. After much comparing, combining, and refining of the wording in many of the items, a composite working list of fifty-nine principles or factors was compiled. This list could be grouped generally under six major subject headings, namely:

1. Leadership principles and factors which operate to bring about school desegregation (role of school officials, press, community leaders, civil rights leaders, etc.)

2. Physical principles and factors (physical condition of schools, distances children live from schools, etc.)

3. Financial and administrative principles and factors (cost of operating dual facilities, federal financing of schools, how school board members are selected, etc.)

4. Coercive principles and factors (legal action and pressures from governmental or civil rights forces)

5. Preparation principles and factors (community and special group preparation for desegregation by school or community groups or press)

6. Other principles and factors (miscellaneous items on community social and political climate, urbanization, racial ratio, communication between races, economic and educational levels of various groups, etc.)

In order to cut the list to a workable size, it was submitted to a panel of eight social scientists and educators who have done research and published articles or monographs relating to desegregation. The panel included three sociologists, one educational sociologist, one educational psychologist, one

---

communication, prejudice and personality, and the minority community) ; Herbert Wey and John Corey, *Action Patterns in School Desegregation* (a guidebook to desegregation, listing and discussing various principles and factors as described by school leaders in seventy southern school districts where desegregation had occurred).

social psychologist, one educator, and one political scientist. Among them were Ernest Campbell, Kenneth B. Clark, Dan W. Dodson, Leslie Dunbar, H. Harry Giles, Joseph Himes, Melvin Tumin, and William Van Til.

The panel of judges was asked to assign one of four categories to each of the fifty-nine principles or factors on the list, using research findings and their experience as criteria for such selection. Each category was to be indicated by a numerical weight, as follows: 1—not important or relevant in the local school desegregation situation; 2—slightly important; 3—fairly important; 4—very important. On the basis of these weightings assigned by the national panel, the following twenty-five principles or factors relating to the school desegregation process were chosen for testing in selected communities:

Item no. BRIEF DESCRIPTION OF ITEM

1. leadership from school board
2. leadership from school superintendent
3. clear policy statement from school board
4. clear policy statement by law enforcement officials
5. firm support from press
6. firm support from religious and civic leaders
7. firm support from business and industry leaders
8. firm support from power structure leaders
9. firm support from political leaders
10. firm support from black leaders
11. federal funds requiring nondiscrimination
12. threat of legal action
13. federal court order
14. pressure from federal agencies
15. pressure from civil rights groups
16. community preparation by human relations groups
17. community preparation by press
18. other existing desegregation in community
19. high educational level of white community
20. high educational level of black community
21. good communication between races
22. moderate or liberal social climate

23. low black population ratio
24. moderate or liberal political climate
25. legislation favorable to desegregation

This list was later used in a questionnaire in interviewing local leaders in the two communities selected for this study.

Selection of Communities

The next problem, also a procedural one, was to select two southern communities in which to study the process of school desegregation. If ten, twenty, or thirty communities could have been included in the study, the findings about the operative forces in such a social change would have provided far greater reliability. However, in order to keep the study within workable limits, it seemed wisest to limit the study to two communities, but to select communities between which a number of comparisons as well as contrasts could be drawn.

Geographically, the selection was limited to urban communities or urbanized areas[11] in North Carolina and South Carolina. These limitations were set for three reasons. First, the frequency of school desegregation in southern urban areas seemed to be considerably higher than in rural areas, thus offering the possibility of a greater selectivity of communities for study. This conclusion was made on the basis of a preliminary survey of reports issued by the Southern Regional Council, the U. S. Commission on Civil Rights, and the Southern Education Reporting Service.

orth Carolina, with its moderate-liberal approach to racial change, and South Carolina, with its conservative-reactionary approach, seemed to offer something of a microcosm of the

[11] For purposes of this study, urban communities or urbanized areas refer to communities of twenty thousand or more population as of 1960 or to those counties or other areas in both states which the U. S. Census labels as "urbanized areas." See United States Bureau of the Census, U. S. Census of Population, 1960 and U. S. Census of Housing, 1960.

South's varied reactions to desegregation.[12] Thus the study of one community in each state seemed likely to provide findings which might be relevant in a variety of other southern urban areas. These two states were in proximity to each other and were more readily accessible to the researcher than other parts of the South.

The data for this selection problem consisted of information relative to the following criteria for all urban communities in North Carolina or South Carolina:

1. communities in which some school desegregation took place between 1954 and the end of the 1964–65 school year.

2. communities in which schools had been desegregated for at least one year or more by the end of the 1964–65 school term.

3. communities similar to each other and to a number of other southern communities in size, racial ratio, economic and religious framework, so that whatever might be learned from this study would be relevant in a generalized way to other southern urban areas.

4. communities with available background studies or reports concerning the power structure, leadership, attitudes on racial matters, community organization, minority groups, etc.

5. communities readily accessible to the researcher.

6. communities in which the co-operation of necessary leaders and other interviewees in doing this study would least likely be marred by idiosyncratic factors such as negative relationship between researcher and certain key persons resulting from the researcher's earlier role as social action participant in such communities.

There were four major sources for such information. First, the *United States Census of Population, 1960* provided a primary source for data on population size, racial population

[12] This contrast in racial patterns in the two states is borne out extensively in several studies, including V. O. Key, *Southern Politics in State and Nation;* Carll Ladd, *Negro Political Leadership in the South;* Melvin M. Tumin, *Desegregation: Resistance and Readiness;* and William H. Nicholls, *Southern Tradition and Regional Progress.*

ratio, educational and economic conditions in state and community.

For information on community school desegregation, the monthly *Southern School News,* and the annual *Statistical Summary of School Desegregation* were invaluable.[13] Other helpful related sources included various summary and analytical reports from the Southern Regional Council, the U. S. Commission on Civil Rights and its state advisory committees in the Carolinas, and the American Friends Service Committee.[14]

For background data on power structure, racial attitudes, leadership patterns, or other relevant subjects relating to urban communities in the two states, several research studies proved to be helpful. These included Tumin's study of racial attitudes in Greensboro and Guilford County just before school desegregation began, Ladd's study of Negro leadership in Greenville and Winston-Salem, Burgess' study of Negro leadership in Durham, Quint's study of race relations in South Carolina in the 1950s, and Waynick's collection of reports on the racial scene in fifty-five North Carolina communities in 1963.[15] A research article on community and racial problems

[13] *Southern School News* was published monthly 1954–65 by the Southern Education Reporting Service, Nashville, Tennessee. The *Statistical Summary of School Desegregation,* giving detailed statistical data on school desegregation, state by state, was published each year, 1957–66, by the Southern Education Reporting Service.

[14] The Southern Regional Council issued its *Special Report on Charlotte, Greensboro and Winston-Salem, N. C.,* in September, 1957. Several annual and special reports were published by the U. S. Commission on Civil Rights from 1959 to 1965. In 1962 its North Carolina Advisory Committee published an extensive report, *Equal Protection of the Law in North Carolina.* These various publications include reports on desegregation in several cities in the two Carolinas. The American Friends Service Committee has operated community relations programs relating to school desegregation and other racial problems in the Southeast since the early 1950s. Numerous unpublished staff and field reports, committee minutes, memoranda, and correspondence from its files provide an excellent firsthand staff observation and experience source in several Carolina communities.

[15] Tumin, *Desegregation: Resistance and Readiness;* Ladd, *Negro Political Leadership in the South;* Elaine Burgess, *Negro Leadership in a*

in Greenville in the 1950s and a similar one on Winston-Salem in the 1960s also provided background data.[16] Other sources of information on communities in the two states included social scientists in several universities, officials in various agencies, and key persons in various leadership roles whom this researcher had known from personal or professional relationships while living in each state and while doing field work in school desegregation from 1958 to 1965 in one hundred or more communities in the two states.

Data sheets were prepared for the eighteen North Carolina and eight South Carolina communities and urbanized areas which had populations of twenty thousand or more in 1960. Data, including population, racial ratio, economic and geographical factors, the year school desegregation began, and the availability of background studies about the community were compiled. Interviews were conducted with social scientists at the University of North Carolina, North Carolina College at Durham, Furman University, and the University of South Carolina in order to learn about research studies relating to any of the communities considered for this study. School officials in several of the communities were consulted in order to learn whether their co-operation would be given if the study should involve their school district.

On each data sheet an indication was made to show whether the community was easily accessible to the researcher for an extended period of study and whether any idiosyncratic factors existed which would make the study especially difficult in particular communities because of the researcher's past experience as a social action participant in such places.

By applying the six criteria, two communities were selected:

Southern City; Howard Quint, *Profile in Black and White: A Frank Portrait of South Carolina;* Capus Waynick, *North Carolina and the Negro.*

[16] "Greenville's Big Idea," *New South,* 5:1–32; May 1950, and Clarence H. Patrick, "Lunch Counter Desegregation in Winston-Salem, N. C.," an unpublished study made in July, 1960, for the city's biracial committee by a local sociologist from Wake Forest College.

Greensboro, North Carolina, and Greenville, South Carolina. These two communities are demographically similar in many ways, such as in racial population ratio, economic and religious life, and geographic location. The selection of these two communities was made somewhat on the premise also that the social scene in each would be found to reflect the strongly contrasting racial and social climates in the two states. At the same time, the selections were made with the realization that no community in either state was likely to be a complete microcosm of that state.

Determination of Presence and Importance of Principles and Factors

The central problem in the study was to determine if any or all of the twenty-five intergroup principles and factors were present and involved in the school desegregation process in Greensboro and/or Greenville and, if so, in what way and to what degree. The data for this problem included the general background and setting of the two communities, the historical experience of school desegregation in each, and the nature of and relationship to each other and to the overall pattern of community interaction involved in the desegregation process. The two major sources used were interviews with key persons in each community and information from various printed materials. A case study method was used primarily.

To set up an interview schedule, the names of potential interviewees in Greensboro and Greenville were compiled from news stories about school desegregation in the two places, from lists of local government officials in 1954 and at the time of desegregation, from lists of officials of various local civic, religious, human relations, and civil rights organizations in 1954 and at the time of desegregation, from the names of black parents whose children were involved in desegregation, and from the names of local social scientists.

It was decided that a feasible number of interviewees in

each community should include at least fifteen persons and probably not more than twenty-five. These limitations were set in view of the time to be involved in each interview (one to two hours), of the fact that several other types of data were to be used, and of the time and resources available to the researcher.

After preliminary consultation with several local leaders, a list of twenty-five potential interviewees in each community was compiled. These lists were based on two criteria. The person should have lived in the community during most of the period 1954–65, or at least during the time immediately preceding and following the beginning of school desegregation in the community and should have had some rather direct relationship to the school desegregation process, either as a school official, as a business or civil rights leader whose organization was involved in the desegregation action, or as a parent whose child was directly involved.

Another factor which had some influence in the final selection of interviewees was the knowledge and experience of the researcher, a participant-observer in desegregation activities in both communities for several years, who made an effort to have the final list representative of a diversity of socioeconomic groups, as well as of a variety of viewpoints about desegregation. A total of forty persons, twenty in each community, were interviewed. They included:

CATEGORY BY	GREENSBORO	GREENVILLE
Vocation:		
Public school leaders (board members, superintendents, principals, and teachers)	7	7
Civil rights leaders	6	6
Business leaders	3	2
Mass media leaders (editors and reporters)	1	2
Religious leaders	6	6
Civic leaders	8	10

Social scientists	2	2
Attorneys and physicians	3	2
Social agency workers	3	2
Political leaders	3	4
Human relations workers (volunteers or agency staff personnel)	7	6
Sex: Women	5	4
Men	15	16
Race: Black	8	7
White	12	13

The categories often overlap with a particular interviewee. For example, one black businessman was also a political leader and a civil rights leader. Several ministers were civic and human relations leaders as well.

To avoid as much overlap as possible and to still have a set of racial and vocational groups which would be large enough for purposes of comparison and correlation, the interviewees in each community were consolidated into the five following subgroups:

CATEGORY	GREENSBORO	GREENVILLE
White leaders	12	13
Black leaders	8	7
School leaders	7	7
Religious leaders	6	6
Business leaders (includes businessmen, doctors, lawyers, and editors)	6	6

In a combination semistructured and open-ended interview with each of these key persons the investigator sought to obtain three types of data. First, in informal conversation the researcher tried to gather pertinent background information about the community, the interviewee's personal bias regarding desegregation, and his role in the local desegregation. Next, the interviewee was asked, during a semistructured conversation, to give his own account of how the local school desegregation came about, what events and factors led to the official decision to desegregate, and what factors seemed to be involved in the implementation of the decision. For this part of the interview, a questionnaire was used by the researcher to record pertinent information.

Finally, a list of the twenty-five intergroup principles and factors selected earlier by the national panel of judges was given to each local interviewee. The interviewee was asked to assign one of four categories to each principle and factor on the list, depending on the relative presence and importance, if any, of each item in the local desegregation situation. The list contained space for the interviewee to add and assign a category to any other principles or factors which he thought should be on the list. This form was completed during the interview. Afterward, the ratings were totalled by the investigator.

Most of the interviews lasted from an hour to an hour and a half each and were concluded in one appointment. A few lasted for as much as two hours, and two involved second appointments. Each interviewee was assured that no statements from the interview would be attributed directly to him in the research report and that his name would not occur in the report at all unless he should be quoted from already published materials.

To supplement the interview data and to serve as a check, four types of printed materials were searched for information about the two communities. These included official records and documents, mass media publications, research and background studies and reports, and public statements on desegregation by local and state leaders and groups. As each of the printed sources was searched, the investigator kept at hand the set of questions posed to the interviewees about these subjects as a guide.

Among the official records and documents searched were the minutes of school board meetings in both communities from 1954 to 1965. The Greensboro *Minutes* report extensively on board discussions and actions about desegregation and related matters from 1954 until after the desegregation began in 1957. In contrast, references to any discussion of desegregation from 1954 to 1965 are very few and extremely formal and legalistic in the Greenville *Minutes*.

In Greensboro, the records of the 1957 state litigation by a group of white parents to prevent desegregation ("In re: Application for Reassignment; Josephine Ophelia Boyd from Dudley High School to Senior High School; etc.") and the 1959 federal court records for the *McCoy* v. *Greensboro City Board of Education* case were scanned. In Greenville, the federal court records of the 1963–64 *Whittenberg, et al.* v. *The School District of Greenville, South Carolina*, were scanned.

Reports of the official "Segregation Committees" of the two states were read also. These include the South Carolina School Committee's *Interim Reports* from 1954–66, and the North Carolina Advisory Committee on Education's occasional *Reports* from 1956–60. Both provide good background on the political thinking of state leaders at varying times during the period covered by this study.

The mass media publications of this period which were read included the *Greensboro Daily News* and the *Greenville News*. Both daily newspapers, in their news stories and editorials, provide a wealth of information about the historical experience of school desegregation in the two communities. Their editorials are helpful in providing an interpretation and reflection of factors related to the desegregation process. Two other local daily newspapers, the *Greensboro Record* and the *Greenville Piedmont*, were scanned for the same period, 1954–65, for any different news or editorial coverage which they might give to specific events. Regional publications which provided considerable background and interpretation include the *Southern School News* (1954–65), the *New South* (1950–65), and the *Race Relations Law Reporter* (1955–65).

A number of scholarly studies and background reports on racial attitudes, desegregation, community organization, leadership patterns, political factors, and educational factors relating to Greensboro and Greenville and areas around them were studied. These included research studies relating to one or both of the communities by Tumin, Ladd, Wey and Corey, and state or regional studies by Ashmore, Key, Quint, Clark, Van Woodward, Myrdal, and Nicholls.[17] Background, analytical and summary data was obtained from various reports by the Southern Regional Council and its affiliates in the two Carolinas,[18] the Southern Educational Reporting Service,[19] the *United States Census,*[20] the United States Commission on Civil Rights and its state committees in North and South Carolina,[21] and the North Carolina Mayors' Co-operating Committee.[22]

---

[17] Tumin, *Desegregation: Resistance and Readiness;* Ladd, *Negro Political Leadership in the South;* Wey and Corey, *Action Patterns in School Desegregation;* Ashmore, *The Negro and the Schools;* Key, *Southern Politics in State and Nation;* Quint, *Profile in Black and White;* Clark, *The Emerging South;* C. Vann Woodward, *The Strange Career of Jim Crow;* Gunnar Myrdal, *An American Dilemma;* and Nicholls, *Southern Tradition and Regional Progress.*

[18] *Special Report on Charlotte, Greensboro and Winston-Salem, N. C.* (September 1957).

[19] *The Statistical Summary of School Desegregation,* a detailed annual report on school desegregation, state by state, including significant events, legal actions, and statistics.

[20] The *U. S. Census* for 1950 and 1960.

[21] Data on school and other desegregation action in Greensboro and in the region was obtained from several annual and special reports published by the commission from 1959 to 1965. Its report on the *Education Conference (Nashville, 1959)* is especially helpful for its detailed account of Greensboro's school desegregation action. The 1962 report by its North Carolina Advisory Committee, *Equal Protection of the Law in North Carolina,* contains background material on various aspects of education and racial matters in Greensboro. A report by the commission's South Carolina Advisory Committee on "South Carolina Cities Meet the Challenge" (August 1, 1963) provides a brief description of desegregation action in Greenville.

[22] A detailed account of varied desegregation activities in many North Carolina communities, including Greensboro, is provided in Capus Waynick's (ed.) *North Carolina and the Negro,* published in 1964 by this

Public statements about racial matters from the early 1950s to 1965 by local leaders and groups in Greensboro and Greenville and by selected state leaders and groups were found in the local or national press, and a few appeared in such official documents as local school board minutes. These public statements helped provide background information concerning community and leadership attitudes towards school desegregation, the political and social climates relating to racial and educational matters, the historical experiences of desegregation, and the factors involved in this social change. Among the persons and groups making such statements were school board chairmen and school superintendents in both communities, various religious leaders and groups, the governors of both states, several legislators, business and industrial leaders, professional and civic groups, and civil rights leaders and organizations.

A third source, though not a major one, was provided by various unpublished reports and records related to this researcher's professional experience as a participant-observer in desegregation activities in the Southeast from 1958 to 1965.[23] Such experience and related observations as a field worker for a national human relations organization are recorded in numerous staff reports, field reports, committee minutes, and miscellaneous memoranda and correspondence. The data relating to his experiences and observations as a participant-observer was not collected to provide a major body of information for this study but was intended for use in corroborating information from other sources and for supplying supplemental facts and observations not included in other

special volunteer group meeting under the sponsorship of Governor Terry Sanford.

[23] As director of a regional community relations program for the American Friends Service Committee, the researcher was involved in various local education and action projects in most of the one hundred or more communities in the Carolinas and Virginia in which some school desegregation occurred during the time covered by this study.

material but considered to be pertinent by the investigator. The data collected from these sources were grouped under three subject headings. These include: (1) general background of the two selected communities; (2) the historical experience of school desegregation in each community; and (3) data regarding the intergroup relations principles and factors involved in the desegregation process in these communities. It seemed logical to consider each of these three groups of data as the subject for one or more chapters in the final research report.

Under the heading of community background, Chapter I helps to place the two selected communities in the general context of their states and area. This includes information regarding population and economics, religion, education, race, and political and leadership factors.

The experiences of school desegregation in Greensboro and Greenville offer so much contrast, and the data on the subject is so extensive, that separate chapters for the two communities were prepared. The course of desegregation in each community seemed to fall generally into the following subdivisions: reaction to the 1954 Supreme Court ruling, development of resistance, pressures for desegregation, decision to desegregate, preparation for desegregation, desegregation begins, and later developments.

The intergroup relations principles and factors involved in the school desegregation process in the two communities has been co-ordinated and analyzed in a separate chapter. The material for this chapter came from all major sources used in the study, including interviews, mass media, official records, other research studies, public statements, and the participant-observer experience of this researcher. The chief body of data, however, consists of interview material, primarily from the questionnaire. Information from the other major sources has been used to corroborate, supplement, or, if necessary, to refute the questionnaire findings.

The material from each community was analyzed separately

at first. Later, the findings for the two communities were compared and analyzed jointly. The techniques used include the development of a series of rank order lists and simple frequency distributions and the computation of rank order correlations between various groups and subgroups of interviewees. The use of such techniques is based primarily on the weightings assigned to each of the questionnaire's principles or factors by the interviewees. The weightings on each item have been totaled for the twenty interviewees within each community, as well as for five subgroups of interviewees within each community.

Chapter V summarizes the findings, sets forth such hypotheses or null hypotheses as seem to result from these findings, and makes recommendations concerning further research needed in the field.

Chapter I

BACKGROUND

To understand the setting and the conditions in which the school desegregation process takes place in the two selected communities in this study, it is necessary to examine the significant characteristics of each place. In the following pages such an examination is made by analyzing similar as well as contrasting forces which appear to be important in the two communities.

POPULATION AND ECONOMY

Both Greenville and Greensboro are cities of the "New South." They both owe their life and development to the industrial movement which belatedly reached that part of the nation in the 1890s and which has mushroomed there since the 1940s.[1]

At the turn of the century both communities were small cities with populations of about ten thousand.[2] From rural oriented agricultural and trade centers they were slowly undergoing the metamorphosis which was to remake and reshape

[1] For discussion of industrial development in the Southeast, see Harry Ashmore, *The Negro and the Schools*, pp. 13–30; V. O. Key, Jr., *Southern Politics in State and Nation*, pp. 135 ff. and 205 ff.; William H. Nicholls, *Southern Tradition and Regional Progress*, pp. 22–26; Thomas Clark, *The Emerging South*, pp. 104–23; and Chamber of Commerce brochures from Greenville and Greensboro, 1960–65.

[2] United States Bureau of the Census, *U. S. Census of Population, 1900*. Greenville's population was 11,860 and Greensboro's was 10,035. Over 40 percent of the population in each was Negro.

the whole inland Piedmont area of the Confederacy into one of the important industrial regions of the twentieth century. Beginning in the 1880s several southern leaders had begun to call for a "New South" approach toward creating an economy to replace the one which had disappeared with the Civil War and which had left the area impoverished in many ways. As one prominent Greenvillian in the 1880s described this new approach, it involved the necessity "to educate the masses, industrialize, work hard, and seek Northern capital to develop Southern resources."[3]

By 1900 several factories, almost without exception textile mills, had been built both in Greenville and Greensboro.[4] By 1917 Greenville had twenty-two cotton mills, was home of the biennial Southern Textile Exposition, and called itself the "Textile Center of the South."[5] From 1900 to 1940, both communities developed as industrial centers in their states and in the Southeast. There was little diversification in their industry, however, most of it being the manufacture of textile goods or textile equipment. At the same time both retained a close relationship to the rural economy which dominated the surrounding counties. In doing this they developed as wholesale and retail trading centers for several counties. Greensboro also came to be known as the "Insurance Center of the Southeast" with home offices of three large southern firms and numerous regional offices of national firms.

During these forty years Greensboro grew nearly 600 percent to be a city of almost 60,000 people. In contrast, Greenville officially increased only 300 percent during this period, its 1940 population being just under 35,000.[6]

[3] From 1882 speech by Benjamin F. Perry, local editor and former South Carolina governor, as referred to by Albert N. Sanders, "Greenville and the Southern Tradition," *Furman University Bulletin*, 7:136, No. 5, November 1960.
[4] See Chamber of Commerce brochures from both cities, 1960–65.
[5] Sanders, "Greenville and the Southern Tradition," pp. 139–42.
[6] *U. S. Census*, 1900 and 1940. Actually there was probably much less difference in the growth of the two cities than the census figures indicate.

With the industrial surge during and following World War II, the entire Piedmont area of the Southeast began to grow very rapidly in population and industry. By 1960, the three hundred-mile "Piedmont Industrial Crescent" of the two Carolinas had a population of more than two million people or about one-third of the total population of the two states. One newswriter described this area as "already the nation's largest producer of textiles, tobacco products and furniture and there are predictions that it someday will rival industrial areas such as that betwen Norfolk, Virginia and New York."[7]

Greenville and Greensboro mushroomed in population, industry, and trade as the area became urbanized and industrialized. By 1960 each city had doubled its urban area population to about 125,000[8] and showed retail sales of more than $200 million annually. Blacks in Greensboro made up about 26 percent of the population while in Greenville they comprised about 30 percent. The rapid development of the two cities brought growth also to the counties in which they are located and for which they are county seats. By 1960, both counties were listed in the *U. S. Census* as "metropolitan areas," Guilford County having nearly 250,000 people and Greenville County having 210,000. The black population in both counties was about 20 percent.[9]

This growth of population in the two cities as well as

Greensboro's city limits expanded much more in accord with the community's urbanization than did Greenville's. Much of Greensboro's industrial area was annexed to the city. In Greenville there has been strong resistence to this, and even today most of Greenville's industrial area is not officially a part of the city.

[7] See special edition of the *Greenville News*, September 29, 1965, and an editorial in the *Greensboro Record*, January 8, 1963.

[8] *U. S. Census, 1960*. By 1960 Greensboro had a city population of about 120,000, plus 4,000 living in the city's urbanized, nonannexed suburbs. This gave it an urbanized area population of 123,334. In comparison, Greenville had an urbanized area population of 126,877 by that time, which included about 66,000 people in the city and another 60,000 in the city's nonannexed suburbs.

[9] *Ibid.*

urbanization of the surrounding counties has been closely related to the movement of new industries and expansion of old ones. From a few cotton mills in the early 1900s, each city by 1960 claimed to have over 250 industrial plants in its incorporated limits or environs. About 30 percent of Greensboro's adult workers and 40 percent of those in Greenville were engaged in manufacturing.[10]

Greensboro's industry has become rather diversified, 130 different products being manufactured. Textiles still form an important segment of the economy, nearly 50 percent of the industrial workers being in textile firms. Other industry includes the making of cigarettes, furniture, terra cotta, pharmaceutical products, paints, and metal products.

Some diversification has come to the "textile center," but 75 percent of all industrial workers in Greenville are still employed in textile firms. Besides cotton and synthetic textile goods and textile machinery, Greenville produces cottonseed oil, cigars, chemical and metal products, and has plants for meat packing and peanut processing.[11]

Both communities have become major trade centers in their respective states as well as in the Southeast. Greensboro claims to be the retail trade center for a twelve-county area which has 800,000 people and 20 percent of all retail sales in North Carolina. In recent years the city's retail sales have totalled more than $200 million annually, and it has over 1,200 retail and 300 wholesale establishments, with one out of every five workers in the city in a trade occupation.[12] The Greenville

[10] *Ibid.* Of the 50,700 workers in the city of Greensboro, 14,970 (29.5 percent) were engaged in manufacturing in 1960. In the "metropolitan area," which includes all of Guilford County, 39,300 (37.6 percent) out of a total of 104,400 workers were engaged in manufacturing. In the Greenville "metropolitan area" 31,400 workers (38.8 percent) out of a total of 81,000 were engaged in manufacturing.

[11] *Ibid.*

[12] Greensboro Chamber of Commerce brochures, 1960–65, and the *U. S. Census, 1960.* Trade occupations accounted for 18,670 workers or 18 percent of the total work force of 104,400 in the Greensboro "metropoli-

trade picture is similar. The city lays claim to being the retail trade center for a nine-county area having about 550,000 people and 25 percent of all retail sales in the state. Greenville's retail sales in recent years have been $250 million or more annually.[13]

To get a better perspective on economic conditions in the two communities, a look at income levels in both is helpful. In 1960 the median income per family for all families in Greensboro was $5,845, slightly higher than the national family median of $5,660. At the same time, the median income per family in Greenville was $4,754, about $900 less than the national figure. Racially the picture is quite different. In both communities, the median income for black families in 1960 was less than half that for white families. The black family in Greenville earned 25 percent less than did the Greensboro black family.[14]

Economic conditions in the two communities are reflected in their patterns and quality of housing. Housing in the South generally has been the poorest in the nation, and housing in both Carolinas in 1960 was worse than that in 85 percent of the rest of the United States.[15] This meant that one-half of all dwelling units in both states were classified as in "dilapidated" or "deteriorating" condition.[16] In Greensboro and Greenville conditions were somewhat better than in their respective states. In Greensboro, for example, only 16 percent of the hous-

---

tan" area (all of Guilford County). In the city, 20 percent or 10,240 of the total of 50,700 workers, were in trade occupations.

[13] *Greenville News* (hereafter referred to as *GN*), September 29, 1965.

[14] *U. S. Census, 1960.* In Greensboro the white family median income was $6,582 as compared to the black family's income of $3,183. In Greenville, the white family income was $5,250, while the black family's was only $2,434.

[15] U. S. Commission on Civil Rights, North Carolina State Advisory Committee, *Equal Protection of the Laws in North Carolina*, Washington, D. C.: U. S. Government Printing Office, 1963, pp. 155–56. The two Carolinas ranked 44th or lower in a national listing of states in 1960 in the percentage of dwelling units in good condition.

[16] *U. S. Census of Housing, 1960.*

ing fell into the poor category in 1960, while in Greenville the figure was 25 percent.[17]

In this overall scene, the housing occupied by blacks in both states and communities in this study was much worse than that of the whites. Whereas, in both communities, about one out of every ten white dwelling units was rated as being in dilapidated or deteriorating condition in 1960, the equivalent figures for poor black housing were six out of ten in Greenville and four out of ten in Greensboro.[18]

RELIGION

The "Bible Belt" which stretches across the South creates an atmosphere in which religion, meaning Protestant Christianity, becomes an obvious part of the physical landscape with its large number of church buildings. Church membership has high priority throughout the region, with over 50 percent of all whites and 36 percent of all the people in the South having joined a church according to an eleven-state church census in 1952. In South Carolina at the time of this study over 60 percent of all whites claimed church membership.[19] A 1964 county religious survey in Greenville County showed that 67.5 percent of all people in the county were church members.[20]

Protestants account for more than 90 percent of the South's

[17] *Ibid.* Of the 35,508 dwelling units in the city of Greensboro, 4,128 were listed as "deteriorating" and 1,475 as "dilapidated." In Greenville, where there were 20,949 dwelling units in the city, 3,516 were listed as "deteriorating" and 1,848 as "dilapidated." In Greenville County, the percentage of poor housing was about the same as in the city. In Guilford County it was 20 percent.

[18] *Ibid.* In Greensboro, 35 percent of the city's 7,653 black dwellings were listed as being in deteriorating or dilapidated condition, while in the city and surrounding county the figures was 41 percent for poor black housing. In Greenville the black housing in the "poor" category totaled 62 percent, in both city and county.

[19] Clark, *The Emerging South,* p. 266. (See George L. Maddox and Joseph H. Fichter, "Religion and Social Change in the South," *Journal of Social Issues,* 22:44–58, January 1966.)

[20] *GN,* September 29, 1965.

total church membership, although in some areas, such as the Carolinas, the number reaches 97 percent.[21] In Greensboro and Greenville, of the 220 or more churches in each place, more than 95 percent are Protestant. These include fifteen to twenty denominational groups, but Baptists far outnumber all others in both places, with Methodists and Presbyterians occupying weak second and third places. The 1964 Religious Survey of Greenville County provides a striking view of the church scene.[22] It shows that out of every one hundred people in the county, about seventy were church members. Of these seventy, forty-four were Baptists, ten were Methodists, three were Presbyterians, one or two were Lutherans, one or two were Episcopalians, and one or two were Catholics. The other eight or nine represented all the Jews, Greek Orthodox, Bahais, Unitarians, Christian Scientists, and members of some fifteen to twenty minor Protestant groups in the county.

Of the forty-four Baptists in this picture, eleven represented the 25,000 Negro Baptists in the county.[23] The percentage of blacks in other denominations was so small that they would not appear in the picture.

In both Greensboro and Greenville there were separate Protestant ministerial associations for whites and blacks for many years. Finally, an interracial, interfaith Ministerial Fellowship was organized in Greensboro in 1955. This group has given strong public support to school desegregation and other human rights issues since its formation.[24] In Greenville efforts

---

[21] Clark, *The Emerging South*, p. 266.

[22] The results of this survey are described in *GN*, September 29, 1965. Figures for the larger groups show 100,000 Baptists (one-fourth of whom are Negroes), 19,000 Methodists, 6,500 Presbyterians, 4,000 Lutherns, 3,000 Episcopalians, and 3,500 Catholics.

[23] The white Baptists are all members of the Southern Baptist denomination, the largest church group in the South. Negro Baptists are divided among two or three all-black denominations and have no organizational relationship to the Southern Baptist group. See Clark, *The Emerging South*, pp. 267–68.

[24] Public statements on desegregation issues by the fellowship or its leaders have been reported at various times in the press. See the *Greensboro Daily News* (hereafter referred to as *GDN*), July 25, 1957, for

to form an interracial ministers group were unsuccessful until 1962–63, when the white Christian Ministers Association finally opened its membership to blacks. Even though it is now officially interracial, few black ministers have participated in it. The association has limited itself to dealing with "religious issues" and has avoided discussion or action regarding racial issues in the community.[25] All Protestant churches in both communities, with one or two exceptions, were still all-white or all-black as late as 1970. Catholic churches in both have been open to all races since the 1950s. Catholic schools in Greensboro desegregated in 1954 while those in Greenville remained segregated until 1964.

EDUCATION

Both Greensboro and Greenville are looked upon as educational centers in their respective states. Both are college centers, Greensboro having six institutions of higher learning and Greenville three. The public school systems in both cities are among the largest and best in each state, and educational matters generally receive a fair amount of public attention and support in both places.

Greensboro has been a center for educational interests since its earliest days. Quaker and Methodist settlers had both established colleges there before 1840, and by 1903 the community had six colleges, three for whites and three for blacks. Of these there was one state-supported college and two church

---

fellowship statement endorsing the local school board's decision to desegregate schools.

[25] Black participation in the association has been very weak. As one black minister said to this investigator, "I don't have time to fool with any organization which calls itself Christian but refuses to discuss racial issues because someone in the group might be offended or embarrassed." Later interviews in 1970 indicated that the association had become more active regarding social issues in the period, 1967–70. It became involved in a slum clearance effort, as well as in supporting school desegregation.

related colleges for each race.[26] All of them, with one possible exception, remained segregated until 1954,[27] but for several years prior to this there was some student and faculty intercollegiate interracial activity.

Greensboro's public school system dates from before 1900. However, as in most of the South, it was after the turn of the century before the community's public schools received much support. It was 1920 before any school in the city had state accreditation.[28] By 1954 the city school system included eighteen schools, ten for whites and eight for blacks, with one high school for each race. All were accredited. That year student enrollment totalled 14,586, of which about 22 percent was black. The city employed 528 teachers that year, or one for every twenty-eight students.[29] By the time desegregation occurred three years later, the city's student population had grown to more than 18,000, of which 28 percent was black.[30] This considerable increase in the proportion of black students was due to annexation by the city in 1957 of several fringe industrial areas in which there were sizable groups of blacks. Even though the school population increased by less than 30 percent during these three years, the number of schools in-

[26] The colleges founded for white students are Guilford (Quaker, coed, 1834), Greensboro (Methodist, women, 1838), and Women's College of the University of North Carolina (state supported, women, 1891). All are now coed and open to blacks as well as whites. The colleges founded for Negroes are Bennett (Methodist, women, 1873), Agricultural and Technical (state supported, coed, 1891) and Immanuel (Lutheran, coed, 1903). The first two are now officially open to both races. Immanuel was closed about 1960 for lack of financial support.

[27] Bennett College has had an interracial faculty for many years and it is reported to have had one or more white students enrolled prior to 1954.

[28] *Education Directory of North Carolina*. Raleigh: State Department of Instruction, 1958, pp. 63–64.

[29] *GDN*, May 18, 1954. The student population included 11,436 whites and 3,150 blacks.

[30] *Statistical Summary of School Segregation in the Southern and Border States* (1959), p. 14. There were 13,211 white students and 5,287 black students enrolled in the fall of 1957.

creased by 70 percent to thirty-one schools. The increase in schools benefited white students primarily, because of the thirteen schools added to the system, only one was for blacks.[31] This occurred even though the black students had increased 60 percent during the intervening years while the whites had increased only 30 percent.[32] Greensboro's school system is governed by an appointed school board of seven members. Six are appointed by the Greensboro City Council and one by the Guilford County Board of Education.[33] By 1954 the city school board had one black member, the president of a local black college.[34]

The Greenville public schools, which also date from before 1900, were in a city system until 1951. At that time, as part of the major effort in South Carolina to "equalize" schools and to upgrade the state's entire educational system, a number of school districts were consolidated. The eighty-seven school districts in Greenville County were merged into one unit, Greenville School District Number 520. The new district had a student population of nearly 40,000 by 1954 and a faculty of 1,300, or one teacher for every thirty students. Of the students, about 22 percent were black.[35] Ten years later, by the time desegregation came to the district, the student popu-

---

[31] *Education Directory*, pp. 63–64. From 1954 to 1958 the number of schools in the system grew from eighteen to thirty-one. The white schools increased from ten to twenty-four and the black ones from eight to nine.

[32] The black students had increased from 3,150 in 1954 to 5,287 in 1958 while the white students increased from 11,436 to 13,211. (Figures from *GDN*, May 18, 1954, and from *Statistical Summary* (1959), p. 14.)

[33] U. S. Commission on Civil Rights, *Education Conference* (*Nashville, 1959*), pp. 103–104. The county has a representative on the city school board because at an earlier time the geographical area of the city school system extended beyond the city limits into the county, and some county children attended the city schools.

[34] Even though the first Negro board member resigned for health reasons in 1956, he was succeeded by another black member, a token policy continued ever since.

[35] *Greenville Piedmont* (hereafter referred to as *GP*), May 17, 1954. An overall news story on Greenville schools on the day of the Supreme Court ruling indicated that the school system had a total of 38,916 students, about 8,300 of whom were black. The system had 1,291 teachers.

lation had increased by one-third to more than 52,000. Of this total, the proportion of blacks was still about 22 percent. The faculty ratio had increased to one teacher for every twenty-nine students.[36]

The job of consolidating and "equalizing" facilities in Greenville was a tremendous one. Most of the school buildings in the city school system as well as in several of the urban areas in the county were in good to fair condition. However, the county as a whole included one-, two-, and three-room buildings, many in poor condition. From 1951 to 1964, 108 such school buildings had to be abandoned because it was "impractical to try and patch them up," as one school official described the situation.[37] During the same period, seventy-nine major renovation or building expansion projects were completed.[38]

To carry out this major development program, Greenville received considerable funds from the state. However, it was necessary to float two local school bond issues in 1959 and 1963 for a total of $15 million.[39] The amount of this overall building program allotted for black schools was not available to this investigator. However, from a report of the local school board in 1954, over 60 percent of the building funds received from 1951 to 1954 by the school system had been channeled into school construction for blacks although less than 25 percent of the system's students were black.[40] The Greenville school system is governed by a seventeen-member, elected school board representing various subdistricts within the system. All of the board members are white. One black ran for election in the early 1950s but was defeated.

Besides its public school system, Greenville has three colleges and one industrial training school. The colleges are

[36] *Ibid.*, April 28, 1964. The student population included 40,676 whites and 11,677 blacks, for a total of 52,353. The faculty totalled 1,748.
[37] *GN*, September 29, 1965.
[38] *Ibid.*, April 28, 1964. This gave the county a total of ninety-five schools.
[39] *Ibid.*, September 29, 1965.
[40] *Ibid.*, May 18, 1954. See also Greenville School Board, *Minutes*, May 17, 1954.

church-supported liberal arts schools and were established for white students. One of them accepted its first black student in 1965.[41] The industrial school, supported by state and federal funds, opened on a desegregated basis in 1963.

Even though both Greensboro and Greenville are looked on as education centers in their own states, the quality and influence of the education in these communities need to be kept in perspective. The public school systems of both rank among the best in the Carolinas. However, on a national level the educational systems of all the southern states rate poorly. This shows up in high functional illiteracy rates (about 20 percent for all southern states in 1950), high dropout rates (in 1950 the percentage of adults who had dropped out of school before high school was twice as high in the South as that for the rest of the nation), and poor showing by southern students on various national tests (military, college entrance, achievement, etc.).[42]

In any of these statistics the southern black citizen and his segregated school system are at the bottom of the list. For example, in Greensboro in 1960, about 10 percent of all adults in the community were functionally illiterate. Among white adults, however, only 7 percent were illiterate, whereas 20 percent of all black adults were illiterate. For the state of North Carolina all these illiteracy percentages were from 50 to 75 percent higher.[43] At the same time, Greensboro's illiteracy rates were about three times higher than the comparable

[41] The colleges are Furman University (Baptist, coed, 1827), Bob Jones University (interdenominational, coed, moved to Greenville in the 1940s), and Holmes Theological Seminary (Holiness). Furman desegregated in 1965, although the issue of admitting black students was approved by student poll in 1956 and officials urged desegregation as early as 1963. The other two schools have remained all-white as far as this investigator has been able to ascertain.

[42] U. S. Commission, *Equal Protection . . . North Carolina*, pp. 127–52.

[43] *U. S. Census, 1960*. Functional illiteracy is the term used to describe adults with less than five years of schooling. For the state of North Carolina, the illiteracy figures in 1960 were 16.5 percent for all adults, 12.2 percent for whites, and 31.5 percent for blacks.

national figures.[44] In Greensboro more than 25 percent of all adults had less than eight years of school. This included 22 percent of the white adults and 42 percent of the blacks. Here again, the comparable state figures were about 50 percent higher.[45]

The 1960 educational statistics for Greenville and South Carolina present an even poorer picture. Greenville's adult functional illiterates numbered about 15 percent. One out of every three adult blacks in Greenville was illiterate. On the state level, 20 percent of all South Carolina adults were illiterate as compared to 16.5 percent of North Carolina adults. The state illiteracy figures for blacks were 41 percent in South Carolina as compared to 31 percent in North Carolina.[46]

The Greenville figures for adults with less than eight years of schooling are again higher than in Greensboro. Whereas 26 percent of all Greensboro's adults were in this category in 1960, the Greenville figure was 35.7 percent. In Greensboro this included 42 percent of all black adults. In Greenville it included 63.3 percent of all black adults. In median years of schooling completed, Greensboro ranked above the national median of 10.6 years and Greenville ranked below it. The Greensboro figures for all adults was 11.7 years as compared to 9.8 years for Greenville adults. Greensboro blacks had completed 8.8 years as compared to 6.8 years for Greenville blacks.[47]

Education in the Carolinas

To understand the poor educational showing of these two Carolina communities as well as their respective states it is

[44] U. S. Commission on Civil Rights, North Carolina State Advisory Committee, *Equal Protection of the Laws in North Carolina*, p. 140. The national figures for adult illiterates in 1960 were 2 percent for whites and 8 percent for blacks.
[45] *U. S. Census, 1960*. The state figures were 41 percent for all adults, 35.5 percent for white adults, and 62 percent for black adults.
[46] *Ibid.*
[47] *Ibid.*

helpful to look briefly at the history of education in the southeastern region of the United States.

Public education in this area "is largely an accomplishment of the 20th century," according to historian Thomas Clark. He explains this by adding that "historically, wealthier Southerners, for economic and social reasons, favored reduced taxation and private schools. Poorer Southerners, for religious and prejudicial reasons, likewise favored private education."[48]

North Carolina made provision for "a statewide publicly supported system of free common schools for all white children" in 1839, but it was never successful and was abolished when the Civil War began.[49] In fact, "unlike the rest of the nation, . . . the ante-bellum South had shown little interest in universal education." By the time of the Civil War, "there was no effective state system of public education anywhere in the region, and only a few of the large cities maintained 'free schools.' There was no schooling at all for Negroes; indeed in several of the Southern states (including the two Carolinas) teaching slaves to read and write was officially a crime."[50]

South Carolina had some free public schools as early as 1710.[51] In 1811 a state system of free schools was set up by the legislature, but, as in North Carolina, it was never given strong support or implementation and ceased at the time of the Civil War.[52]

Public school systems were established for the first time in most southern states by the Reconstruction governments. Most were set up on a dual basis, except in South Carolina and Louisiana, where the state constitutions adopted immediately after the Civil War prohibited racially separate public schools

[48] Clark, *The Emerging South*, pp. 150–51.
[49] U. S. Commission, *Equal Protection . . . North Carolina*, pp. 128–29.
[50] Ashmore, *The Negro and the Schools*, pp. 5–6.
[51] Mary Sims Oliphant, *Simms History of South Carolina*. Columbia, S. C.: The State Co., 1932, p. 259.
[52] *Ibid.*, p. 177.

and even extended this policy to institutions of higher learning. The South Carolina Constitution of 1868, in providing for "free public schools, . . . declared that all public schools and colleges of the state, supported in whole or in part by public funds, should be free and open to all youths of the State, without regard to race or color."[53]

Actually, there were some "mixed" schools in South Carolina for a while, but "they survived only briefly and the closest the races came to mixing was while attending classes in separate rooms of the same buildings."[54]

In North Carolina the "radical Republican" government "manifested a striking interest in public education, . . . devoting an entire article to education in the 1868 Constitution." This "provided for an elective superintendent of public instruction and required the General Assembly . . . to provide, by taxation and otherwise, a general and uniform system of free public schools for all children between the ages of 6 and 21." Even though the system was set up theoretically without any mention of race or segregation, available records indicate that blacks and whites attended separate schools from the beginning.[55]

The public school systems of the Reconstruction era with their principles of universal education survived even after the southern whites returned to power, and they form the basis of today's educational systems in most of the South.[56] However, with the development of local segregation in all phases of life in the South, the school systems fell prey to these laws too.

---

[53] U. S. Commission on Civil Rights, *Equal Protection of the Laws in Public Higher Education*, p. 10.

[54] Ashmore, *The Negro and the Schools*, p. 7. For further discussion of education during the Reconstruction period, see Joel Williamson, *After Slavery: the Negro in South Carolina During Reconstruction, 1861–1877*. Chapel Hill: University of North Carolina Press, 1965, pp. 232–33; and George Brown Tindall, *South Carolina Negroes, 1877–1900*. Baton Rouge: University of South Carolina Press, 1966, pp. 227–28.

[55] U. S. Commission, *Equal Protection . . . North Carolina*, p. 129.

[56] Ashmore, *The Negro and the Schools*, p. 9.

North Carolina legalized school segregation in 1875. It was twenty years later, however, in 1895, before South Carolina took this step.[57]

Even though southern public schools may be said to date from the Reconstruction era, there was actually little support, financial or otherwise, given to such schools before 1900. Many blame this on the postwar poverty of the South plus the whites' fear of "mixed" schooling. Two North Carolina historians, Lefler and Newsome, disagree, stating that "the real explanations" for this poor education situation in North Carolina and even in the South "were a colossal general indifference to public education and a sterile, reactionary political leadership. . . ."[58] As Woodward described southern schools at the turn of the century, they were "miserably supported, poorly attended, wretchedly taught, and wholly inadequate for the education of the people. Far behind the rest of the country in nearly all respects, Southern education suffered from a greater lag than any other public institution in the region."[59] In 1900, the national expenditure per public school student was $21.14. The South spent about one-fourth of this amount for its children, North Carolina's average being $4.56 and South Carolina's being $4.62. The amount spent per black child in each of these states was less than one-half that spent per white child.[60]

Education in the South began to receive more favorable attention and support in the early part of the twentieth century. Several factors were responsible for this. First, a new and more vigorous money economy came to the poverty-ridden South as the industrial revolution moved belatedly into the region in the 1890s and early 1900s. Textile mills and many light industries began to dot the Piedmont area. Both Greensboro and Greenville began their growth as cities as a result of

[57] U. S. Commission, *Equal Protection*, pp. 9, 10.
[58] Hugh T. Lefler and Albert R. Newsome, *North Carolina: The History of a Southern State*. Chapel Hill: University of North Carolina Press, 1954, pp. 304, 381–82.
[59] C. Vann Woodward, *Origins of the New South, 1877–1913*, p. 398.
[60] U. S. Commission, *Equal Protection . . . North Carolina*, p. 136.

this development.[61] With this improvement in the economy, advocates of education found it easier to secure funds for public schools.

By the early 1900s the racial turmoil of the post–Civil War era had subsided, the white Southerners were in control of state and local government again, the Negro had been disinfranchised, and segregation had been legalized in nearly every area of southern life. This had been done by state law, with federal approval. The threat of "mixed" schools had been removed by the United States Supreme Court's 1896 *Plessy* v. *Ferguson* decision, making "separate but equal" facilities legal. Leading Negro spokesmen of that period, such as Booker T. Washington, argued in support of this philosophy.[62] Under these conditions, it became easier to gain white support for public schools than earlier.

A third factor was the financial contribution made to the area's schools by philanthropists such as Rockefeller, Peabody, Rosenwald, and Jeanes. The latter two gave direct support to "Negro education" in the South.[63] By 1935, for example, Rosenwald funds had been a major factor in the construction of nearly one out of every three black schools in North Carolina and one out of every two in South Carolina.[64]

In North Carolina, public education received a strong push at the turn of the century with the election of Charles B. Aycock, the "education" governor. He went into office pledging to fight illiteracy and to develop public schools for all of the state's children, white and Negro. During his term of office, North Carolina made major strides toward giving public education the significant role which it has occupied there ever since.[65]

[61] Ashmore, *The Negro and the Schools*, p. 13.
[62] *Ibid.*, pp. 13–23.
[63] *Ibid.*, p. 17.
[64] Gunnar Myrdal, *An American Dilemma*, p. 1,418.
[65] U. S. Commission, *Equal Protection* . . . *North Carolina*, pp. 130–31. In 1959 another gubernatorial candidate, Terry Sanford, won election on a similar platform in North Carolina and did much to give leadership to the educational forces and forces of racial moderation in the state.

From a current expenditure of less than $5 per student in 1900 in the Carolinas (less than 25 percent of the national per student expenditure),[66] these two southern states increased their spending to $40 per student in 1940 (45 percent of the national average). By 1950, the figure was $153 for North Carolina (73 percent of the national average) and $137 for South Carolina (66 percent of the national average).[67] By 1960, the figures had jumped to $240 in North Carolina (62 percent of the national average) and $223 in South Carolina (57 percent of the national average), but the national figure had also surged upward to nearly $400.[68]

The percentage of children attending school in the Carolinas has increased considerably in this century. In 1890 over 35 percent of the white children and over 50 percent of the black children in the two states were dropouts before the age of ten. By 1960 only about 15 percent of all children aged five to seventeen years in both states were out of school.[69]

Even though considerable educational progress has been made in the two Carolinas in the twentieth century, there has been a major difference in the kind and quality of education available to white and black children. The 1896 "separate but equal" ruling of the Supreme Court, even if it could have become a physical reality, remained a meaningless term in regard to schools for nearly half a century. It was not until 1935 that the *Plessy* doctrine was literally applied by Court order. From then through the 1940s, however, in a series of decisions relating to schools and other facilities, the federal courts began to push harder and harder for proof of equal treatment on the basis of race.[70]

---

[66] *Ibid.*, p. 136.

[67] Ashmore, *The Negro and the Schools*, pp. 152–53.

[68] U. S. Commission, *Equal Protection . . . North Carolina*, pp. 130–31.

[69] *Ibid.* p. 141. The 1960–61 figures actually vary slightly for the two states, North Carolina's public school enrollment being 87.6 percent of the population aged 5–17 years, and the South Carolina figure being 84.4 percent.

[70] Ashmore, *The Negro and the Schools*, pp. 31–39.

Impelled by this legal action and probably hoping to avert, or at least to stall, the trend of the courts toward even more drastic racial rulings, political and educational leaders in several southern states, including the two Carolinas, began a major drive in the late 1940s and early 1950s to "equalize" schools. Governor James F. Byrnes of South Carolina was a leader in this move. As he explained the situation in 1951, "We are forced to do now what we should have been doing for the past 50 years. . . . It is our duty to provide for the races substantial equality in school facilities. We should do it because it is right. For me that is sufficient reason."[71]

To get a view of the discrepancy in black and white schools in the Carolinas, a look at a few comparative figures is helpful.

At the time of the *Plessy* ruling all the southern states were spending about 50 cents per black child for every dollar spent on a white child.[72] By 1940 the figure in North Carolina was 65 cents per black child as against one dollar per white child. South Carolina dropped, however, to 30 cents per black child for every one dollar per white child. By 1950 the North Carolina figure for black children was 85 cents against every dollar spent on white children, and the South Carolina figure was 60 cents.[73] In 1957 the figures had risen to 91 cents per black child in North Carolina and 80 cents per black child in South Carolina. In both states the expenditures in urban school districts have been consistently higher than in rural districts and the discrepancy between races less. In 1957, for example, in North Carolina urban areas such as Greensboro the annual expenditure per child was about $35 to $40 more than in the state's rural areas. At the same time, expenditures per child for white and black children in such urban areas were almost equal, whereas on the state level the black child's share was only 90 percent that of the white child. In South

[71] Clark, *The Emerging South*, p. 173.
[72] Patrick McCauley and Edward Bell (eds.), *Southern Schools: Progress and Problems*, p. 32.
[73] Ashmore, *The Negro and the Schools*, pp. 152–53.

Carolina in the same year the expenditures per child in urban areas such as Greenville was about $30 more than in rural areas. In such urban areas, however, as well as throughout the state, the annual expenditure for a black student was still only 80 percent of that for each white student.[74]

In capital outlay for school buildings, both states made major progress after 1940. In that year, North Carolina spent over three times as much per white child as per black child for buildings, although the state's school property value per child was already 3 to 1 favoring the white child. By 1952 the state was spending almost the same for each child although the school property value was still almost 2 to 1 favoring the white child. By 1954 the school property value gap had been narrowed to only 1.3 to 1 favoring the white child.[75]

In South Carolina in 1940, nine times as much per child was being spent for white schools as for black schools. By 1952 the state was still spending over twice as much per child for white schools although the school property value gap was over 3 to 1 favoring the white child. From 1952 to 1954, however, the school property value gap was dramatically narrowed to only 1.4 to 1 favoring the white child.[76]

To carry out this massive "equalization" effort in North Carolina, two bond issues totalling $100 million were passed in 1949 and 1953, and a major part of each was channeled into school construction for blacks.[77] In South Carolina, under Governor Byrnes's leadership, a 3 percent sales tax was imposed in 1951 for "school equalization." By 1954, out of $100 million income from this, $65 million had been put into Negro school construction throughout the state.[78] In the Greenville school district, for example, 60 percent of all building funds

[74] McCauley and Bell, *Southern Schools*, pp. 111, 118, 120.
[75] U. S. Commission, *Equal Protection . . . North Carolina*, p. 104.
[76] McCauley and Bell, *Southern Schools*, pp. 148, 150. See also Ashmore, *The Negro and the Schools*, p. 156.
[77] Albert Coates and James Paul, *The School Segregation Decision.* Chapel Hill: University of North Carolina, Institute of Government, 1954, p. 20. See also *GDN*, May 7, 1954.
[78] *GN*, May 21, 1954.

in the district from 1951 to 1954 were allocated for black schools although only 25 percent of the school population was black.[79]

Teacher salaries in both states rose greatly from 1900 to 1950. In 1900, the average annual salary for white teachers in the South was $200 and for black teachers $100.[80] In North Carolina, the figures were $148 for whites and $105 for blacks.[81] By 1940, North Carolina's average black teacher still made only 73 percent as much as a white teacher.[82] Four years later, however, in the face of a court test, North Carolina equalized its teacher salaries,[83] and by 1950 black and white teachers were receiving an average salary of $2,900. By 1957 the average for both was $3,500 in metropolitan districts such as Greensboro. In South Carolina the black teacher's average annual salary was less than half as much as that of the white teacher in 1940 ($938 for whites, $338 for blacks). By 1950 the gap had been narrowed, but still the black teacher received only 75 percent as much as the white teacher ($2,644 for whites, $1,985 for blacks). By 1957 the salary gap was about 3 percent in urban school districts such as Greenville ($3,300 for whites, $3,200 for blacks).[84]

RACE

On the racial scene, many changes have come to Greensboro and Greenville in recent years. By the mid-1960s both had some school desegregation, their public accommodations and

---

[79] *Ibid.*, May 18, 1954. See also Greenville School Board *Minutes*, May 17, 1954.

[80] Ashmore, *The Negro and the Schools*, p. 18.

[81] Coates and Paul, *The School Segregation Decision*, p. 19.

[82] Ashmore, *The Negro and the Schools*, p. 159. The average annual salary for black teachers was $717 in contrast to a $988 average annual salary for whites.

[83] U. S. Commission, *Equal Protection . . . North Carolina*, pp. 101–102.

[84] Ashmore, *The Negro and the Schools*, p. 159; McCauley and Bell, *Southern Schools*, pp. 142, 144.

many job opportunities were open to all, and there was no discernible discrimination in voter activities. The pattern of change varied considerably in the two communities, however. Many of these changes came several years earlier in the North Carolina community. School desegregation, for example, began in Greensboro in 1957, several years before there was any desegregation of public accomodations or employment opportunities. Greenville schools were not desegregated until 1964, some time after public accommodations and numerous local employment opportunities had become open on a nonracial basis.

To discern the patterns of racial change it is helpful to look at the background of each community, particularly with regard to the racial profile of the population, the history of racial attitudes and actions in each community, and the patterns of discrimination and desegregation in community organization, public facilities, voting, employment, education, housing, law enforcement, and other local matters before and after the *Brown* v. *Board of Education of Topeka* ruling.

Racial Population Ratio

The black-white population ratio is very similar in both places, being about 1 to 4 in each city and about 1 to 5 in the surrounding county areas.[85] This means that in North Carolina, Greensboro's black population ratio is about the same as that for the state average which is just under 25 percent.[86] This same ratio exists in most of the industrialized "Piedmont Crescent" area of North Carolina. Actually, the state's black

---

[85] *U. S. Census, 1960.* The black population in Greensboro was 30,817 or 26 percent, while in Guilford County as a whole, it was 51,536 or 20.9 percent. Blacks in the city of Greenville numbered 19,658 or 29.7 percent while in the county as a whole they totalled 36,842 or 17.6 percent.

[86] *Ibid.* North Carolina's 1,116,021 blacks in 1960 comprised 24.8 percent of the state's total population of 4,556,155.

population varies from over 50 percent in several coastal area counties to less than 10 percent in much of its western mountain and hill country.[87] In South Carolina, where the overall black population is nearly 35 percent, Greenville ranks below the state's average, with blacks consisting of less than 30 percent of the city's total population. In Greenville County the black percentage is only one-half that of the state average. The Greenville city and county black populations are similar in size and percentage to other cities and counties in the industrialized Piedmont area of South Carolina.[88]

The percentage of blacks in both Greensboro and Greenville and their surrounding areas has steadily decreased since 1900. At that time the black population of Greensboro was above 40 percent while the black population for the surrounding county was almost 30 percent. Greenville's black population at that time was 45 percent for the city and just over 35 percent for the county.[89] By 1950, however, blacks in both places, although they had increased numerically, had declined in proportion to the total local populations. In the city of Greenville five out of eleven persons in 1900 were black, but by 1950 the figure was only three out of eleven. In the surrounding county, where four out of every eleven persons were black in 1900, the figure was only two out of eleven by 1950.[90] In Greensboro the black proportion of the population dropped from 41 percent in 1900 to

---

[87] Coates and Paul, *The School Segregation Decision*, p. 32.

[88] *U. S. Census, 1960.* South Carolina's 831,962 blacks in 1960 comprised 34.9 percent of the state's total population of 2,383,594. Greenville County's black population was only 17.6 percent of the county's total population.

[89] *Ibid., 1900.* Greensboro at that time had 4,086 blacks. This was 40.7 percent of the city's total population of 10,035. Guilford County's black population was 28.4 percent. Greenville at that time had 5,414 blacks in the city, 45.6 percent of the city's total population of 11,860. Greenville County had 19,491 blacks, or 36.4 percent of the county's total population of 53,490.

[90] *Ibid.,* 1900 and 1950. The black percentage in the city dropped from 45.6 percent in 1900 to 27.6 percent in 1950. In the county the drop was from 36.4 percent to 18.7 percent.

25 percent in 1950. The surrounding county had a drop from 28 percent in 1900 to 19 percent in 1950.[91] Thus by 1950 both communities and their surrounding counties had quite similar racial ratios.

Several factors account for this proportional decline in the black population of the two areas at a time when the overall population was increasing rapidly. One was the curtailment of agricultural pursuits in the Carolinas and particularly in the Piedmont areas, as the growing of cotton became less and less profitable. In the two Carolinas, for example, the cotton acreage decreased more than 50 percent from 1929 to 1955. As this decline in agriculture removed the black citizen's chief livelihood in the South, job opportunities for blacks remained extremely limited until the 1960s. More than one million blacks left the South from 1940 to 1950, while the region's gain in black population was less than 150,000.[92]

From 1950 to 1960, the percentage of blacks in both Greensboro and Greenville became somewhat stabilized, varying in each instance less than two percent in their relation to the total local population from the beginning to the end of the decade. This means that as a racial factor, the proportion of blacks in both communities and in their surrounding counties is fairly low for the South, only about 20 to 30 percent of the local populations. Also, these two communities are more similar to each other and to other Piedmont area communities in racial ratios than they are to much of the rest of their respective states, where blacks often are a majority of the population.[93]

[91] *Ibid.*

[92] Clark, *The Emerging South*, p. 50.

[93] *U. S. Census, 1960.* In North Carolina, the black population in about one-third of the state is over 40 percent and in ten large coastal counties it is over 50 percent. In South Carolina over one-half of the state has more than a 40 percent black population and over one-third of the state has from 50 to 75 percent black population.

Housing Patterns by Race

Most blacks in both communities live in segregated ghettoes, in housing which is in considerably poorer condition than the housing of white areas. In Greensboro about 93 percent of the 31,000 black citizens live in the southeast corner of the city within six of the community's twenty-nine census tracts. Within this older area of the city, the population is almost entirely black, except in one tract which is in a state of racial transition and was still about 60 percent white as of 1960.[94] The city's other 3,700 blacks live in small clusters scattered throughout the rest of the city.[95]

The scene in Greenville is similar in that the city's 20,000 blacks live in segregated areas. However, instead of there being one black community, there are several subcommunities, interspersed throughout the older residential sections of the city and varying in size from sixty city blocks to only a few dwelling units. This fragmented housing pattern has tended to hamper any strong spirit of unity among the city's black citizens. In newer residential sections in both communities, segregation is almost complete, in that new areas are developed either "for whites" or "for Negroes."[96] In the metropolitan area or county surrounding each of the cities, there are scattered groups of blacks, but no large population concentrations.[97]

These patterns of ghetto housing are the result of many factors, not the least of which is prejudice, but much credit

[94] *Ibid.* It was in this "transition" area that Greensboro's first elementary school desegregation occurred in 1957.

[95] *Ibid.* These small groups of blacks comprise less than 10 percent of the population in any area in which they live, except for one tract which has about 15 percent black population.

[96] Carll Ladd, *Negro Political Leadership in the South*, pp. 55–56. See also U. S. Commission, *Equal Protection . . . North Carolina*, p. 178.

[97] *U. S. Census, 1960.*

for encouraging and supporting them over the years must go to the forces of government, according to a 1962 civil rights report. It mentions such actions as "the requirement of racial restrictions in deeds where FHA and VA loans were to be insured, city ordinances compelling racial segregation by blocks and zones," and "court enforcement of deed restrictions on transfers of property to Negroes." The report adds that even though such governmental action has been discontinued officially, its effects will last for many years.[98]

The quality of black housing in both communities, as well as throughout the Carolinas, the South, and the nation, is generally poorer than that for whites. Indicative of this are statistics from a 1960 report on Greensboro showing that, whereas 26 percent of the city's citizens were black, they occupied only 17 percent of the city's "good" dwelling units, 48 percent of the "deteriorating" ones, and 62 percent of the "dilapidated" ones. To emphasize the poor conditions, the director of the Greensboro Redevelopment Commission reported that these figures "do not begin to indicate the much poorer environmental conditions that generally exist in black areas as contrasted with white areas."

Factors helping to create such conditions in both Greensboro and Greenville include the blacks' lower incomes, limited job opportunities, inferior training, poorer health, and general nonparticipation in voting and government.[99]

Employment Patterns by Race

Economically, blacks in both communities have fared poorly, compared to their white neighbors. The median annual income

---

[98] U. S. Commission, *Equal Protection . . . North Carolina*, pp. 178, 211. The housing segregation ordinance in Greensboro was repealed in 1929, after being on record for fifteen years. In Greenville, however, a similar ordinance was still in effect as late as 1962 (see Ladd, *Negro Political Leadership*, p. 55).

[99] *U. S. Census, 1960*, pp. 157, 178.

for black families in both places was less than half of that for white families as late as 1960, and the black family in Greenville earned 25 percent less than did the Greensboro black family. This great discrepancy in income by race is largely accounted for by the fact that up to 1960 most jobs in both communities, except for menial and unskilled work, were closed to blacks.[100] According to the U. S. Census for 1960, about 50 percent of all black workers in both places were employed in household and service jobs or as day laborers.[101] Another 20 percent were listed as operative and kindred workers. Most of these were employed in nontextile firms, for the textile industry throughout the South has had a notably negative attitude about employing blacks in any capacity.[102] One South Carolina law, dating from 1915 and still existing in recent years, prohibited textile factories from "permitting laborers of different races from working together in the same room, or using the same entrance, pay windows, exits, doorways, stairways, drinking water buckets, pails, cups, dippers or glasses at any time."[103] In the area of professional, technical, clerical, and sales work blacks in both communities have occupied a low place in the total work force, but in Greensboro they rated considerably better than in Greenville by 1960. In the South Carolina community only 3 percent of the blacks were in professional or technical jobs at that time, whereas the figure for the North Carolina community was twice as much.[104] In sales and clerical jobs the Greenville per-

---

[100] From interviews with community leaders. See also Ladd, *Negro Political Leadership*, pp. 54–58.

[101] *U. S. Census, 1960.* In Greenville 55.4 percent of the employed blacks were in such jobs, while the figure for Greensboro was 49 percent.

[102] See Myrdal, *An American Dilemma*, pp. 285–86, 289, 382, 1,110–11; Charles S. Johnson, *Patterns of Negro Segregation*, New York: Harper, 1943, p. 84; Ladd, *Negro Political Leadership*, pp. 56–58, 63.

[103] C. Vann Woodward, *Strange Career of Jim Crow*, p. 83.

[104] In Greenville 3.5 percent of the blacks in 1960 were engaged in professional or technical work. In Greensboro, the figure was 8.3 percent for the city and 6.2 percent for the "metropolitan" or county area (from *U. S. Census, 1960*).

centage was 1.7 percent, as contrasted to a figure three times as high in Greensboro.[105] From 1960 to 1965 changes occurred in the Greenville employment scene. A number of businesses and industries, including textile firms, began token employment of blacks. Much of this was due to federal pressures, although threats of demonstration from the black community, the desegregation of the local industrial training school, a series of visits to employers by a citizen group from the Greenville Human Relations Council, and negotiation by the city's semiofficial biracial committee helped to influence these changes.[106]

In Greensboro progress toward nondiscriminatory employment practices has been several years ahead of that in the South Carolina community. There was token employment of blacks in Greensboro industry by 1960.[107] In early 1962 a number of the leading downtown businessmen publicly declared their support for adding blacks to their sales and clerical staffs.[108] A year later the mayor, in a forthright public appeal for complete desegregation of all public facilities, cited the city government's policy of hiring "on the basis of merit alone."[109] In a press conference the following day President John F. Kennedy commended the Greensboro mayor's speech as an example for the nation.[110] A 1964 report by the North Carolina Good Neighbor Council included the statement that

[105] Only 1.7 percent, or 234 blacks in Greenville held sales or clerical jobs in 1960, whereas in Greensboro the figure was 741, or 6 percent, in the city and 961, or 4.7 percent, in the "metropolitan" or county area (from *U. S. Census, 1960*).

[106] Interviews with community leaders corroborate references to these changes found in Ladd, *Negro Political Leadership*, pp. 62, 81–82; *GN*, September 29, 1965; Harold Martin, "A New Era for the Old South," *Saturday Evening Post*, October 9, 1965, pp. 23–25; and Greenville Human Relations Council *Minutes* (1960–64).

[107] American Friends Service Committee, *Field Reports* (unpublished), 1954–60.

[108] *Greensboro Record* (hereafter referred to as *GR*), February 20, 1962.

[109] *GDN*, June 8, 1963.

[110] *New York Times*, June 9, 1963.

"in Greensboro, where there are 75,000 employees, 50 percent of all jobs are controlled by employers who have racially equal employment policies."[111]

History of Race Relations to Early 1900s

Both Greensboro and Greenville date their settlement to the 1700s when groups of Scotch-Irish and other European Protestants moved into the Piedmont region of the Carolinas. Most of these early settlers "were small freeholders whose zeal for religious, economic and political freedom dotted the region with churches, wrested prosperity from the wilderness and helped win independence from the British." There were Scottish Presbyterians from Northern Ireland and German Lutherans and Calvinists who came to both communities. A few French Huguenots who moved into the Greenville area, and English and Welsh Quakers gave Guilford County a strong flavor of their "peaceful, honest ways" which remains even today.[112]

For various reasons neither Greensboro nor Greenville were strongholds of the Old Bourbon South, philosophically or economically. Both were much more a part of the upland Piedmont region where most farms were too small to make slavery a profitable institution, as contrasted to the coastal area where slaves and large plantations were vital to the ante-bellum way of life in the South. With this economic heritage, a strong religious and moral tradition which emphasized democracy and freedom, and an antipathy against landed aristocracy, it is easy to understand how the antislavery and antisecession

[111] Capus Waynick, *North Carolina and the Negro*, pp. 255, 261. The Good Neighbor Council, set up by executive action by Governor Terry Sanford on January 18, 1963, was a statewide biracial group "to encourage the employment of qualified people without regard to race, and to encourage youth to become better trained and qualified for employment."

[112] Blackwell P. Robinson, *North Carolina Guide*, Chapel Hill: University of North Carolina, 1955, p. 205.

movements gained strong spokesmen in the Piedmont.[113] Greenville had several pro-Union leaders, some of whom gained state and national importance and whose influence probably kept the state from leaving the Union earlier than it did. They were eventually overwhelmed by the movement toward war, but one of them, Benjamin Perry, regained leadership later as state governor immediately after the Civil War and became one of the region's strong proponents of the development of a "New South."[114]

In Greensboro and surrounding Guilford County, the Methodists and Quakers, who had founded the community's first two colleges in the 1830s, expressed strong antislavery sentiment. Several Methodist leaders were imprisoned in the 1850s for speaking and distributing literature opposing slavery. North Carolina Quakers as a group took a firm stand against slavery as early as 1774. Many of them left the state because of the slavery issue, but those who remained continued to seek changes in North Carolina's slavery laws until the time of the Civil War.[115] A group of Greensboro Quakers is credited with being instrumental in developing the famed "under-

[113] Key, *Southern Politics*, pp. 3–15. For excellent analysis of the factors and conditions encouraging and perpetuating the segregation concept in the South generally, see James W. Silver's *Mississippi: The Closed Society.*

[114] Laura Smith Ebaugh, "A Social History," *Furman University Bulletin*, 7:14–17, (November 1960), No. 5. See also unpublished speech by Marion W. Wright, "Fall-Out," given at a meeting of the Greenville Human Relations Council, May 15, 1958. Other prominent Greenvillians who opposed the secession of their home state were Joel R. Poinsett, Waddy Thompson, and William J. Grayson, all of whom had records of service in national government positions.

[115] For a discussion of antislavery and antisecession movements in Greensboro and the Piedmont area of North Carolina, see "Anti-Slavery Crusade Begins Here," *GDN*, June 14, 1964; *Ante Bellum: Writings of George Fitzhugh and Hinton Rowan Helper on Slavery.* Ed. by Harvey Wish. New York: G. P. Putnam's Sons, 1960 (Capricorn Books), pp. 23–35; Southern Regional Council, *Special Report on Charlotte, Greensboro and Winston-Salem, N. C.*, September 1957, p. 7; and an unpublished address by Floyd Moore, "Friends in the Carolinas," given at High Point Friends Meeting, October 27, 1963.

ground railroad" system through which thousands of slaves were aided in escaping from the South.[116] Following the Civil War, neither Greensboro nor Greenville had as difficult a period of readjustment as did the coastal plantation areas of their states.[117] However, there is a record of some Ku Klux Klan activities in both places during the Reconstruction period.[118]

The present-day public school systems in both Carolinas got their start from the new state constitutions drawn up just after the Civil War.[119] In South Carolina there was no official school segregation until 1895, although very little actual desegregated schooling existed prior to that time.[120] In fact, in such areas as Greensboro and Greenville the public school systems really did not become operative until after 1900.[121] From 1865 to 1900, however, church groups established schools for blacks in Greensboro. Quakers set up several schools which later closed or became public schools.[122] Methodists established Bennett College in 1873. In 1891 North Carolina set up the Agricultural and Technical College (for Negroes).

In commenting on race relations in Greensboro in the post-

[116] Moore, "Friends in the Carolinas." Records on the "railroad" are scanty because of the sub rosa nature of its operation, but several historians seem to agree, according to Moore, that Greensboro was one of the first stops on it and that Quakers there were leaders in the overall project. Levi Coffin, a Greensboro Quaker who migrated to the Midwest, came to be known as the "president" of the "railroad."

[117] See Ebaugh, "A Social History," p. 17; and Key, *Southern Politics.*

[118] Southern Regional Council, *Special Report*, p. 7; Lerone Bennett, "South Carolina: Post Bellum Paradise for Negroes," *Ebony*, 21:116–22, No. 3, January 1966. Klan activities became so militant in South Carolina in several counties adjoining Greenville that President Grant sent federal troops to take control in 1871. Over one thousand whites, including many prominent local persons, were arrested as a result.

[119] U. S. Commission, *Equal Protection*, p. 10.

[120] Ashmore, *The Negro and the Schools*, p. 7.

[121] Ebaugh, "A Social History," p. 28, discusses the early years of the Greenville school system. See U. S. Commission, *Equal Protection . . . North Carolina*, pp. 100, 130–31, for the early history of North Carolina schools.

[122] Moore, "Friends in the Carolinas."

Civil War period, two local news reporters in an article in 1943 stated " 'there is no record of any trouble between the Negroes and white people of Greensboro during Mayor Sloan's administration or since,' the reference being to a mayor who was elected in 1869."[123]

The host of rigid segregation laws which came to be the trademark of the South until recent years did not exist until almost the end of the nineteenth century. A black New York newspaperman and "radical champion of his race" visited South Carolina in 1885 and wrote glowingly of conditions there. "I feel about as safe here as in Providence, Rhode Island. I can go into saloons and get refreshments even as in New York . . . and be more politely waited upon than in some parts of New England." About the same time a white Northerner, who was a strong antislavery advocate, visited the Carolinas and reported that he found no evidence of blacks being oppressed.[124]

As late as 1897 an editorial in the *Charleston News and Courier* referred to a proposed "Jim Crow" law as "unnecessary and uncalled for . . . a needless affront to our respectable and well-behaved colored people. . . . We have no need for a Jim Crow system."[125]

Blacks continued to occupy various official and public offices in both Carolinas until about the end of the century. Often they held somewhat minor positions as "trial justices, jury commissioners, and members of county and state commissions," but several held legislative seats, and one was a United States congressman from North Carolina until 1901.[126]

---

[123] Quoted by the Southern Regional Council, *Special Report,* p. 7, from an article by Cecil and Nellie Rowe Jones in the *Greensboro Daily News.*

[124] Woodward, *Strange Career of Jim Crow,* pp. 16–17, 20–22.

[125] *Ibid.,* p. 18.

[126] *Ibid.* pp. 35. See Richard Bardolph, *The Negro Vanguard.* New York: Rinehart and Company, Inc., 1959, p. 146. George H. White, who represented a district in eastern North Carolina, was the last of the twenty-two black post-Civil War congressmen who represented southern

By 1900 the white segregationists had again seized control of the South, and any strides made by blacks after the Civil War or any hopes they might have had for a "free society" in the South were destroyed. Woodward argues that this "adoption of extreme racism was due not so much to a conversion as it was to a relaxation of the opposition." Racial fears and hatreds had long been present, he says, but their surge of strength and domination in the 1890s and early 1900s was due to the "almost simultaneous" weakening of liberal forces, such as the "Northern liberal opinion in the press, the courts, and the government," and the discrediting of the influence of southern moderates and liberals. He specifically cites (1) the "acquiescence of Northern liberalism in the Compromise of 1877," when the federal government returned control of southern states to local white leaders; (2) the "weakening of resistance to racism" in Supreme Court decisions, including the Civil Rights Cases of 1883, the *Plessy* v. *Ferguson* "separate but equal" decision of 1896, and the 1898 *Williams* decision approving Mississippi's plan to deprive Negroes of the franchise; and (3) America's "plunge into imperialistic adventures" in 1898 in Cuba and the Philippines, which brought under American control "some eight million people of the colored races, 'a varied assortment of inferior races,' as the *Nation* described them, 'which of course, could not be allowed to vote.' "

In both Carolinas, as well as in other southern states, the rise and fall of the Populist party in the 1890s and the resulting strengthening of the Democratic party, which had strong anti-Negro elements in it, coincided with these trends encouraging the bitter surge of racism which swept the region by 1900.[127]

---

states at one time or another from 1869–1901. See also Lerone Bennett, *Before the Mayflower*. Chicago: Johnson Publishing Company, 1962, p. 241.

[127] Woodward, *Strange Career of Jim Crow*, p. 51–57. See also Key, *Southern Politics*, pp. 6–9.

In a rapid series of legal acts, blacks were disenfranchised, first by passage of the "grandfather" and "good character" clauses (South Carolina, 1895 and North Carolina, 1900), then by the establishment of the "all-white primary" (South Carolina, 1896 and North Carolina, 1915).[128] A vast number of "Jim Crow" laws, establishing racial segregation in almost every phase of life, came into being in all southern states by the early 1900s.[129] Among those passed in the two Carolinas were laws requiring segregation on trains, streetcars, steamboats, and buses; segregation in public schools and all state-supported institutions such as orphanages, homes for the aged, mental and other hospitals, penal institutions for adults, and reform schools for young people; segregation in parks, the National Guard, factories and businesses, fraternal orders, and in crafts and trades. Toilets and drinking fountains were required to be segregated in all public places, whether governmental or business or industry. South Carolina passed a law requiring that only Negro nurses could attend Negro patients in a hospital, North Carolina required that school-owned textbooks be segregated while such books were being stored between school terms. The tax books in North Carolina were segregated as to white, Negro, and Indian, and in several North Carolina areas where the three races lived, there were three sets of toilets, drinking fountains, and public schools until recent years. Marriage between whites and blacks was forbidden by both states. In North Carolina marriage between whites and Indians was illegal until 1961.

Many municipalities had ordinances requiring segregation in residential areas, motels, hotels, restaurants, theaters and other places of amusement, libraries, and cemeteries. Some

[128] Woodward, *Strange Career of Jim Crow*, p. 67.

[129] For references to the many and varied segregation laws in the two Carolinas, see: *ibid.*, pp. 81–86; Waynick, *North Carolina and the Negro*, pp. 232–44; Myrdal, *An American Dilemma*, pp. 578–82; and U. S. Commission, *Equal Protection . . . North Carolina*, pp. 203–25.

required separate Bibles for use in courtrooms. Both Greenville and Greensboro adopted a number of these ordinances.[130]

Patterns of Discrimination Before 1954

By the 1940s the patterns of racial discrimination and segregation were so well established throughout the South that, as Gunnar Myrdal observes in his classic study, *An American Dilemma*, "the white Southerner practically never sees a Negro except as his servant and in other standardized and formalized caste situations." Myrdal's view applied to both Carolinas and to the communities involved in this study. The only major difference between the two states and communities was that racism did not become the continuous political force in North Carolina which it did in its southern neighbor. A reputation for "fair dealing" with its black citizens, even if on a segregated basis, developed in North Carolina along with the state's strong emphasis on business and industrial growth and development.[131]

This helps to explain why Greensboro could have a semiofficial interracial commission as early as 1926 whereas such did not develop in Greenville until 1963. It also helps to show why there is no record of major racial violence in the North Carolina community in the 1900s, whereas its neighbor to the south was the scene of a lynching as late as 1947[132] and of

---

[130] For specific reference to segregation in these two communities see Woodward, *Strange Career of Jim Crow*, p. 85; Ladd, *Negro Political Leadership*, pp. 55, 75–83; U. S. Commission, *Equal Protection . . . North Carolina*, pp. 168, 206–209, 211; Waynick, *North Carolina and the Negro*, pp. 87–92.

[131] Key, *Southern Politics*, p. 206.

[132] In February, 1947, Willie Earle, a Greenville black, was lynched by a mob of armed white men after he allegedly had stabbed a local white taxicab driver. A total of thirty-one men, several of whom admitted to being Ku Klux Klan members, were arrested for his murder. In a nationally publicized trial, all were acquitted. (See Rebecca West, "Opera in Greenville," *New Yorker*, June 14, 1947; *Life Magazine*,

other incidents of violence during the 1950s.[133] Overall, it shows why the state of North Carolina, and particularly its Piedmont area, was several years ahead of South Carolina and its Piedmont area in accommodating to racial changes in the 1950s and 1960s.

In Greensboro, for example, several community organizations were already desegregated by the time of the 1954 Supreme Court ruling. The local YWCA and the Council of Church Women began interracial activities as early as the 1940s. In the period 1950–54 the Community Council of Agencies became interracial,[134] the city hired its first black policeman,[135] a black physician was elected as a city councilman,[136] and a black educator was appointed to the school board.[137]

In contrast, most of the equivalent facilities and organizations in the South Carolina community were not desegregated until the 1960s. Exceptions were the YWCA, which began interracial activities in the early 1950s, the city hospital, where local black physicians had some staff privileges as early as 1951,[138] and the local Donaldson Air Force Base, which desegregated its base operational facilities about 1950.[139]

June 2, 1947; and various issues of the *Greenville News* in February and June, 1947.)

[133] See Southern Regional Council, *Intimidation, Reprisal and Violence in the South's Racial Crisis*, 1959, pp. 26–27.

[134] Greensboro Interracial Commission, *Minutes*, November 21, 1955.

[135] "Negro Police in the South," *New South*, October 1953, p. 6. The city had nine black policemen in 1953.

[136] U. S. Commission, *Equal Protection . . . North Carolina*, p. 64. The physician, William Hampton, was elected to the city council in 1951 in a city-wide election. Since that time there has been at least one black member on the council every year.

[137] U. S. Commission on Civil Rights, *Education Conference (Nashville, 1959)*, p. 114. David Jones, President of Bennett College, was appointed to the school board in 1953. Since that time there has been a black member on the board continuously.

[138] Ladd, *Negro Political Leadership*, pp. 80–81.

[139] See Lee Nicholls, *Breakthrough on the Color Front*, for the story of desegregation of military bases as a result of executive order by President Harry S Truman in 1948.

Racial Change—1954 and After

In Greensboro from 1954 until public schools desegregated in 1957, several other changes took place. The Catholic high school began to accept blacks, an interracial ministerial association was formed, and desegregation began on city buses, in the railway station waiting room, at the public library, and at the local campus of the state university.[140] In 1960 the city's public eating and overnight facilities began to desegregate as a result of the student "sit-in" movement, which originated in Greensboro that year.[141] In 1963, after a turbulent period of protest demonstrations marked by the arrest of more than 1,800 persons, an official biracial committee was set up and most public facilities were desegregated. By 1963 much progress was made in job opportunities for blacks, the public schools had moved beyond the "tokenism" of their first five years of desegregation, and "open housing" had begun in the city's low rent housing units.[142]

In Greenville, where protest demonstrations also occurred in 1960, the public library was the only facility to desegregate at that time.[143] At last, in 1963, after the formation of two biracial committees of local leaders, most public facilities desegregated quietly.[144] As one leader said, these changes took place peacefully because "the power structure was afraid that Greenville would be another Birmingham, . . . and they couldn't afford that. . . . They are trying to bring new busi-

[140] Southern Regional Council, *Special Report*, p. 6.

[141] *New York Times*, February 3 and July 26, 1960. See also *Southern School News* (hereafter referred to as *SSN*), March–August 1960.

[142] Waynick, *North Carolina and the Negro*, pp. 87–92, 261. See also *GDN*, September 15, 1963. About 220 black students were enrolled in ten previously all-white schools by the fall of 1963. The "open housing" policy was announced in July 1963 by the Greensboro Housing Authority. By 1964 at least one black family had moved into a previously all-white housing unit with no incidents involved.

[143] See *GN*, September 29, 1965.

[144] For good description of these changes, see *ibid; GP*, September 30, 1965; and Ladd, *Negro Political Leadership*, pp. 75–83.

ness in, and racial conflict is bad for that sort of thing."[145] About the same time the city's ministerial association became interracial. In 1964 the local Catholic schools desegregated at the same time as did the public schools.[146]

By 1965 job opportunities for Greenville blacks were somewhat improved, though not as much as appears to have occurred in Greensboro by that time. Greenville hired its first black policeman in 1964 but still had no blacks in local government as late as 1965.[147]

POLITICS

There has been less voter participation in the South than in other parts of the nation, especially prior to the 1960s. This was the result of such factors as "the one party system and the thousands of Negroes who do not or cannot vote."[148] In the 1956 presidential elections, for example, when the voter participation in some states was as high as 75 percent of the potential, all southern states ranked near the bottom in a national listing. North Carolina was 39th, with 47.6 percent of voting age casting ballots, and South Carolina was 47th, with only 24.5 percent of its adults voting.[149]

To give some indication as to the voting scene in the two communities of this study, the statistics for the 1956 and 1960 elections are helpful.

Voter records for the Greensboro metropolitan area, which includes all of Guilford County, show that in 1956 and 1960 only about one-half of the adults in the total population were

[145] Ladd, *Negro Political Leadership*, pp. 73–74. Similar opinions were expressed by several Greenville interviewees.
[146] *GN*, September 1, 1964.
[147] Ladd, *Negro Political Leadership*, pp. 62, 81, 278; *GN*, September 29, 1965; and Harold Martin, "A New Era for the Old South," *Saturday Evening Post*, October 9, 1965, pp. 23–25.
[148] Margaret Price, *The Negro and the Ballot*, p. 10.
[149] *Ibid.*

registered to vote. Racially, however, this included two-thirds of the potential white voters but only one-third of the blacks. This meant that there were about 82,000 white voters and 10,000 black voters.[150]

Comparable figures in 1958 for the Greenville metropolitan area, including all of Greenville County, show that slightly more than one-third of the adults were registered to vote. Racially, this included between one-third and one-half of the potential white voters but only one-sixth of the blacks, or 47,000 whites and 4,000 blacks.[151] Five years later, by the fall of 1963, the number of registered black voters was still only about 4,500.

In this picture, the black voter makes a poor showing when compared with his white neighbor. The reasons grew out of the South's pattern of racial segregation. There has been little political leadership among blacks, who have seen little use in participating in a political system where the voter's only choice was between two or more "white segregationist" candidates. Most blacks have been "severely disadvantaged in education and socioeconomic characteristics," and in the two communities of this study they comprise only a small part of the overall population.[152]

For many years also there was a strong effort throughout the South by whites to prevent or limit black registration. Little of this abridgment of black voter rights has been reported in recent years in the two Carolinas and none in the two communities of this study.[153] At the same time the overall scene in North Carolina has been much more favorable for

[150] U. S. Commission, *Equal Protection . . . North Carolina,* p. 27. See also Southern Regional Council, *Special Report,* p. 6.

[151] Percentages estimated on the basis of population and registration statistics can be found in Price, *The Negro and the Ballot,* pp. 72–73.

[152] See Ladd, *Negro Political Leadership,* pp. 91, 101, 277, 303–306; and Price, *The Negro and the Ballot.*

[153] See Ladd, *Negro Political Leadership,* p. 85; and U. S. Commission, *Equal Protection . . . North Carolina,* p. 46.

black voter participation than that in South Carolina, especially prior to the 1960s.[154] V. O. Key, in his classic study of southern politics, pointed out in 1948 that "Negroes have encountered stubborn opposition to even a gradual admission to the Democratic primaries in South Carolina," adding that prior to the federal court order outlawing the white primary that year, "virtually no Negro voted."[155] They were not barred from the state's Republican party, but it was so weak that it was not a significant factor in politics at that time.[156] North Carolina, however, "practices the doctrine of gradual enfranchisement. It is nowhere written into the regulations, but it seems to be the guiding principle of state authorities in their informal advice to local registration and election officials."[157]

Even with the abolishment of the white Democratic primary, the black vote in South Carolina and in Greenville remained relatively insignificant in size and effect.[158] As evidence of this,

[154] Ladd, *Negro Political Leadership*, pp. 27–43. In the 1960s there was considerable change in many parts of the South, including the two communities of this study, as the black vote increased to the point of being influential. For example, in the eleven states of the Confederacy, only about 1,000,000 blacks were registered in 1952. By 1962 the figure was still only 1,414,000, but by the fall of 1964 the figure had jumped to 2,250,000, and the black vote was perhaps the key factor in several states and communities in keeping the Democrats in power in 1964.

[155] Key, *Southern Politics*, p. 522. The white primary was declared unconstitutional in the 1944 Supreme Court decision *Smith* v. *Allwright*. It was four years, however, before the decision affected South Carolina. Then, in a heatedly debated trial, J. Waties Waring, a district judge and native South Carolinian, ruled that the state's Democratic primary was unconstitutional since it kept blacks from participating. Because of this ruling and his 1951 decision against school segregation in the Clarendon County case, Waring and his wife were harassed so much that he gave up his position and left the state. (See *ibid.*, pp. 621–32; and J. W. Peltason, *Fifty-eight Lonely Men*, p. 10.)

[156] Key, *Southern Politics*, pp. 288–89.

[157] *Ibid.*, pp. 650–51.

[158] Ladd, *Negro Political Leadership*, pp. 94–95, 303–306. In 1964 this picture began to change. As a result of a highly successful Negro voter registration drive that year, the number of black registrants in Greenville County almost doubled from about 4,500 to 8,000. That year, for

blacks have generally been excluded from both the local Republican and Democratic party organizations, and white political candidates have made only slight overtures, if any, toward local black voters. Less than 25 percent of the eligible black voters have been registered and only a small part of these have usually actually participated in elections. There are no all-black precincts in Greenville and none in which more than 40 percent of the registered voters are black, and local black citizens have not held elective office or occupied any policy-making positions in city or county government in this century.[159]

On a "potential political participation scale" used by Ladd in his study of "Negro political leadership in twenty-four major Southern cities," he shows Greenville as ranking near the bottom of the scale with regard to such factors as income, education, and job skills of blacks. Greensboro ranks highest among the cities on the same scale.[160] Ladd explains this difference by pointing out several factors already mentioned, and he adds that in the South Carolina community blacks are still "confronted with a denial by whites of the legitimacy of their electoral participation."[161] In North Carolina's Piedmont cities, such as Greensboro, quite a different race relations situation exists. Active black political participation is accepted by whites as quite "legitimate." He cites as evidence there the

the first time since Reconstruction days, a local black leader entered the race for the state legislation. He was defeated, but his bid for election added a significant new element to local politics. Also, that year, the black vote probably kept the Democrats from losing control of the county delegation. This may represent the beginning of a new period politically in Greenville, when the black vote may possibly become a balance of power factor.

[159] *Ibid.*, pp. 90–91, 101–102, 278, 303–304. In 1969, according to later interviews, a local black physician, Dr. E. L. McPherson, was elected to fill an unexpired six-month term on the city council. He was not re-elected.

[160] *Ibid.*, pp. 66–70.

[161] *Ibid.*, p. 279.

presence of black members on city councils, school boards, and various city boards and commissions.[162]

The political climate of the two communities during the 1900s has strongly reflected the state pattern in each instance. This has been true despite the facts that both Greenville and Greensboro by history, location in the Piedmont region, racial ratio population, and twentieth-century economic development have been much more similar to each other than to the "Old South" areas of either Carolina.

This means that Greenville has been caught up in the conservative, racially oriented climate of South Carolina politics. From the 1890s to the 1960s the "race issue" has overwhelmed all other issues. It has been used by almost every major winning political figure as an assured technique for vote getting during this period. A major factor in perpetuating this kind of climate has been the overwhelming influence in South Carolina politics of the rural, "black-belt" areas of the state.[163]

In North Carolina, Greensboro has been a part of the Piedmont industrial area which has exerted a major influence over state politics.[164] Here, elections have often been dominated by such issues as public education, industrial development, honest government, and a balanced state economy. This does not mean that racism has been forgotten. Potentially it has existed, sometimes becoming a vital issue, even as late as the 1960 and 1964 gubernatorial elections, but it has usually been overshadowed by other matters. This has helped to give the state a reputation of being moderate on the racial issue, a reputation which, in turn, has influenced the growth of business and industry, thus helping to strengthen support for a political climate of moderation.[165]

Both communities, as well as their respective states, have

---

[162] *Ibid.*, p. 280.

[163] Key, *Southern Politics*, pp. 130–31.

[164] *Ibid.*, pp. 205–206.

[165] See Key, *Southern Politics*, pp. 130–31; Nicholls, *Southern Tradition*, pp. 117–19; and *SSN*, December 1959, p. 9.

voted traditionally for Democratic candidates. There have been small Republican groups in each community, but until the 1950s and 1960s they were weak and ineffective. In recent years, with the civil rights issue often being the focal point for division and realignment, there has been considerable flux in the politics of both communities, particularly with regard to national elections. Richard Nixon in 1960 and Barry Goldwater in 1964 drew strong support from both places. Democrats have continued to take the lead in local and state races although there are indications that changes may be developing here, too.

LEADERSHIP

To study the process of desegregation in a community setting, it is important to know something of the forces of leadership and power which operate there. Of the various theories and concepts used to describe these forces, one of the most simple is Floyd Hunter's classic "pyramid" view in which there are various layers of power or leadership, dominated by one or more "top leaders." Another, more complex view is that of several power forces operating side by side, acting in various interrelationships at different times.[166]

This latter view seems to more nearly portray the power-leadership scene in both of the communities in this study.[167] As industrial and commercial centers, both have the strong influence of economic power. At the same time, such forces of power as organized politics, education, religion, labor, and the press must be given consideration, and the power of the black community cannot be omitted, although this often overlaps

[166] Floyd Hunter, *Community Power Structure*, pp. 60–113. See Edward Suchman et al., *Desegregation: Some Propositions and Research Suggestions*, pp. 21–31.

[167] See Ladd, *Negro Political Leadership*, p. 51, for comments on the leadership pattern in Greenville. Observations about leadership in Greensboro can be found in Tumin, *Desegregation: Resistance and Readiness*, pp. 149–70; and *GDN*, June 7, 1963.

with each of the other forces. As pointed out by Suchman, people high in these hierarchies have power or leadership corresponding to the strength of the institutions they represent.[168]

Economic Leadership

Economically, Greensboro and Greenville have many similar characteristics, as was pointed out earlier in this chapter. Both are industrial centers, predominantly textile manufacturing, and both are trading points for several surrounding counties. In such industrial-commercial areas, which are typical of much of modern-day America, one can expect to find "business power" as one of the dominant, if not the most important, power force according to Suchman.[169]

This view that "business and industry" represent the major power forces in both communities was expressed in one way or another by almost all of the local leaders interviewed for this study. There was some variation among the interviewees as to names of firms or individuals holding such power positions. At the same time, such names as Burlington Mills, Cone Mills, Jefferson Standard Insurance, Western Electric, and Vick Chemical appeared often in the Greensboro interviews. In Greenville the most frequently heard names were those of Daniel Construction Company and its top official, Charles Daniel, the Alester Furman family and its real estate-brokerage firm, and the Liberty Life Insurance Company.

In neither community does there appear to be as clearly defined a view of this "business power" as, for example, in Winston-Salem, another Piedmont area city, where three major firms "have dominated the economic and to a large extent the political life of the city."[170] On the other hand, Greenville has "a fragmentation of economic and political

---

[168] Suchman et al., *Desegregation*, p. 26.

[169] *Ibid.*, pp. 25–26. See also Hunter, *Community Power Structure*, p. 76.

[170] Ladd, *Negro Political Leadership*, p. 50.

power," which is the result of absentee ownership of many of its textile and other industrial firms, the lack of any large "consumer-oriented industries selling highly publicized national brands," and other factors.[171]

In Greensboro a somewhat similar situation exists in the realm of economic power. There may be more home ownership of industry than in the South Carolina city. However, the considerable diversity of leadership in the business world makes the formation of a tightly knit power structure, as in nearby Winston-Salem, difficult and undesirable.[172]

As one Greensboro editor described his city's leadership in 1963, "it does not have the kind of 'big mule' power structure of some Southern cities. . . . There is no one group which can press a button and produce miraculous cooperation." Then, in referring to a racial crisis facing the city at that time, he proposed that "the time, indeed, may have come when Greensboro's top executives in the business world should combine their leadership resources to assist the political leadership in meeting issues which can no longer be evaded."[173] This diverse pattern of leadership in Greensboro is indicated by the variety of persons selected as top "white leaders" by Tumin during his study of the city in 1957–58.[174]

Political Leadership

Political leadership in both communities has usually been the voice through which community decisions have been expressed. However, as several interviewees suggested, such de-

---

[171] *Ibid.*, pp. 51–52. Ladd contends that the Reynolds Tobacco and Hanes Hosiery firms, both of which manufacture national brand products and are major power forces in Winston-Salem, are very concerned about maintaining good public images and that they have helped to influence changes, such as desegregation, in Winston-Salem.

[172] From community interviews. See also Tumin, *Desegregation*, pp. 154–55; and *GDN*, editorial, June 7, 1963.

[173] *GDN*, editorial, June 7, 1963.

[174] Tumin, *Desegregation*, pp. 154–55.

cisions had the endorsement of economic leaders, and often the political expression was only implementation of decisions made by economic leaders.

This should have led to much more similarity in the pattern of racial change in the two communities. However, as pointed out earlier in this chapter and emphasized by several interviewees, the two communities are integral parts of states which have had quite different political leadership since 1900 or earlier. In North Carolina, Greensboro has been a part of the urbanized Piedmont industrial area, which with its low Negro population, its emphasis on economic development, and its concern for education, has exerted a dominant influence on state politics.[175] In South Carolina, Greenville is at the heart of a Piedmont industrial area which is similar in many ways to that in North Carolina. However, South Carolina politics since the 1890s have been dominated by the rural, former plantation, eastern area of the state, where townsmen and the remnants of an earlier landed aristocracy have been largely in control and where a large, often voterless, black population has influenced the mood of racism.[176]

In these contrasting state scenes, local political leaders in the two communities have tended to reflect the overall political mood of their respective states. Thus, Greensboro leaders have found it expedient to promote economic growth and development and to ignore or de-emphasize issues which might discourage new industries from moving there. A small but well-organized black vote in Greensboro has also helped to promote a tone of racial moderation in politics,[177] as well as to

[175] Key, *Southern Politics*, pp. 204–28.

[176] *Ibid.*, pp. 130–55.

[177] As evidence of the power of the local black vote and the danger in any form of political racism, several interviewees mentioned a 1962 election in which a longtime local Democrat leader lost his state senate seat to a Republican newcomer because the local black vote, ordinarily almost solidly Democratic, swung over to support the Republican. Interviewees accounted for this by citing a speech during the campaign in which the Democrat made remarks which offended local black leaders,

bring blacks a share in the community's political leadership.[178]

In Greenville, where industrial development has been a vital issue also, local political leaders have not appealed to racist sentiments in their public statements as much as political leaders from other parts of South Carolina, although until the early 1960s the degree of difference was often slight. As one interviewee explained it, the economic power structure in Greenville and the Piedmont area of South Carolina "saw little harm in the exploitation of the racial issue by political leaders until the early 1960s, when the economic losses of Little Rock, Birmingham, and other racial crisis areas shocked them into realizing that South Carolina was headed in the same direction. That was when the economic leaders took the political leaders into tow and the state's whole political climate began to acquire a tone of racial moderation."[179]

Black political leadership, and the black vote, in Greenville has been negligible. There are some indications that this situation is beginning to change slightly, but up to 1968 no black citizen held elective office in Greenville during this century and none occupied a position on any governing body in the city.[180]

Educational Leadership

Both communities have been looked on as educational centers in their areas. Each is a college center and the public school system in each is among the best and largest in their state.

Several interviewees in Greensboro thought the six local

---

who reacted by openly denouncing him and urging black voters to support the opposition candidate.

[178] There has been at least one black city councilman since 1951, and several other blacks have held local political positions.

[179] Variations of this view were expressed by several interviewees in Greenville. See also Ladd, *Negro Political Leadership*, pp. 73–74; and *SSN*, May 1963, p. 14.

[180] Ladd, *Negro Political Leadership*, pp. 94–95, 303–306.

colleges were influential in providing training for community leadership among both whites and blacks. They also credited the colleges with being helpful in preparing the community for social change. Ladd's study makes a particular point of the fact that it has been in communities having black colleges that the strongest civil rights leadership for change has come. He cites Greensboro as a good example.[181]

Some Greensboro interviewees said that the appointment of local school board members by a nonpartisan city council helped to provide the community with a more qualified and more liberal board, at least up to 1954. At the same time, most of these same interviewees expressed the view that school board members represented the city's economic power structure by being business or industrial officials themselves or because they had the stamp of approval of such leaders. Several of these board members in the early 1950 were described as being liberal on racial matters, a factor that was evidently acceptable at that time in a community which had a reputation for being "progressive and advanced in race relations." The appointment of a black member to the board in the early 1950s was seen by some as a move by leaders to help maintain this "good race relations" image.

In this setting, the school board, under the leadership of a superintendent who had been in his post for many years, acted with firmness and without hesitation in 1954 to endorse the Supreme Court ruling on school desegregation just as it might have acted regarding other educational advances.[182] There is also some indication that leadership for the 1957 off-the-record, tri-city conferences in Greensboro, Charlotte, and Winston-Salem came from the Greensboro School Board.[183] With the retirement of the superintendent and two of the "most liberal" board members a year later, Greensboro's

[181] Ladd, *Negro Political Leadership*, p. 195.
[182] *GDN*, May 19, 1954.
[183] Two school leaders in Greensboro expressed this opinion in interviews.

school leadership took on a conservative tone regarding racial matters and for several years afterward no progress was made in desegregation.

Greenville is also a college center, but its three colleges admitted "whites only" until 1965, and there is little evidence that the presence of these schools provided any substantial leadership for social change in the community. Furman University probably had some influence in preparing the local climate of opinion among whites for change in that it has been the training center for many local white public school teachers, Baptist ministers, and other community leaders. The complete absence of any black colleges "within 100 miles of Greenville" is credited as being a major reason for the lack of local black leadership.[184]

Greenville's public school system has been looked upon as one of the leaders in the state for many years in various "educational activities." This has been particularly true of its administrative officials. In fact, there is some reason to believe that two or more of the top officials were ready to begin school desegregation soon after 1954 if such action had been permitted by the board and by state law.

As for the school board itself, there is some indication that before the city-county school merger in 1951, the city board represented a "much more progressive" view on various issues than did the county board. After 1951 the seventeen-member elected board, representing city and county districts, spent much of its efforts on "equalizing" school facilities for blacks and whites.[185] Four or five of the members are reported to have favored desegregation some years prior to the board's change of policy in 1964. However, as one of them expressed it, "most of the board favored doing nothing about desegregation until we were forced to do so." There has never been a black member on the school board, although one ran an un-

[184] Ladd, *Negro Political Leadership*, pp. 195–96.
[185] Greenville School Board, *Minutes* (1951–54).

successful race for such a position in the 1950s. The weak political position of blacks in Greenville helps to account for this.[186]

L. P. Hollis, one local school superintendent, had retired by 1954. He had played a leading role in local and state educational development for many years and continued to be outspoken regarding racial progress as well as other school issues after his retirement. Hollis has been credited by some as being a key figure in bringing together community leaders to form the biracial committee in 1962–63 which led to desegregation of much of Greenville's public facilities.[187] Several Greenville interviewees labeled him as a "maverick leader" whose influence was based on his long years as a "respected and beloved educator" and his close friendships with local industrial leaders.

Religious Leadership

The forces of organized religion in the two communities are similar in that both are overwhelmingly Protestant and predominantly Baptist and Methodist. Among these forces, individual churches, groups of churches, and ministerial associations have often shown community leadership in combatting alcoholism, pornography, and obscenity in publications and movies and sometimes have taken the lead in dealing with mental health or other health or welfare problems.

So far as racial matters have been concerned, most religious organizations in both communities have been segregated throughout the 1900s. Annual one-day or one-week "brotherhood programs" represented the leadership in race relations of most such organizations prior to 1954 and often even afterwards.

[186] Ladd, *Negro Political Leadership*, pp. 66, 94–95, 303–306.

[187] *GP*, September 30, 1965. See also U. S. Commission on Civil Rights, South Carolina Advisory Committee, "South Carolina Cities Meet the Challenge" (unpublished report), August 1, 1963, p. 2.

In 1955 an interracial ministerial association was formed in Greensboro, followed by one in Greenville in 1962–63. The North Carolina group soon gave support to or sponsored various community desegregation efforts. The South Carolina one, however, adopted a policy of not getting involved in "controversial issues."[188]

Individual ministers and lay leaders in both communities have shown leadership over the years on race relations and desegregation. Some of these leaders have been members of the school board or other official boards. Others have been leaders in various community organizations such as civic clubs, civil rights and human relations groups, and social agencies. In both communities several white and black religious leaders have occupied positions on the local official or semiofficial biracial bodies. Individual black ministers have been among the chief black leaders in various activities in both communities, including civil rights.[189]

Overall, religious groups and leaders in both communities probably can be legitimately credited with helping to prepare the social climate for racial change, through their work in organizing human relations activities and through some emphasis on "moral values."

Labor Leadership

The forces of organized labor in both communities in this study, as in many other places in the South, have been so weak as to be hardly relevant in a discussion of community leadership.[190] At the same time, the threat that unions might be

[188] This stance changed somewhat in the late 1960s when the association became active in promoting a low-income housing program as well as in supporting school desegregation.

[189] Ladd, *Negro Political Leadership*, p. 238. In Greenville seven of the twenty-five blacks selected as local leaders by Ladd were ministers. According to interviewees, black ministers have been among the top leaders in civil rights activities in both places.

[190] For a good study of the textile labor movement and why it has been so weak in the South, see Glenn Gilman, *Human Relations in the In-*

organized has had a considerable influence in upgrading living and working conditions and wages of industrial workers in both Greensboro and Greenville.

On the national level the Textile Workers Union of America took an early stand in support of the Supreme Court's school desegregation decision. In Greensboro the local chapter, even though it was one of the largest unions in the city, had taken no official stand on the matter as late as 1958 "because its parent state body had not, and because its local position" was "too weak, organizationally, and in terms of member-ship." At the same time, because of some liberal leadership in the local union, its union hall was desegregated and it had "several Negro shop stewards representing both white and Negro workers in their plants."[191]

In Greenville efforts at union organizing have been largely unsuccessful, one reason being the strong opposition from local industrial leaders. One Greenville social scientist described local industrial leaders as being "far more anti-labor than anti-integration."

Leadership of the Press

The press in both communities was described by several interviewees as being part of the local power structure or at least as being the voice for local power leaders. In each com-munity the two daily newspapers, morning and afternoon, are owned jointly. At the same time, each of these newspaper firms owns or controls the leading local radio and television stations in their communities, so that there is a virtual mo-nopoly on news in each place.

In Greensboro both daily newspapers have reflected and

---

dustrial Southeast: A Study of the Textile Industry; and Ladd, Negro Political Leadership, p. 58.

[191] Tumin, Desegregation, p. 159. See also Southern Regional Council, Special Report, p. 9.

supported editorially the moderate to liberal view on social issues and racial matters which have prevailed in the North Carolina Piedmont urban industrial area. Both newspapers endorsed the 1954 Supreme Court desegregation ruling and supported the local school board in its statement at that time as well as the board's desegregation action in 1957.[192]

In contrast, the Greenville newspapers have faithfully reflected the views of South Carolina political leaders on racial and other social issues, at least since the early 1950s.[193] The *Greenville News,* edited by a member of the state's official segregation committee, gave strong leadership to the "absolute segregation" view until 1962–63, when state policy was altered to permit some desegregation. The *News* then became a strong "law and order" advocate. Both Greenville papers have strong "anti-union," "anti-federal government," and "anti-communist" policies.

Black Leadership

In many ways black leadership in such southern communities as the two in this study is interwoven with the various other leadership or power forces. At the same time there is a distinctly separate black "community" or "subcommunity" with its own leadership and power forces which are closely related to, if not determined by, racial issues.

The black population in Greenville and Greensboro is similar in size, but vastly different in accomplishment and leadership. This is due largely to factors such as income, education, job skills, and population distribution, as well as state and community race relation patterns. For instance, in Greensboro

---

[192] *GDN,* editorials, May 19, 1954, and July 24, 1957.

[193] From interviews. See also studies of the local press made by Alfred S. Reid, "Literature in Greenville," *Furman University Bulletin,* 7:124–25, November 1960, and "Recent Literary Developments in Greenville, 1959–1963," *Furman University Bulletin,* 12:24–30, November 1964.

18.7 percent of the blacks had some college education as of 1960, whereas in Greenville, the figure was only 5.1 percent. At the same time, 23 percent of Greensboro's black families earned $5,000 or more per year, while the figure was only 9 percent in Greenville. A relatively scattered black population in the South Carolina community has left it with much less political power than exists in the North Carolina city, where over 90 percent of the blacks live in one area.[194]

Because of this political power which Greensboro blacks have, a black leader has been on the city council since 1951 and several others have held positions on various city boards. In contrast, no black citizen in Greenville held any elective or appointive position in government in this century prior to 1969.[195]

Black leadership in both communities has come primarily from the professional groups, and the potential has been considerably larger in the North Carolina city as indicated by economic and educational information. Ministers, doctors, and lawyers have provided the bulk of this professional leadership.

In Greenville only one civil rights organization, the National Association for the Advancement of Colored People (NAACP), has been active for any length of time, and even it has been primarily an "umbrella" for individual leaders, groups, and actions. Several voter registration and political action organizations have had sporadic lives, and the Congress on Racial Equality (CORE) operated for a few months in the early 1960s.[196]

The absence of any black college facilities in the Greenville area, the scarcity of human resources, the rigid pattern of segregation, and internal disagreement are other factors which have helped to create a black leadership that has often been fragmented and ineffective.[197]

[194] Ladd, *Negro Political Leadership*, pp. 2–4, 55–56, 68–69.
[195] *Ibid.*, pp. 278, 280.
[196] *Ibid.*, pp. 108–109, 263–65, 270.
[197] *Ibid.*, pp. 197, 270.

In Greensboro civil rights action has been carried out under the leadership of several organizations, including NAACP, CORE, and the Greensboro Citizens Association. The groups sometimes operate jointly, but often independently. In the North Carolina city, there also has been considerable fragmentation of black leadership. However, the presence of three black colleges for many years, a fairly high educational and economic level among blacks as compared with other southern cities, acceptance of black political participation by whites, and the presence of a moderate racial climate in the overall community, plus factors already mentioned, have helped to create a situation in which black leadership has been encouraged to develop and to participate in overall community matters.[198]

SUMMARY

The two communities selected for this study offer a number of striking similarities as well as some strong contrasts in general background and in manner of reacting to social changes such as desegregation.

Located about two hundred miles apart in the Piedmont area of the Southeast, both are population centers for their respective states. Each has a population of about 125,000 in its "urbanized area" and both are county seats for "metropolitan area" counties of over 200,000 population each. The population is about 25 percent black in each community and about 99 percent "native born."

Both communities rank as leading industrial and trade centers for their states and for the Southeast, each having about 250 industrial plants and annual retail sales of $250 million or more.

Both are education centers in their states with several colleges and outstanding public school systems.

[198] *Ibid.*, p. 280; *GDN*, September 15, 1963; and Waynick, *North Carolina and the Negro*, pp. 87–92.

Both are strong religious centers, with over two hundred churches each. The religious population in each place is 95 percent or more Protestant and predominantly Baptist.

They have similar histories, having been settled in the 1700s by European Protestants, small farmers, and merchants. Neither was a strong plantation or slave-holding area. Both have some strong liberal elements in them.

However, there are strong contrasts between the two. Both have been strongly influenced by the political and social climate in their respective states. Greenville has reflected generally the racism which has pervaded South Carolina life and politics since the 1890s. Greensboro, on the other hand, has been a leading representative of North Carolina's more moderate approach to racial problems in a setting where economic and educational development of community and state have been emphasized to the curtailment of racism. As evidence of this, racial changes in the direction of desegregation came several years earlier and with less opposition in the North Carolina community. A specific example of this is seen in the Greensboro move to "voluntarily" desegregate public schools in 1957, whereas it was seven years later under court order that the first school desegregation occurred in Greenville.

Chapter II

GREENSBORO AND SCHOOL DESEGREGATION

REACTION TO *BROWN* v. *BOARD OF EDUCATION OF TOPEKA*

The immediate reaction by North Carolina political leaders to the Supreme Court's 1954 desegregation decision was described by the local press in Greensboro as follows:

> Governor Umstead today said he was "terribly disappointed" by the Supreme Court decision ruling public school desegregation unconstitutional. . . .
> W. Kerr Scott, former governor and candidate for the U. S. Senate, issued a statement saying he did not approve of the decision, but urged everyone regardless of race "to remain calm, and work together in an orderly fashion to avoid disruption of our pattern of school life. . . ."
> The reaction on the part of North Carolina legislators who could be reached was basically temperate. . . .[1]

Somewhat in contrast, the local reaction from city and school officials in Greensboro appears to have been positive, as reported by one of the local newspapers:

> Greensboro today appeared to be accepting the Supreme Court's invalidation of segregation in the nation's public schools in the mood of sober consideration that has won the city's race relations an outstanding reputation throughout the United States. . . .
> City and county educational and civic leaders . . . were seemingly unanimous in agreeing that North Carolina would abide by the high court decision, probably without resorting to legal subterfuges to circumvent the law. . . .

[1] *Greensboro Daily News*, May 18, 1954 (hereafter referred to as *GDN*).

Greensboro Public School Superintendent Ben L. Smith said, "It is unthinkable that we will try to abrogate the laws of the United States of America, and it is also unthinkable that the public schools should be abolished."

D. E. Hudgins, chairman of the Greensboro School Board, also declared that the City School System "will abide by the rule of the law."[2]

On the following day, May 18, the Greensboro School Board, at its regular monthly meeting, adopted a resolution recognizing "that the decision of the Court constitutes the law of the land and is binding upon the Board," and instructing the superintendent "to study and report to the Board regarding ways and means for complying with the Court's decision."[3] The resolution was adopted by a vote of six to one, the sole dissenter stating that he was not opposed to the content of the resolution but to its timing.

The board chairman, in introducing the resolution, said that it "would let the community, the state, the South, and if necessary the nation, know that we here propose to live under the rule of law." The school superintendent urged adoption of the resolution, stating that "there are certain officials in the South who have said that they will abolish the public school system if the decision of the Court should stand. That, I think, would be disastrous. Others have said that they will evade the law. That sort of thing is open defiance. Therefore, it could possibly be assumed that we might not abide by the decision. For that reason, you should adopt the resolution."[4]

The local press also gave strong endorsement to the Supreme Court's ruling, as indicated by its first editorial comments:

This is no time for demagoguery, emotionalism or political explosiveness. Rather there is a grave need for statesmanship, for

---

[2] *Ibid.*
[3] Greensboro School Board, *Minutes*, May 18, 1954.
[4] *GDN*, May 19, 1954.

perspective. . . . So far as North Carolina is concerned, the *Daily News* is confident that it will accept the opinion in the faith, the spirit, and the meaning of its deliverance, that statesmanship will assert itself, that we shall meet the problem as we have other trying problems in North Carolina, with fairness, fortitude and courage. . . . North Carolina has an unbroken record of never turning backward; and that record, we strongly feel, is not going to be shattered now. . . .

The Court's unanimous decision is grounded in the essential philosophy of the American system—the doctrine that all citizens are entitled to similar treatment before the law and that any infringement of these rights denies the spirit and letter of the Constitution. There will be many Southerners who deny the logic of this contention. As for the *Daily News*, we believe that the principle which the Court enunciates, under current conditions in the United States, is a valid one. The intangibles of public education cannot be made equal when division of pupils is based on race. . . .[5]

The next day the *Daily News* editors succinctly expressed that "we are faced with reality. . . . How one felt or what one did about segregation before May 17, 1954 has become relatively academic now. Segregation has been ruled out and the responsibility now is to adjust to that reality with a minimum of friction, disruption and setback to the public school system and our children." The editors commended the school board for its stand:

The Greensboro School Board followed a course of sanity and good sense when it adopted a resolution instructing its superintendent to begin a study "regarding ways and means for complying with the Court's decision." Every school board, we think, should move in the same direction.

We think, for instance, that a city like Greensboro may assume leadership in working out a formula for integration which could be a model for other areas. Here we face fewer tensions, fewer frustrations.[6]

The editors pointed out that "in a city like Greensboro, where the races are generally separated by residential loca-

5 *Ibid.*, editorial, May 19, 1954.
6 *Ibid.*, editorial, May 21, 1954.

tion, the proportion of Negroes to whites is not large, and the level of education of Negroes is fairly high, the problem will probably not be too difficult to solve, given time."[7] At least two major community organizations, openly endorsed the school board's action. They were the Community Council, representing most voluntary and United Fund-supported agencies in the city,[8] and the Jaycees.[9]

The school board's action, which was unique in the South, received widespread praise outside the region, as noted in the local newspaper:

Nationally and locally there has been a favorable reaction to the Greensboro School Board's resolution ordering a study of ways and means to end school segregation. . . . Editorials and news stories concerning the board action have appeared in newspapers from coast to coast. . . . In almost every instance the tone of the editorials has been enthusiastic.[10]

At the 1954 North Carolina Democratic Convention, the keynote speaker, Irving Carlyle, a leading attorney, was applauded roundly by the delegates when he observed that "as good citizens, we have no other course except to obey the law as laid down by the Court. To do otherwise would cost us our respect for law and order. . . ." The delegates then adopted a platform containing the statement that "we believe in the supremacy of the law for all citizens, and that the law must

[7] *Ibid.*, May 20, 1954.
[8] See Greensboro School Board, *Minutes*, June 21, 1954.
[9] *GDN*, May 21, 1954.
[10] *Ibid.*, editorial, May 26, 1954. It is interesting to note that of the three public school districts in Guilford County, all of which are funded by the County Board of Commissioners, only the Greensboro school district officials made a forthright statement supporting the Supreme Court ruling. The other two districts, represented by the Guilford County School Board and the High Point City School Board, both made statements saying in essence that they would wait to see what leadership state officials would give (see *ibid.*, May 28 and 30, 1954). High Point did not begin desegregation until 1959 and the county system remained segregated until 1964.

be enforced fairly and impartially. We condemn, without reservation, every effort of men, singly or in organized groups, to set themselves above the law."[11]

DEVELOPMENT OF RESISTANCE (1955–57)

It was three years later, however, before the Greensboro School Board actually began desegregation. Why the delay? What factors intervened to delay the action?

The restraining hand of state officialdom seems to have been a significant factor in discouraging any desegregation action by the local school officials. Two former school officials in Greensboro expressed such a view when interviewed by this researcher, one of them stating that "our board was ready to begin desegregation in 1954 or 1955, but we were told in a letter from a top state official that Greensboro could not move alone to desegregate but that we must wait until the state as a whole was ready to move on this issue."

This is in accord with off-the-record remarks made to the researcher by school superintendents in two other North Carolina communities. Both officials spoke quite critically of what one of them called "the effort of state officials to prevent desegregation as long as possible."[12]

An Associated Press writer within a week following the Supreme Court decision made a prediction that history has sustained:

Eight states seem prepared to accept the verdict. . . . The remaining nine are seeking ways to circumvent the ruling. . . . Apparently resigned to compliance are Kansas, Oklahoma, Texas, Arkansas, West Virginia, Kentucky, Missouri and Maryland. . . . In addition to Georgia, apparently willing to circumvent it are Louisiana, Tennessee, North Carolina, South Carolina, Mississippi, Virginia, Alabama and Florida.[13]

[11] *Ibid.*, May 21, 1954. See also *New York Times*, May 23, 1954.
[12] American Friends Service Committee, *Field Reports* (unpublished), 1959–64.
[13] *GDN*, May 23, 1954.

North Carolina's Governor Umstead offered no support for such actions as that taken by the Greensboro School Board. In a public statement two weeks after the Court ruling he was still talking about the "great strides made in equalizing public educational facilities" in North Carolina. He berated the Supreme Court for reversing itself and declaring segregation unconstitutional. He added, "In my opinion, the Court's previous decisions on this question were correct. The reversal of its former decision is a clear and serious invasion of the rights of the sovereign states. . . ."[14]

This negative attitude on the part of state officials was encouraged by the grave lack of leadership from national officials, especially President Dwight Eisenhower. Three days after the Supreme Court ruling a major wire service story, reporting on a White House press conference, stated that "President Eisenhower side-stepped giving any advice to the South on how it should react to the Supreme Court's ban on segregated schools today. At the same time he pointed to the temperate approach used by Governor James Byrnes of South Carolina as an example of a 'very fine statement'."[15] Eisenhower referred to the statement made by the governor on May 17, when he said, "I am shocked to learn that the Court has reversed itself. . . . I earnestly urge all of our people, white and colored, to exercise restraint and preserve order."[16]

Even the *Greensboro Daily News* lost some of its ardor and support for desegregation by the end of May, 1954. Its editors called Governor Umstead's attitude "a reasonable one, temperately stated," and they berated "these extremists on either side—the Talmadges and the NAACP," advising them to "remember the moderate views held by most Southerners" and warning that "they cannot be pushed too fast."[17]

---

[14] *Ibid.*, May 30, 1954.
[15] *Ibid.*, May 20, 1954.
[16] *Southern School News* (hereafter referred to as *SSN*), September 1954, p. 12.
[17] *GDN*, editorials, May 30 and 31, 1954.

Officially, the record shows that just a month after the Court decision, Greensboro's school superintendent reported to the school board "that because of the Court's ruling that it will hold further hearings in the fall and because of the recent action of the State Board of Education in establishing bi-racial schools for 1954–55, the only practical solution for Greensboro would seem to be to continue a bi-racial organization for the time being."[18] However, as the same official later reported at a conference of educators convened by the U. S. Civil Rights Commission, he began soon after the *Brown* decision to make some administrative changes and to carry on a personal campaign of school and community preparation for desegregation. Even though his statement was made in 1959, five years after the Court ruling and two years after pupil desegregation actually began in Greensboro, the following excerpts reveal the strength of character which he possessed and the leadership which he exerted in Greensboro. Many of the local leaders interviewed by the researcher corroborated Superintendent Smith's activities as he described them:

We began at once to make some changes. . . .
The reference in the handbook to biracial organization was eliminated. The schools were listed in the directory alphabetically instead of by races as had been done previously. Joint meetings of white and Negro principals and supervisors were now held regularly instead of occasionally as had been done prior to this.
I talked with individuals and small and large groups: principals, teachers, parents, ministers, lay citizens. I said over and over again that the decision had overthrown a long standing tradition, . . . that the decision was inevitable in the leading nation in a world where two-thirds of the population is colored, that the decision is law and there is no probability of its reversal nor of the adoption of a constitutional amendment to the contrary. I stated that I did not think the decision incompatible with the ideals of democratic government and the ideals of the Judeo-Christian religion. I pointed out that we were accepting desegregation in trade, transportation, the Armed Forces, in higher education, in sports, in entertainment,

---

[18] Greensboro School Board, *Minutes*, June 22, 1954.

etc.; and that more than 30 states had for years operated desegregated schools. I said that there would be disillusionment on both sides—it would not bring the millennium for the Negro, nor signal doomsday for the white. I pointed out that there were no precedents to follow, but appealed for the observance of law and order and said that a solution could be formed to the problem, however difficult, by the exercise of common sense, patience, and good will.[19]

On the state level, immediately after the Court ruling Governor Umstead asked the University of North Carolina's Institute of Government to make a study of the implications of the decision. The study results were reported in August, 1954, the stated purpose of the report being to review the "School Segregation Cases" and "the legal problems presented by some of the proposals for preserving the substance of separate schools within the framework of the decision."[20] Three possible courses of action were suggested for North Carolina:

1. It can take the course that the Supreme Court has made its decision—let it enforce it; and meet the Court's efforts to enforce it with attitudes ranging from passive resistance to open defiance.

2. It can take the course that the Supreme Court has laid down the law, swallow it without question, and proceed in the direction of mixed schools without delay and in unthinking acquiescence.

3. It can take the course of playing for time in which to study plans of action, making haste slowly enough to avoid the provocative litigation and strife which might be a consequence of defying the decision, avoid the possibility of friction and strife which might be a consequence of precipitate and unthinking acquiescence, and yet make haste fast enough to come within the law and keep the schools and keep the peace.[21]

[19] U. S. Commission on Civil Rights, *Conference on Education* (*Nashville, 1959*), p. 113.
[20] Albert Coates and James C. W. Paul, *The School Segregation Decision*, p. 1.
[21] *Ibid.*, p. ii–iii.

A U. S. Civil Rights Commission study, in commenting on this phase of North Carolina history, states that "there was never any serious thought given to the second choice of 'unthinking acquiescence'. The only question was whether to put the initiative on the Court, with 'passive resistance' or 'open defiance,' or to 'play for time'. As it turned out, the last course of action was adopted, with overtones of passive resistance."[22]

Upon receiving the institute's report, Governor Umstead immediately appointed an eighteen-member, biracial advisory committee to deal with finding a policy and a program that would "preserve the State public school system by having the support of the people."[23] Within six months this committee reported "that the mixing of the races forthwith in the public schools throughout the State cannot be accomplished and should not be attempted."[24] However, it urged that efforts be continued to try to find ways for the state to live with the ruling and maintain its school system intact. It recommended that the legislature set up a special committee for this task and that legislation be enacted to transfer all authority for enrollment and assignment of public school pupils from the State Board of Education to local school boards.

Governor Umstead died in the fall of 1954 and was succeeded by former industrialist, Luther Hodges. The newly inaugurated governor endorsed the committee report and recommendations and turned them over to the legislature. In April, 1955, this body established a continuing advisory committee on education under the chairmanship of Thomas Pearsall and enacted a pupil assignment law, transferring all authority for the enrollment, assignment, and transfer of pupils to local school boards. The new law did not mention the word "race" but suggested that local boards assign pupils on the basis of "the best interest of the child involved," the

[22] U. S. Commission on Civil Rights, *Civil Rights U.S.A.: Public Schools Southern States, 1962*, p. 64.
[23] *SSN*, September 1954, p. 10.
[24] *Ibid.*, February 1955, p. 14.

"orderly and efficient administration of the school," the "effective instruction of the pupils," and "the health, safety and general welfare of the pupils." The law included a provision permitting requests for reassignment and providing for local administrative and judicial appeals by individual applicants whose transfers might have been denied.[25]

When the new law was explained to a statewide meeting of 150 school superintendents, one schoolman was reported as commenting enthusiastically that "if this stands up [in court] it is all we need. Schools can continue as they are [segregated]."[26] The *Daily News* endorsed the law, calling this "a wise, moderate approach to a great problem, where saving the public school system is of gravest importance."[27]

On May 31, 1955, the Supreme Court issued its long-awaited implementation order regarding the 1954 desegregation decision. This follow-up ruling, containing the phrase "with all deliberate speed," required "that the defendants make a prompt and reasonable start toward full compliance" and remanded to the lower federal courts "the authority to enter such orders and decrees . . . as are necessary and proper to admit to public schools on a racially nondiscriminatory basis. . . ."

The decision, according to the *Greensboro Daily News*, "was warmly received by Southern leaders, who interpreted it as a means of indefinitely extending the touchy problem." Actually, as the newswriter expressed it, "the Court passed the problem back to school authorities and lower federal courts but specified that segregation end as soon as feasible." He explained that "opponents of racial integration viewed this as meaning long delays, perhaps years, would be sanctioned by the high tribunal if local conditions indicated a need."

[25] North Carolina General Statutes. 1955, Chapter 366. For a good discussion of North Carolina pupil assignment law, see U. S. Commission, *Civil Rights: Southern States*, pp. 65–67.

[26] *GDN*, June 25, 1955.

[27] *Ibid.*, editorials, June 23 and 25, 1955.

North Carolina political leaders seemed to agree that the decision offered no immediate threat to the state's equilibrium. As one legislative leader commented, "I don't think integration is going to prove either feasible or practicable in North Carolina. . . ."[28]

Somewhat in contrast, the editors of the *Daily News* viewed the ruling as creating "a more favorable climate of opinion . . . for working out the problem, . . ." adding that "there should be localities in the South with a not too large proportion of Negroes who yet have a reasonably good educational foundation, and such localities might well try the experiment of non-discriminatory schools."[29] In another editorial headed "Go Slow, But Go," the editors digested the school problem to one sentence: "The question now is this: Is the South willing to go at all?"[30]

In support of the new ruling, Greensboro's Superintendent Smith was reported as saying that "the directive was about what he had expected," and that on the basis of it, "integration can be accomplished peaceably and with good will." The chairman of the local school board was more cautious, commenting that "we still need considerable study, but I hope we can proceed in an orderly fashion. . . . The decision comes suddenly and at a time when plans are pretty well jelled for next year, but we will certainly give it most careful study."[31]

Within a few days, the *Daily News* applauded two other North Carolina school boards, those of Asheville and Charlotte, for their statements supporting the desegregation ruling and indicating a readiness to move toward compliance.[32] Concurrently, North Carolina's attorney general expressed the legal view that the state's "communities seem free to operate segregated schools during the coming year if they begin studies of

---

[28] *Ibid.*, June 1, 1955.
[29] *Ibid.*, editorial, June 2, 1955.
[30] *Ibid.*, June 4, 1955.
[31] *Ibid.*, June 1, 1955.
[32] *Ibid.*, editorial, June 10, 1955.

desegregation 'with dispatch'."[33] In accord with this opinion, a number of school boards, including the Guilford County School Board, appointed special committees "to study the effects of the Supreme Court's desegregation decisions."[34]

Three events related to the federal ruling evoked fanfare in North Carolina that summer and helped to point up the racial tension and poor communication between the races which existed, even in that "moderate" state. One was a civic club speech made near Greensboro by Assistant Attorney General I. Beverly Lake, who advised "every community in the state to be prepared to operate private schools to avoid integration." The *Daily News* was highly critical of the speech and the state NAACP leaders protested to the governor, calling for the firing of the official.[35]

Governor Hodges immediately defended his staff member by stating that "it is my intention to use every means at my command to retain for the State the services of this distinguished lawyer." However, he did not stop there. He unleashed an attack on the NAACP, declaring that "agitation for integration in the schools is being brought by a bunch of misguided white people in New York," that NAACP policies "are determined by its national office in New York," that it "does not actually represent any substantial portion of our Negro citizens," and that as for suits by the NAACP, "let them file. They will have to file suit against every school board in the state." In this same speech, he declared that the state would "seriously consider abolishing schools rather than integrate" and that steps had been "taken to prevent integration for this coming school year."

The governor was reprimanded for his remarks by at least one state political leader, who commented that "it is easy to fan the fires of prejudice and become a temporary hero. It's

---

[33] *Ibid.*, July 20, 1955.
[34] *Ibid.*, July 17, 1955.
[35] *Ibid.*, July 16 (editorial) and 17, 1955.

more difficult to be an educational statesman like [Charles] Aycock."[36] The *Daily News* held that it was

> a distinct disservice for anybody to stir up prejudice or project an extremism which makes settlement all the more difficult and costly for those whom it directly affects. . . . North Carolina cannot follow its announced middle course by catering to either extreme. . . . Somewhere within the bounds of moderation, of earnest study, of good will among men and the realization of our basic obligation to our children, North Carolina can and will work out a saving solution.[37]

The governor, evidently realizing that he had spoken too sharply and too quickly, made a feeble attempt to back out of his "school closing" statement by saying that North Carolina was "not yet ready to seriously consider abandoning public schools," but added that "this is a course of action which is and has always been available as a last resort." His parting comment, however, left no doubt of his feeling about such groups as the NAACP: "I do not propose to be forced around by pressure groups."[38]

The second issue which helped to expose the vast gap between the races in understanding of the racial issue was the plea for "voluntary segregation" which Governor Hodges and other white leaders began to champion but which was rejected openly by black leaders. The governor, in one of his first comments on the 1955 Supreme Court decree, declared "that the great majority of our citizens—both races included —prefer to keep our schools separate."[39] On August 8, 1955, in a statewide radio-television address, he called for support of the public schools, urging "voluntary separation" of the races. He appealed to "our Negro citizens" to "take pride in your own race by attending your own schools," adding a thinly

[36] *Ibid.*, July 18–20, 1955.
[37] *Ibid.*, editorial, July 19, 1955.
[38] *Ibid.*, July 20, 1955.
[39] *Ibid.*, June 23, 1955.

veiled threat that the state would make it very difficult for any citizens who sought desegregation.[40] At the annual meeting of the all-black North Carolina Teachers Association, he called upon its members "as educational leaders of your race" to either co-operate in maintaining a system of voluntary separation in the schools or be responsible for destroying the public school system. The teachers, in a strong reply, rebuffed the governor:

> We heartily endorse the Supreme Court decision. . . as being just, courageous and timely. All good citizens have a solemn obligation to abide by the law. As professional educators, our obligation in this regard is even more impelling. We do not now nor have we ever subscribed to voluntary segregation, but as good citizens we have abided by it because it was the law of our state. Now that the Supreme Court has ruled that this law is in conflict with the Constitution of the United States, it is our conviction that it is in conflict with our obligation.[41]

The *Daily News* accepted the "voluntary separation" plea, although its editors continually tried to balance their view with comments on behalf of "the Negro's aspirations and rights under the law."[42] The editors seemed to have some better understanding of the changed relations which had come about between the races since 1954 than did the governor and many other white leaders.

Historian Thomas Clark offers an interesting comment on these changes in *The Emerging South:*

> No longer did the Southern Negro come into the Governor's presence or into court as a suppliant defendent who waited for patriarchal justice to take its leisurely course. He now came as a militant plaintiff accompanied by a competent legal staff. . . . If not arguing his case in court he could draft effective resolutions

---

[40] *Ibid.*, August 9, 1955.
[41] *Ibid.*, August 27 and 28, 1955.
[42] *Ibid.*, editorials, June 17, July 21, and August 16, 1955.

setting forth his views and position in clear forceful language. It was a breaking away from the old tradition where a few Negroes met a few white intellectuals in discussions of the educational needs of the two races. . . .[43]

The third issue to stir racial feelings that summer was the filing of the first school desegregation suit in North Carolina. This occurred in a county west of Greensboro, in an area where black children had to travel a long distance to attend a segregated school. The attorney general at once announced that his office would assist the county school board in fighting this suit "in which Negroes are seeking to force admittance into the white public school system."[44]

In commenting on the case, the *Daily News* called for "a spirit of moderation on the part of Negroes and an absence of vindictiveness and coerciveness on the part of whites" and predicted that "where special hardships and the convenience of school patrons is involved, citizens on both sides may anticipate some desegregation." It urged that all school boards and state educational boards include black members, arguing that it was no longer satisfactory to have only one race make all the decisions.[45]

In the face of these developments, the Greensboro School Board, at its meeting in August, 1955, agreed not to make any immediate moves on the desegregation issue. They heard Superintendent Smith report that he had been "gathering all possible information relative to the desegregation order from the Institute of Government, *Southern School News*, etc. and that some local studies were being carried on." He told about a statewide meeting of schoolmen and state officials which he had just attended, and he suggested that "in view of recommendations made at that meeting and the circumstances in which we find ourselves at this time, it seems wise

---

[43] Thomas Clark, *The Emerging South*, pp. 197–98.
[44] *GDN*, August 16, 1955.
[45] *Ibid.*, editorials, August 17 and 19, 1955.

to continue a segregated system for another year." When one board member questioned whether this "could be considered a prompt and reasonable start in complying with the . . . Supreme Court's instructions to implement integration," the board chairman and attorney agreed that the action represented compliance and that the federal ruling "seemed to indicate that a year of study would not be out of line with the decree."[46]

Evidently still anticipating some early action toward desegregation, Superintendent Smith at a school board meeting in January, 1956, told a delegation of local black leaders that it did not seem wise to do any major repairs or altering on black schools until the issue of desegregation was settled. He pointed out that "if and when students go to their nearest school, the need for classrooms might be changed in some districts."[47]

By April of that year, however, state pressure to maintain segregation became evident with the publication of the Pearsall Committee's strongly worded official report recommending the authorization of tuition grants and the permitting of local option on school closing as a means to meet the school crisis. Excerpts from the report's conclusions follow:

1. We are of the unanimous opinion that the people of North Carolina will not support mixed schools. . . .

2. The saving of our public schools requires action now. . . .

3. The white race has been almost wholly responsible for the creation, development and support of an educational system which has been and is now educating the Negro children of the State, all of them. . . .

4. The educational system of North Carolina has been built on the foundation stone of separation of the races. . . .

5. The Supreme Court of the United States destroyed the school system which we had developed, a segregated-by-law system.

[46] Greensboro School Board, *Minutes*, August 16, 1955.
[47] *Ibid.*, January 31, 1956.

Our problem is to build a new system out of the wreckage of the old. . . .

6. The decision of the Supreme Court, however much we dislike it, is the declared law and is binding upon us. . . .

7. Defiance of the Supreme Court would be foolhardy. . . .

8. No Federal Court has said that there must be a mixing of the races. . . .

9. The Supreme Court has said just this, a law barring a child from a public school because of color and nothing else is invalid; but an administrative body may well find . . . that under existing local conditions it may not be feasible or best for a particular child to go to a particular school with children of another race. An understanding and tolerant Court may well recognize that difference. . . .

10. We believe that members of each race prefer to associate with members of their race and that they will do so naturally unless they are prodded and inflamed and controlled by outside pressure. . . .

The report concluded by recommending that the state's pupil assignment law be continued and that a state constitutional amendment be adopted which would authorize tuition grants for children who objected to attending desegregated schools and permit local communities to close their public schools if a majority of local citizens should so desire.[48]

Action on the report came quickly. A special session of the legislature was convened on July 23. The lawmakers were given the Pearsall Committee's report, plus a packet of proposed legislation to implement the report. These proposals were "the result of joint efforts of the Committee, the Governor's office, the Attorney General's office, the office of the Superintendent of Public Instruction, and members of the

[48] North Carolina Advisory Committee on Education, *Report to the Governor, the General Assembly, the State Board of Education, and the County and Local School Boards of North Carolina (April 5, 1956)*, pp. 1–14.

General Assembly."[49] The delegates adopted the proposed legislation and adjourned in four days—probably the shortest legislative session in North Carolina history.

The "Pearsall Plan," as the tuition-granting, local option school-closing plan came to be known, was debated extensively before being voted on in a special state election. Most political leaders endorsed the proposal, either because they believed in segregation, or because they valued it "as safety-valve, stop-gap, and time-buying legislation" as Irving Carlyle, a state political figure and opponent of the "Pearsall Plan," termed it.[50] He added that the plan "does not settle the legal problems of school segregation," but "it merely postpones the solution." School leaders were divided in their view about the proposal, and most of them were cautious about speaking their views publicly. In Greensboro, Superintendent Smith spoke openly against it.[51] At the same time, the Greensboro press endorsed the plan as "an honest and painstaking effort to walk a narrow path between outright defiance of the Supreme Court mandate and outright defiance of Southern folkways and customs." A local editor admitted that the plan had inherent dangers, but he added that "no wiser course of action has been proposed."[52]

On September 8, 1956, the state's voters approved by a four to one vote the constitutional amendments making the "Pearsall Plan" into law. The amendments were favored in every one of the state's one hundred counties, the total vote being 471,657 to 101,767, the largest voter turnout for a special election in North Carolina history.[53]

As political pressures to maintain a segregated school system mounted, the Greensboro School Board fell into line by abolishing all school area attendance lines as a legal safety measure and by appointing a special committee to formulate

[49] *Ibid.*, (July 23, 1956), p. 1.
[50] *Winston-Salem Journal,* December 1, 1956.
[51] *Greensboro Record* (hereafter referred to as *GR*), August 27, 1956.
[52] *GDN*, editorial, July 16, 1956.
[53] U. S. Commission, *Civil Rights: Southern States*, p. 69.

rules and regulations to comply with the requirements of the new legislation and the "Pearsall Plan."[54]

PRESSURES FOR DESEGREGATION (1956-57)

If the resistance to change appeared to be stiffening among Greensboro's white leaders, the reverse is true among its black citizens. In the fall of 1956, Omer Carmichael, superintendent of the Louisville, Kentucky city schools, which had desegregated successfully the year before, was invited to speak at a meeting of black teachers in Greensboro to describe the desegregation situation in his city.[55]

Also, by the time the "Pearsall Plan" became effective that fall, black parents in four communities in the central and western parts of North Carolina had unsuccessfully asked for the transfer of their children to white schools.[56] Before the end of the year, federal court suits had been filed by three of these groups seeking desegregation and challenging the state's pupil assignment law and the "Pearsall Plan," which one Greensboro newsman described as "the base of North Carolina's legal foundation to sidestep the . . . Supreme Court's desegregation mandates."[57] The stage was set, as this newsman predicted, for 1957 to be "a year of decision" in the state's "efforts to maintain racial segregation in Tar Heel classrooms."

One major aspects of each of these court cases as well as later ones was the attempt by NAACP attorneys to prove that state officials were responsible for the lack of desegregation

[54] Greensboro School Board, *Minutes*, June 19 and July 30, 1956.

[55] While Carmichael was in Greensboro, a special unpublicized meeting was arranged for him also with local white school principals and supervisors (see Greensboro School Board, *Minutes*, November 20, 1956).

[56] *SSN*, August 1957, p. 5; *GDN*, January 1, 1957. The school systems involved were Swain County, Montgomery County, Caswell County and McDowell County.

[57] *GDN*, January 1, 1957. For a discussion of each court case, see Southern Education Reporting Service, *Statistical Summary* (1963-64).

by local school boards. Thurgood Marshall, a national civil rights attorney and advisor in several of the North Carolina cases, made this accusation publicly in 1957, declaring that at least six communities had been ready to desegregate their public schools when the state stopped them by legislative action at the urging of the governor.[58] The accusation was included in a court appeal which cited as evidence several speeches by the governor urging "voluntary segregation" and warning Negroes of legal entanglements if they pressed for desegregation through the courts.[59] The accusation mentioned also a booklet defending segregation, entitled "The Segregation Problem in the Public Schools," which had been issued by the governor's office.

Other top officials were accused also of being involved in what black plaintiffs termed "the legislative and administrative design of the State of North Carolina, as expressed by legislative and administrative enactments and administrative orders, directives and utterances . . . to maintain the school systems of the state . . . on a racially segregated basis. . . ."[60] The state's education superintendent and his official board were accused of influencing local boards to resist desegregation and of conferring with the Pearsall Committee on various segregation policy matters. The Pearsall Committee was accused of having conducted a series of regional meetings in 1956 to advise local school boards about ways to maintain segregation, of having sent letters to all school boards advising discontinuation of any discussions on admission policies, and of having pledged advice and assistance to any school board facing a court test.

State officials replied to most of these charges in general terms, saying that under North Carolina law, no state agency had any power to tell any local school board how to deal with assignment matters and that therefore such charges were ir-

[58] *Winston-Salem Journal*, February 15, 1957.
[59] *GDN*, August 21, October 17, and December 23, 1958.
[60] *Ibid.*, August 21, 1958.

relevant.[61] The state's education superintendent denied that either he or his official board had given any advice on desegregation to local school boards.[62] The Pearsall Committee's chairman held that the committee had done nothing to prevent any local school board from beginning desegregation. He denied that the committee had sent letters to local school boards recommending inaction on desegregation matters, even though copies of such letters bearing his signature were presented in court.[63]

With regard to the state's desegregation policies, Harry Jones, director of the North Carolina Human Relations Council, commented as early as 1956 that his contacts throughout the state had led him to believe that there was "a willingness and a readiness on the part of many school boards to begin desegregating their schools in September, 1956." He chided the Pearsall Committee for trying to prevent local school boards from "honestly and sincerely attempting to formulate plans which will meet the requirements of the Supreme Court, but which will cause the least amount of friction and dislocation in the operation of their schools."[64]

This dissatisfaction with the status quo was expressed well by John H. Wheeler, prominent black business and civic leader, in a public speech in the spring of 1957:

Many North Carolinians felt that our state would be one of the first of the Southern states to move toward compliance with the decision

[61] *Ibid.*, January 15 and May 19, 1957; August 21, October 17, and December 23, 1958.

[62] *Ibid.*, January 15, 1957. This is in accord with a statement which the state's top education official made to a small group of human relations leaders in 1958 when he said that "education is the business of my department, and since desegregation is a political issue and not an educational issue, we have nothing to do with it." (As quoted from American Friends Service Committee, *Field Reports*, unpublished, 1958.)

[63] *GDN*, May 19, 1957; August 21 and October 17, 1958. In interviews by this investigator, two former Greensboro School Board members mentioned such a letter, but a top school official in Greensboro said that if any such letter was ever received by his office, he knew "nothing about it."

[64] *New South*, March 1956, p. 5.

of the Court. Those of us who were hopeful that this would be the case were not unduly alarmed that no real progress was made prior to May 31, 1955, at which time the Court handed down its decree indicating the manner in which the decision should be implemented. . . . Since 1955 however, it appears that pro-segregationist forces in North Carolina have worked with determination, and with some degree of success, to create a number of mechanisms or devices which may be used to slow down, or prevent entirely, integration of the races in our public schools.

Wheeler implied that any "legislative" devices would be "subjected to a full court test of their constitutionality." He added that "our Negro population has been educated to believe implicitly in the principle of equality," and "even now it is increasingly difficult if not impossible to convince a Negro citizen who has served in an integrated army . . . that he is anything less than a full-blown American citizen."[65]

The first court rulings on the cases attacking the state's "segregation policies" found the pupil assignment law and the "Pearsall Plan" to be "not unconstitutional on their face." State leaders praised these decisions as being endorsements of North Carolina's "moderate" approach to the school issue.[66]

However, many lawyers and state officials came to be convinced that some desegregation in North Carolina schools would be essential if the statutes were to continue to withstand legal tests, particularly as being constitutional in their administration.[67] This view was expressed aptly in an address before the North Carolina Bar Association by W. T. Joyner, vice-chairman of the Pearsall Committee:

Some mixing in some of our schools is inevitable and must occur. I do not hesitate to advance my personal opinion and it is that the admission of less than 1 percent, for example one-tenth of 1 percent,

[65] *GDN*, May 18, 1957.
[66] *Winston-Salem Journal*, March 26, 1957.
[67] *SSN*, August 1957, pp. 3, 5. See also U. S. Commission, *Civil Rights: Southern States*, pp. 72–73, for a discussion of this matter by Richard Day.

of Negro children to schools heretofore attended only by white children, is a small price to pay for the ability to keep the mixing within the bounds of reasonable control. One of the nightmares which besets me on a restless night is that I am in a Federal Court attempting to defend a school board in its rejection of a transfer requested by a Negro student, when a showing is made in that court that nowhere in all of the State of North Carolina has a single Negro ever been admitted to any one of more than 2000 schools attended by white students.[68]

BOARD ANNOUNCES DESEGREGATION POLICY (1957)

The first public indication that North Carolina's record of no school desegregation was about to be broken came in a news story in May, 1957. The story, uncovered accidently by a Greensboro reporter, told of a series of off-the-record joint meetings between officials and board members of three school systems—Greensboro, Charlotte, and Winston-Salem. The meetings, as one official described them, were for the purpose of discussing "mutual problems" such as "the segregation matter."

This announcement was followed by a fast-moving series of events. Within a few days an official of the Pearsall Committee, in a public statement, emphasized that local school boards "are on their own. . . . If they don't say so, they are mistaken or trying to shift the responsibility."[69]

On May 21, at its regular meeting, the Greensboro School Board routinely adopted three resolutions spelling out its assignment policy. The resolutions pointed up specifically the provisions of the state's pupil assignment law and "Pearsall Plan." This meant that the board would take no initiative to assign students except as it had been assigning them, but any student not satisfied with his assignment could seek reassign-

---

[68] *GDN*, October 26, 1956. This widely circulated speech was one of the items introduced into several court cases against school boards as evidence of the state administration's effort to maintain segregation.
[69] *Ibid.*, May 14, 16 (editorial), and 20, 1957.

ment by following certain procedures. It also indicated that if any desegregation should occur, any student not satisfied with being in a desegregated school could ask for reassignment to a school attended only by members of his own race. If a time should come when there were no "unmixed" schools, the segregationist student could, if he so desired, ask for a tuition grant to attend a private school.[70]

As one local editor assessed the school board's action:

> The stage is set for decisions which may be far reaching. On the one hand those decisions could ultimately test the validity of the pupil assignment act; on the other they could authorize some racial breakthrough in the public schools next fall. . . . The *Daily News* urges all parties to recognize the challenging nature of these decisions. . . . This is a time for statesmanship in Greensboro and North Carolina.[71]

The *Daily News* during the following weeks printed several editorials arguing in support of the necessity for protecting the "North Carolina approach," even if it meant beginning some school desegregation.

Black parents added impetus to these efforts. Even before the school board announced its revised policy, two black families notified Superintendent Smith that they wanted their children to attend "a white school" during the next school term. By the time the school board met in June, transfer requests had come from nine black students. The board postponed action on the matter until July even though an attorney representing four of the students urged an immediate decision and even though one white parent sought "early action so that he could ask for funds to send his children to a private school if the board should desegregate the public schools."[72]

The next meeting of the school board was July 23, the same date as that set for board meetings in Charlotte and Winston-

---

[70] Greensboro School Board, *Minutes*, May 21, 1957.
[71] *GDN*, editorial, May 23, 1957.
[72] Greensboro School Board, *Minutes*, June 18, 1957.

Salem. All three school bodies had received transfer requests from black students, as had the boards in Raleigh, Chapel Hill, Bryson City, Old Fort, and Mecklenburg County. Altogether, 128 black students had requested transfer to "white schools" in eight North Carolina school districts that year.

The Greensboro School Board met for what the *Daily News* predicted "may be the most important meeting in the history" of that body. About seventy-five spectators, including a few blacks, tried to crowd into the board's small meeting room but some had to stand outside and look through windows.[73]

The meeting was a turbulent one. A local attorney, speaking on behalf of "the Patriots of North Carolina and its thousands of members" spent forty minutes telling the board that it had "no right or obligation to force integration on the people." If it took such action, he declared, the board would be "vilified, condemned and cursed by millions of people in North Carolina and beyond." He was applauded noisily by most of the audience, particularly when he shouted, "If you board members want to mix with the colored people, do it yourselves. Go and live with them if you want to. . . . But don't force the rest of our people." The board then took up each of the seventeen transfer requests from white and black students, voted on each, and approved the transfer of six blacks to two previously all-white schools.[74]

In a prepared statement, the board chairman said, "Each board member has given much thought and prayerful study" to this matter and has acted in "support of the laws of the United States, as well as those of the State of North Carolina." He called for "the understanding and cooperation of all people

[73] *GDN*, July 21, 22, and 24, 1957. See also *SSN*, August 1957, p. 3.

[74] Greensboro School Board, *Minutes*, July 23, 1957. Of the nine transfer requests from black students which had been reported earlier, one was withdrawn, one was denied by the school board for "geographical reasons," and one which involved application to a "demonstration school" operated jointly by the school board and the Woman's College of the University of North Carolina was referred to the latter's officials for disposition.

whom we are conscientiously trying to serve." Two local religious leaders, a Protestant minister and a Jewish rabbi, asked to be heard before the meeting adjourned. Each commended the group for its action and expressed the view that "the ministers of the city would support the board in the stand taken."[75]

That same night, the school boards in North Carolina's two other largest cities—Charlotte and Winston-Salem—acted in concert with the Greensboro board. Charlotte voted to transfer five black students; Winston-Salem approved transfer for one.

As one national press service reported it, this was "the first break in racial school segregation in the Southeast." It added that prior to the North Carolina action, "almost 700 'Southern' school districts have desegregated since the 1954 decision," but all of them were located in the "border states."[76]

REACTION TO DECISION (1957)

The action of the three school boards was acclaimed nationally by numerous governmental and other leaders as evidence of North Carolina's "moderate approach." In the state, the chairman of the Pearsall Committee and the chairman of the State Legislative Committee on Education expressed the view that the move would strengthen the "Pearsall Plan" by showing that "we have nondiscriminatory laws, administered by local boards."[77] Other state leaders, including national representatives, refused to comment or gave evasive answers when queried by the press as to their reaction to the desegregation move.

Governor Hodges, who was away from the state on vacation at that time, issued a brief statement a few days later which said "in effect, that he neither approves or disapproves the

[75] *Ibid.*

[76] *GDN*, July 24, 1957. In Charlotte, thirty-five other applications were denied. In Winston-Salem, two of the three earlier requests were withdrawn before the board took action.

[77] *SSN*, August 1957, p. 3.

actions of the three school boards."[78] The *Daily News* was highly critical of the governor for his "disinclination to comment . . . on the decisions." As one editor expressed it, the governor "must realize that what concerns every community in the state concerns the state; that these three communities which have acted cannot be isolated or abandoned; that local officials are entitled to support for what they have done in accord with their oaths of office. . . ."[79]

The chairman of the Greensboro School Board was quite pointed in his remarks on the opening day of school: "We felt a statement from the governor would have been helpful," but "to my knowledge, the board received no encouragement" from him.[80]

It might be said that the governor gave aid and comfort to the opposition, not only by his refusal to give any support to the Greensboro or other two school boards in their desegregation effort but by his statements in two speeches on the eve of school openings that fall. In a press interview he declared that he did not favor integration but would defend law and order.[81] During a nationwide radio-television address he renewed his earlier plea for "voluntary segregation" and criticized those "few Negro citizens who have refused to go along" with this idea. "Can these few citizens seriously believe," he asked, that "they are helping remove any real or fancied stigma from their race by placing their children in schools formerly attended only by white children? Do they not know that court decisions cannot make or re-make a society? Where are the Negro leaders of wisdom and courage to tell their people these things? Have they none?"[82]

---

[78] *GDN*, July 25 and 26, 1957.
[79] *Ibid.*, editorials, July 27 and August 10, 1957.
[80] *Ibid.*, September 4, 1957.
[81] *Ibid.*, editorials, July 26, August 30, September 1 and 5, 1957.
[82] *Ibid.*, September 4, 1957. See American Friends Service Committee, *Staff Notes*, (unpublished), 1958–59. Governor Hodges maintained this rather typical "southern" stance as long as he was in office. When the "lunch-counter movement" of 1960 developed, he was outspoken in criticizing it. A large restaurant which he owned near Raleigh was one

Also on the state level, Beverly Lake, former state official who had become the chief spokesman for the segregationist forces in North Carolina, denounced the action of the three school boards.[83]

LOCAL OPPOSITION ACTIVITIES (1957)

Aside from the criticism expressed or implied by some state leaders, the Greensboro School Board was soon faced with local opposition. Official reports concerning this period have de-emphasized such factors.[84] However, if one reads the day-to-day press and other on-the-scene accounts, keeping in mind the general southern scene of the summer and fall of 1957, a picture of a very tense and troubled community emerges.

Numerous incidents of intimidation, reprisal, and violence relating to racial matters occurred in other parts of North Carolina and the South earlier that year, several being related directly to school desegregation. Only a few months earlier the high school in Clinton, Tennessee, had been bombed. As the 1957 fall term began, a school in Nashville, Tennessee, was bombed, and the Little Rock, Arkansas, school crisis erupted, with all its tragedy and brutality.[85]

In North Carolina, activities of the White Citizens Council,

---

at which a number of demonstrators were arrested. However, when he became the secretary of commerce under President John F. Kennedy, he spoke as openly for desegregation as did any of the Kennedy team. In a 1959 conference with this investigator and several North Carolina human relations leaders, Hodges commented: "Gentlemen, I suspect that personally I am about as liberal as any of you on this racial matter, but I am in politics and I can't afford to express such views. If the time comes that I leave politics or the political climate changes, and I feel free to express liberal views, I will do so."

[83] GDN, July 25, 1957.

[84] U. S. Commission, Conference on Education (Nashville, 1959), pp. 107–108, 114. See also U. S. Commission, Civil Rights: Southern States, pp. 73–74.

[85] See Southern Regional Council, Intimidation, Reprisal and Violence in the South's Racial Crisis; SSN, September and October, 1957.

the Patriots of North Carolina and the Ku Klux Klan were widespread. All three groups existed in or near Greensboro in 1957. These organizations, or their members, in all probability instigated a series of acts opposing desegregation, beginning with the meeting at which the school board made its decision to desegregate and continuing through several months.

At the July meeting of the board, as already noted, an attorney for the Patriots group spoke vehemently against the decision. A few days later a group of white parents, represented by this same attorney, filed a local court suit against the board seeking an injunction to stop the desegregation move. A hearing in the County Superior Court was set for August 29, just four days before the fall term of school was to begin.[86]

At a regular school board meeting on August 21, a local segregationist spokesman appealed to the officials not to fight the court action, declaring that the suit had the approval of "the majority of the patrons of the Gillespie School," one of the schools scheduled to be desegregated the following month. The board's reaction was to reaffirm its desegregation decision.[87]

When the case came up in court, the injunction was denied on the grounds that the board had acted legally and in good faith with state and federal laws.[88] The white parents appealed the case to the State Supreme Court but lost again.[89] A similar unsuccessful effort to block desegregation in Charlotte was made by the Patriots group there. The *Daily News*, which had criticized the injunction effort, commended the judges in Greensboro and Charlotte for upholding the constitutionality

[86] *GDN*, July 24, August 4, 13, and 29; September 18, 1957. See also U. S. Commission, *Civil Rights: Southern States*, p. 74.

[87] Greensboro School Board, *Minutes*, August 21, 1957. See also *GDN*, August 22, 1957.

[88] *Race Relations Law Reporter*, 2:967–69; October 1957. See also *GDN*, August 30, 1957.

[89] *Race Relations Law Reporter*, 3:174, February 1958.

of the "Pearsall Plan" and North Carolina's "course of moderation and good sense."[90]

In other opposition action, a mass drive was made to get white parents to transfer their children away from the Gillespie School. Mimeographed letters, including directions and a blank form for seeking transfer, were circulated widely in the school area. Even though no person or group was publicly identified as sponsoring the drive, the local press reported that representatives of the Patriots were holding meetings in the area and were known to have requested and obtained a list of patrons of the school.[91] Probably as a result of this drive, the parents of 20 of the 515 white children enrolled at the school requested their transfer to an "all-white school." Before the school year ended, six of these students asked to return to Gillespie and one of them commented that he had not wanted to leave it in the first place but that his parents had insisted that he do so.[92] It was not reported until later, but 18 white students transferred to Gillespie that summer, even though they knew it was to be desegregated.[93]

About the end of July, John Kasper, a roving segregationist agitator and organizer who had been involved in the Clinton, Tennessee, violence, announced that he planned to visit North Carolina to aid in stopping desegregation. The state's leading newspapers, the governor, and school officials decried this suggestion. Even the local leaders of the Patriots voiced strong disapproval of such a visit, saying it "would result in great harm to the cause of segregation."[94]

On August 31, Kasper arrived at the Greensboro Courthouse

[90] *GDN*, August 30 and 31 (editorial), 1957.

[91] *Ibid.*, August 28, 1957.

[92] Herbert Wey and John Corey, *Action Patterns in School Desegregation*, p. 124. See also U. S. Commission, *Conference on Education* (*Nashville, 1959*), p. 114.

[93] U. S. Commission, *Conference on Education* (*Nashville, 1959*), p. 114.

[94] *GDN*, July 27 and 28; August 25 and 26; and September 1, 1957.

where he spoke to an audience of about three hundred for more than two hours on the evils of "race-mixing" and the "low" action of the school officials. Later, in a local meeting of the White Citizens Council, which included students and adults, he urged the adoption of "a campaign of terror against Negro students attending previously all-white schools and a program of harassment against members of the Greensboro School Board." Kasper advocated various student activities such as spilling ink on the books of the black students, elbowing them in school corridors, writing slogans such as "Nigger go home" on school walls, or picking fights with the black students. For the adults, he urged them "to act so as to cause nervous breakdowns, heart attacks and suicide" among the school officials. "If you work on the night shift," he suggested, "pick up the telephone and send a Negro cab to their house. Order a bunch of merchandise from some Jew department store. . . . Send them flowers from one member to another. Call up the undertaker and send him out there."[95]

Many of these and even worse harassing tactics were carried out against the school superintendent, the board members, and several black students during the next few months. A number of anonymous telephone calls and letters, including threats on their lives, were received by the superintendent and several board members. Crosses were burned at Gillespie School and the superintendent's home, and windows were smashed at the superintendent's home several times. Other harassments which one or more of the school officials reported later were the finding of unwanted or unordered taxis, coal and oil, termite exterminators, ambulances, fire equipment, and police at their homes at all hours of day or night.

In commenting later on the Greensboro desegregation experience, the superintendent expressed the view that "as was expected and as will always happen, the superintendent of

[95] *Ibid.*, September 1, 1957.

schools, principal of the school where integration takes place, and the board of education bear the impact of the opposition."[96]

Others were harassed, however. Several black families whose children had been transferred to previously all-white schools reported receiving anonymous telephone calls, sometimes threatening, often insulting, and frequently late at night. An unidentified nighttime explosion in the yard of one black family splattered the front of its house with mud and debris but did not harm anyone.[97] The six black students themselves received many harassments in the form of taunts, jeers, and other heckling from a few fellow students for several months after school opened. There was little or no reported violence directed toward them except for three instances when eggs were thrown during class at the lone black girl at the senior high school.[98]

LOCAL SUPPORT FOR DESEGREGATION (1957)

Despite opposition to the Greensboro School Board's decision, there was also strong community support for the desegregation move, or at least for law and order. This came from the press, religious leaders and groups, human relations and civil rights groups, some civic groups, law enforcement officials, and many parents and students.

The *Daily News* editor called the action "a courageous and sensible one," saying the three boards had "acted after long months of study and deliberation among their joint memberships, with other school officials on the state and local level and after due consideration of other alternatives facing them." The paper added that "nobody can foresee how these experi-

[96] *Ibid.*, August 29 and 30; September 10, 1957. See also U. S. Commission, *Conference on Education (Nashville, 1959)*, pp. 107, 114; and Wey and Corey, *Action Patterns in School Desegregation*, p. 159.

[97] American Friends Service Committee, *Staff Memos* (unpublished), 1957; *SSN.* November 1957, p. 13.

[98] *GDN*, September 16 and 17, 1957.

ments will work. But they do proclaim to the world that North Carolina at least will try to take a first step toward complying with the law of the land." In justifying the action, the editor gave weight to the view that "at the core of the decision" was the belief that "some racial breakthrough somewhere in the state" was necessary to bolster the legal survival of the "state's assignment plan."[99]

The city's other newspaper, the *Greensboro Record,* also commended the board, saying that its action reflected "a sincere purpose to comply with the law of the land in a manner which will . . . recognize . . . social and political factors involved."[100]

The Greensboro Ministers Fellowship, an integrated group of most religious leaders in the city, commended the board for its action and called for "the good people of Greensboro to stand behind the school board in its policy regarding the admission of students to our schools without distinction of race or color."[101] Several leading ministers and church groups encouraged the board in its action and pledged support through their churches.

Other local groups or leaders expressing approval of the policy change were the Greensboro Community Council, a coordinated body representing many of the city's volunteer and nonprofit organizations;[102] the city's Council of Parent Teacher Associations, Greensboro Interracial Commission; and local NAACP leaders.[103]

Greensboro police officials did not make a public statement,

---

[99] *Ibid.,* editorial, July 24, 1957.

[100] *GR,* editorial, July 24, 1957.

[101] *GDN,* July 25, 1957.

[102] Two of these leaders are quoted in the Greensboro School Board, *Minutes,* July 23, 1957. Mention of "several churches, ministers and congregations" which "encouraged the Board to accept the pupils" was made by a Greensboro official in an off-the-record interview in June, 1957, as reported in American Friends Service Committee, *Staff Memos* (unpublished), 1957.

[103] See Wey and Corey, *Action Patterns in School Desegregation,* pp. 25, 30; *GDN,* September 30, 1957.

per se, but in various ways gave indication of a determination "to preserve law and order" in the community.[104]

State or other organizations which issued statements commending the school officials in Greensboro, Charlotte, and Winston-Salem and pledged the support of their local groups and members included the North Carolina Association of Rabbis (the state chairman lived in Greensboro), the American Friends Service Committee (regional office located in Greensboro), the North Carolina Council on Human Relations,[105] and the North Carolina Council of Churches.[106]

Major newspapers throughout the state commended the board's decision, but most of them did so on the premise that such action was necessary to "protect the schools."[107]

PREPARATION FOR DESEGREGATION

Many of these same supportive institutions, groups and individuals played a significant role, along with school officials and staff, in preparing the Greensboro community for the beginning of school desegregation.

Community Preparation

The two local newspapers, the *Greensboro Daily News* and *Greensboro Record*, besides commending the school board for its "courageous and sensible" action, carried a series of editorials for several weeks before and after the actual decision, in what has been described as an effort to create as favorable a community climate as possible for the acceptance of school desegregation.[108] They presented first the legal necessity for

---

[104] U. S. Commission, *Conference on Education* (*Nashville, 1959*), p. 105. See also American Friends Service Committee, *Staff Memos* (unpublished), 1957.

[105] Southern Regional Council, *Special Report on Charlotte, Greensboro and Winston-Salem*, September 1957, p. 9.

[106] *GDN*, January 30, 1958.

[107] *SSN*, August, 1957, p. 5.

[108] *Ibid.*, p. 3.

making the move to protect the state's pupil assignment law and the "Pearsall Plan." After the board's decision was announced, the newspapers emphasized the need for law and order, pointing out the moral, ethical, religious, and educational values in the decision.

The Greensboro Ministers Fellowship, in a statement urging "the good people of Greensboro" to support the desegregation move, gave official voice to the attitude of many of the city's religious leaders.[109] There are no reports available on the extent of preparation for school desegregation which went on within the churches. Annual brotherhood programs had been conducted for several years by the Greensboro Interracial Commission and the Ministers Fellowship.[110] From interviews conducted in the summer of 1957 with local leaders, it seems likely that in most of Greensboro's leading churches there was at least assent to the desegregation move and that several churches had "prayers for peace and brotherhood." In some of the churches sermons supported the action and discussion groups were held for youth and adult groups on "how to make the transition a successful one."[111]

The school superintendent gave credit for much of the city's acceptance of desegregation to "the liberal views of the Friends Society of which there are many members" and "the Jewish element that numbers many of Greensboro's leading businessmen and civic-minded citizens."[112]

Preparation by School Officials

The Greensboro school officials and staff carried on preparation activities of various kinds both within the school system and in the community. The school board itself began to prepare

---

[109] *GDN*, July 25, 1957.

[110] See *Minutes* of the Greensboro Interracial Commission, 1950–60.

[111] American Friends Service Committee, *Staff Memos* (unpublished), 1957. Interviews by this investigator in 1964–65 with community leaders help to corroborate this data.

[112] U. S. Commission, *Conference on Education* (*Nashville, 1959*), pp. 106, 114.

for eventual desegregation as early as 1954, as noted in its statement accepting the Supreme Court's *Brown* decision and instructing the superintendent to begin a study of how to implement the decision locally.[113] During the next three years, the school leaders sought to keep up with developments related to desegregation, as the superintendent reported to the U. S. Commission on Civil Rights. As his report states, "We listened to speeches for and against desegregation. We read everything that came to hand on the question: books, news releases, magazine articles, special leaflets and pamphlets, *Southern School News,* laws, court decisions, etc. We talked with many people who were either for or against the idea of desegregation."

Among those with whom they talked were school officials from two cities which had successfully desegregated—Louisville, Kentucky, and Baltimore, Maryland. In off-the-record meetings with Greensboro school officials and staff the Kentucky and Maryland school leaders discussed the desegregation experiences in their communities.[114]

Even though Superintendent Smith's full statement may be correct, there appears to have been little more than occasional mention of desegregation at official meetings of the Greensboro School Board from June, 1954, until applications for transfer were submitted by nine black students in May and June, 1957. One board member, who joined the official body in 1955, reported in an off-the-record interview in late 1956 that the issue had received very scant attention during his tenure and he really didn't know how various other board members stood on it.[115]

[113] Greensboro School Board, *Minutes,* May 18, 1954.

[114] U. S. Commission, *Conference on Education (Nashville, 1959),* pp. 113, 114. The visit to Greensboro by Omer Carmichael, Louisville's school superintendent, was officially under the auspices of the North Carolina (Negro) Teachers Association (*GDN,* November 14, 1956). While he was in the city, an off-the-record dinner meeting was arranged for him with white principals and supervisors of the local schools (Greensboro School Board, *Minutes,* November 20, 1956).

[115] American Friends Service Committee, *Staff Memos* (unpublished), 1956.

Other preparation which took place within the school system, as reported later by the superintendent, included "workshops on human relations . . . for school personnel," "lessons on 'children of good will' " for pupils, and parent-teacher meetings in which human relations was emphasized "in nearly all the schools."[116]

The only workshop for school personnel on which reports are available was an off-the-record one in May, 1957, sponsored jointly by the American Friends Service Committee and the Greensboro Interracial Commission. The local school officials declined to participate officially but gave approval for teachers or principals to attend voluntarily. The one-day workshop was led by a visiting human relations specialist, and included resource persons from schools in Kentucky and Washington, D. C., where desegregation had occurred.[117] It was attended by an interracial group of thirty teachers from thirteen Greensboro schools, as well as representatives from the local Parent Teachers Association and North Carolina Teachers Association.

At a meeting of the city's school principals and supervisors in August, 1957, the superintendent urged them to "support the policies and position of the Board of Education" and to "withhold adverse comment on the recent board decision" to desegregate. Any "who cannot support these policies," he said, "should sever their connections with the city school system."

To emphasize the role of the school principals and supervisors he told them they were "neither law makers nor policy setters," but added that the principals had a duty to "keep the peace, obey the laws and preserve the schools." In conclusion, he praised the principals and teachers of the two

---

[116] U. S. Commission, *Conference on Education* (*Nashville, 1959*), p. 113.

[117] "Report of the Development of a Seminar on School Desegregation for Teachers in Greensboro, North Carolina" American Friends Service Committee, *Staff Report* (unpublished), 1957. The workshop director was Dan W. Dodson, Director of the Human Relations Center, New York University.

schools to be desegregated for showing "a high sense of duty and finest judgment."[118]

When a principal of one of the desegregated schools was asked about his policies, he commented that "no time will be lost as a result of integration; there will be discipline." Later he emphasized this need for firmness as a primary requisite in the early stages of desegregation, saying that without it failure was likely in many of the "touchy" situations that might arise.[119]

This policy of firmness was adhered to by the school board once it made the decision to desegregate. And when local segregationists were trying to stop the board's move several weeks before the opening of school, one official commented that nothing short of a court order would interfere with the decision to desegregate the local schools.[120]

Another preparatory step was the school system's policy "for several years before desegregation began," of hiring, insofar as possible, only teachers who had "no strong opposition" to teaching in a desegregated situation.

Preparation by Police Officials

A few days before the fall school opening, Governor Hodges made a major radio-television appeal for "law and order" as being the "North Carolina way." At the same time he re-emphasized his own belief in segregation, but conceded that "orderly processes and obedience of the law are other matters."[121]

On the local level police officials did not express their views on desegregation, but they made careful and extensive preparation for the change, envisioning their job as being the maintenance of a firm policy of law and order. Evidence of this

---

[118] *GDN*, August 24, 1957.
[119] Wey and Corey, *Action Patterns in School Desegregation*, p. 164–65.
[120] *GDN*, August 22, 1957.
[121] *Ibid.*, editorial, September 1, 1957.

can be drawn from reports of how they handled numerous situations related to the opening of school, the meetings held by segregation groups and the several reported instances of violence before and after school opening. In the immediate areas around the two desegregated schools full-time traffic officers were kept on duty from 7 A.M. to 5 P.M. for several weeks and patrol cars cruised on a twenty-four-hour basis, policemen in street clothes attended every meeting held by segregationist groups in order to learn of their plans, and a close liaison was maintained constantly with school officials.[122] The police chief urged that "any parent or pupil" who might "be molested" should "report the incident to the teacher of the pupil, the school principal or the police," and that, "under no circumstances" should parents or pupils attempt to settle the matter themselves.[123]

DESEGREGATION BEGINS (SEPTEMBER, 1957)

Despite the preparation for desegregation and the support for it from various groups and individuals, there was considerable tension in Greensboro as the date for school opening approached in the fall of 1957. The fanning of the flames of race hatred by Kasper's visit, the announcement of threats against the school officials, the anxiety surrounding the court appeal to stop desegregation—all occurred within a week before school opened. These events, plus similar ones in nearby Winston-Salem and Charlotte where desegregation was also scheduled to begin, plus the rising tide of violence and potential violence in other southern crisis areas such as Little Rock and Nashville impelled Governor Hodges at last to move out of his "neutralist corner" and speak up for law and order. He declared that "we will not tolerate any lawlessness or

---

[122] Wey and Corey, *Action Patterns in School Desegregation*, pp. 6, 40, 192–25, 201.

[123] American Friends Service Committee, *Staff Reports* (unpublished), August 1957.

violence" in connection with the school desegregation issue, but in almost the next breath he renewed his appeal for "voluntary separation of the races."

For several days consecutively before the school opening date both Greensboro newspapers had editorials calling for law and order. As one editorial writer stated, "There is no place for demagoguery, incitement or violence in North Carolina." Later, he added, "The *Daily News* has sufficient confidence in the people of our community and state to believe that the test will be met. We have in Greensboro and in North Carolina a levelheaded, common-sense and fair-minded citizenry. They believe in education and they are law-abiding. . . ."[124]

The opening for Greensboro's thirty-two elementary and junior high schools was set for September 3, one day earlier than that in the other two North Carolina cities—Charlotte and Winston-Salem—which were scheduled to begin desegregation that fall.

The Greensboro opening received national and international news coverage. An estimated twenty to twenty-five newspaper and magazine reporters, photographers, newsreel and television men were on hand from most of the major news services to record in detail the first desegregation at a public school in the southeastern United States.

Also on hand at the Gillespie Park School that morning was a crowd, mostly white, estimated at 100 to 250 people. Some of the onlookers were undoubtedly from the school's 500-member student body. Others in the crowd were probably curiosity seekers. On hand, however, were several recognized leaders of the White Citizens Council, the Ku Klux Klan, or the North Carolina Patriots.[125] Unknown to most, several plain-clothes men were in the crowd, while twenty additional

---

[124] *GDN*, September 1, 3, and 4, 1957.

[125] *Ibid.*, September 4 and 5, 1957. Later the police chief and the school's principal were quite critical of the media representatives, saying that their presence tended to create incidents and confusion and to encourage the opposition groups who were seeking publicity (See Wey

policemen were on emergency standby two blocks away.[126] As the press reported the event, "there was no violence . . . but hecklers taunted the Negro children with epithets" as they walked into school and several hecklers followed the students into the hallways of the building. At one point the police chief appeared and escorted the segregationist leaders off the school grounds.

Four of the five black students arrived together in one car and were accompanied across the school grounds by a police officer in street clothes. The fifth student arrived and entered the building a few minutes later, accompanied by his father.

The newsmen were told by the police chief that they must leave the school grounds after the students entered the building. As they left they were heckled too, as "a bunch of 'nigger lovers'."

The following day seventeen-year-old Josephine Boyd became the first black student to desegregate an all-white public high school in North Carolina and the Southeast. Along with 1,920 white students she enrolled and attended classes, as the *Daily News* reported it, "without incident" at Greensboro Senior High School. The paper reported that "students appeared to be curious but there were no catcalls or insulting remarks made."[127]

LATER DEVELOPMENTS (1958–65)

Resistance to the Greensboro's school desegregation move continued throughout the school year and afterward. Much of

---

and Corey, *Action Patterns in School Desegregation*, p. 201). One newsman facetiously wrote that "while a large delegation of press representatives" spent two days "recording the integration move" of six students in the public schools, "a private school enrolled 17 Negroes in silence." He was referring to Greensboro's Catholic high school which had begun desegregation three years earlier without fanfare or difficulty.

[126] Wey and Corey, *Action Patterns in School Desegregation*, pp. 194–95.

[127] *GDN*, September 4, 5, and 6, 1957. See also Wey and Corey, *Action Patterns in School Desegregation*, pp. 194–95, 201.

it was passive, or at least quiet. Some was vocal and enough was violent that the police maintained a close watch on key persons and buildings which might be threatened.

One white parent said near the end of the school year that there was "less talk among parents" than at first about the situation, but the "opposed patrons simply are resigned to the fact that there is nothing . . . they can do about it."[128]

There was vocal opposition also, as seen in the organized segregationist groups, such as the White Citizens Council. This group held "public" meetings from time to time at which speakers denounced "integration," "communism" and the "Supreme Court."[129] More aggressive and violent opposition was evident in varied harassments against school officials and the black families and students involved in the desegregation situation.

At the desegregated schools, the prevailing attitude among white students seemed to be that of quiet avoidance of the blacks as much as possible. There was some harassment and a few overtures of friendliness, but for the most part, the black students were ignored.[130] The harassment included catcalls, jeers, occasional pushing or shoving, and three occasions when eggs were thrown at black students. The egg incidents, all of which occurred the first week at the senior high school, provoked a strong reprimand from the school's principal and the *Daily News* editor. "There is no place in any school for such misconduct and for students' inhumanity to students," the editor said. "What reflects upon the high school reflects upon the community," he cautioned,[131] referring to nearby Charlotte where only a few days earlier one black student had withdrawn

---

[128] *SSN*, April 1958, p. 6. This is borne out by interviews reported in American Friends Service Committee, *Staff Reports* (unpublished), 1957–58.

[129] For stories on some of these meetings, see *GDN*, September 18 and 27, 1957, and *SSN*, April 1958.

[130] *SSN*, April 1958, p. 6; *GDN*, June 1, 1958; and the American Friends Service Committee, *Staff Memos* (unpublished), 1957.

[131] *GDN*, September 16 (editorial) and 17, 1957.

under harassment from a desegregated school, bringing national criticism to the school and the community.[132]

If there was a minimum of violence, there was also very little effort shown by white students to welcome the newcomers. At the high school, four white girls invited the black student to have lunch with them in the cafeteria the first week of school. The four girls and their families were chided and threatened by other students and adults, but they continued their gesture of friendliness throughout the year.[133]

At Gillespie Elementary School, the five black students there had a rather lonely year, not being molested seriously, but not being accepted well either.

The black high school student, Josephine Boyd, was on the honor roll several times, and in June, 1958, she became the first black student to graduate from a desegregated school in North Carolina. The Gillespie students made poor to average grades, perhaps reflecting the differences in academic standards in the city's white and Negro schools, as one school administrator suggested in an off-the-record interview.[134]

During the school year there was one significant indication that the citizens of Greensboro and surrounding Guilford County were as committed as ever to education, regardless of the desegregation issue. In December, 1957, they approved overwhelmingly a $7 million school bond issue for capital improvements in the city and county. The vote was 85 percent in favor of the bond issue. One school official in Greensboro interpreted this as a "vote of confidence" for the school board.[135]

Even though the first year of school desegregation in Greensboro and its sister cities of Charlotte and Winston-Salem was heralded by many observers as being the beginning of a major breakthrough in the South's segregation wall, there

---

[132] See *SSN*, October 1957, p. 5, for an account of the Charlotte incident.
[133] *Ibid.*, April 1958, p. 6.
[134] *GDN*, June 1, 1958. See also *ibid.*, April 1958, p. 6; July 1958, p. 12,
[135] Greensboro School Board, *Minutes*, December 17, 1957.

was almost no movement beyond this "beginning" in any of the cities for several years. "Tokenism" came to be the "Greensboro way," as well as that of the State of North Carolina. During the second year of desegregation, for example, only two more black students were transferred into school with whites in Greensboro.[136] By the fall of 1962, as the city's sixth year of desegregation began, the number of blacks in school with whites was still only 35, and all were at one school. By that same fall, out of the state's total of 173 school districts, 16 had begun some desegregation. With only one exception, the "tokenism" of Greensboro was the typical pattern followed by all the others.[137]

In Greensboro, one factor which probably helped to curtail further movement by school officials was the retirement in 1958 of the superintendent and two of the most liberal board members at the end of the first year of school desegregation.[138] Their replacements appeared to be more conservative in their social views and certainly were more cautious in dealing with the racial issue. Political reaction in the community against any major amount of social change helped also to keep desegregation to a minimum, according to some local leaders. At the same time, there was no significant pressure on the school officials from civil rights leaders or groups to move further until 1962 and 1963.[139]

This "tokenism," or "gradualism" approach to desegregation as some preferred to call it, was strongly defended by the state's attorney general. In a 1959 speech, he said that "the people of our state . . . are making a genuine effort to gradu-

---

[136] U. S. Commission on Civil Rights, North Carolina State Advisory Committee, *Equal Protection of the Laws in North Carolina*, pp. 122–23.

[137] *Statistical Summary* . . . (*November 1962*). The exception was Durham, where about 150 Negro students were in school with whites as the result of a federal court order.

[138] See Greensboro School Board, *Minutes,* January 21 and March 24, 1958.

[139] From interviews with two school officials as reported in American Friends Service Committee, *Staff Reports* (unpublished), 1958.

ally adjust themselves to the new, and what seems to them to be revolutionary, requirements imposed by the decisions of the Supreme Court. . . ."[140]

One Greensboro editor called the North Carolina approach "a model for the rest of the South." As he explained it, "On the one hand it did not make for massive integration . . . , on the other the courts accepted it as a 'good faith' start." Thus, "while Virginia and Arkansas fought their futile battles of massive resistance," he added, "North Carolina stuck determinedly to the middle road." The editor clinched his argument by pointing out that this "approach seems level-headed and supremely practical," because "new industry has been pouring into North Carolina, in contrast to a drought in certain other Southern states." He referred specifically to the "divisive race controversy . . . at Little Rock."[141]

In 1963, the Greensboro School Board made a major policy change by adopting a "freedom of choice" plan for the assignment of pupils.[142] As a result, the number of black students in desegregated schools jumped from 35, all at one school in the school year 1962–63,[143] to about 200 in twelve schools in 1963–64.[144]

This policy change by the school board was the result of several factors, one of which was undoubtedly the overall change which had come by that time to North Carolina and the South in the political and social climate regarding racial matters. Related to these changes were the commitments of both the North Carolina and the national political administrations after 1960 to the improvement of the lot of black citizens, the growing national support for civil rights issues growing

---

[140] From a speech by Malcolm Seawell before a U. S. Senate Committee, as reported by the *GDN*, May 27, 1959.

[141] *GDN*, editorial, May 27, 1959.

[142] Greensboro School Board, *Minutes*, May 21, 1963.

[143] *Statistical Summary . . . (1962)*.

[144] From figures given by school superintendent, as reported in the *GDN*, July 17 and September 6, 1963.

out of the student movement and other demonstrations from 1960 to 1963, the slow but steady cracking of the segregation wall in other southern states, and the increasing pressures for change being exerted by civil rights groups from the national and local scene.[145]

Local pressures for an increased pace in racial change in Greensboro began as early as 1961 when the Greensboro Citizens Association, an all-black group representing "many civic clubs," presented to the school board a resolution calling for increased desegregation.[146] This request and a similar one in 1962 was referred to "a committee for study."[147] In March, 1963, this same group appeared before the board again with a "supplementary resolution" calling for geographic assignment of all pupils.[148]

In the meantime two interracial citizens groups, the Greensboro Community Fellowship and the Greensboro Education Committee, both headed by local white businessmen and both formed in the winter of 1962–63 by a number of business, civic, religious, and educational leaders concerned about local racial problems, began a series of activities relating to the school situation. They jointly sponsored a public meeting, to which school officials were invited to discuss pupil assignment policies;[149] they presented a resolution with the signatures of 500 parents to the board requesting the elimination of racial factors in operation of the school system;[150] and the fellowship sponsored a May 26 full-page newspaper advertisement with

[145] By the spring of 1963 school desegregation at some level had begun in all southern states (See *SSN*, February 1963.)

[146] Greensboro School Board, *Minutes*, May 30, 1961. See also *GDN*, May 31, 1961.

[147] Greensboro School Board, *Minutes*, January 16, 1962.

[148] *Ibid.*, March 19, 1963. The board's black member urged that the "resolution" be considered, but the board voted to postpone the matter. Two months later, on May 21, the board adopted its "freedom of choice" plan.

[149] *GDN*, March 7 and 14, 1963. See also American Friends Service Committee, *Staff Report* (unpublished), 1962–63.

[150] Greensboro School Board, *Minutes*, April 16, 1963.

names of 1,300 local white citizens who pledged to support desegregated institutions and businesses.

After the school board's adoption of its "freedom of choice" assignment plan in May, 1963, an extensive program of organization and education was carried on in various parts of the city by members of the Community Fellowship and Education Committee. They conducted an interracial summer program for beginning first graders who would be in desegregated schools,[151] they encouraged and assisted black parents and students in complying with the school board's regulations for filling out and submitting transfer requests, and after the school term began they operated a tutorial program for 100 or more of the black students who were newcomers to the desegregated schools.[152]

By the fall of 1964, with this same "freedom of choice" policy still operating, about 500 Greensboro black students were enrolled in classes with whites in sixteen schools.[153] In that same fall, school desegregation occurred for the first time in Greenville, South Carolina.

[151] From interviews with community leaders and from American Friends Service Committee, *Staff Reports* (unpublished), 1963–64.
[152] *GDN*, June 6, 1963; January 20, 1964.
[153] *Statistical Summary . . . (1964)*.

Chapter III

GREENVILLE AND SCHOOL DESEGREGATION

SCHOOL SEGREGATION ACTIONS BEFORE 1954

In order to understand the reaction in South Carolina and Greenville to the Supreme Court's 1954 school decision it is necessary to examine several significant events and anticipatory actions which occurred in the state as early as three years before the ruling actually occurred. Among these were a massive statewide effort which was initiated in 1951 to "equalize" black and white school facilities, the setting up of an official segregation committee by the 1951 General Assembly, and the abolishing by popular vote in 1952 of the state's constitutional obligation to operate public schools.[1]

The longtime prominence of race in state politics, the Clarendon County school case, and James F. Byrnes's return to state leadership helped to precipitate these early actions.

The prominence of race in South Carolina politics throughout the first half of the twentieth century created a climate in which any racial incident or threat of racial change was likely to be seized upon by politicians and amplified far out of proportion. Key characterizes this situation in *Southern Politics* by labeling his chapter on South Carolina as "The Politics of Color."

The Clarendon school case, which began in 1950 and later became one of the five historic cases involved in the Supreme Court's 1954 *Brown* decision, provided just such a case in

[1] *Southern School News* (*SSN*), September 1954, p. 12.

point. Legally the case had major significance, but politically it offered South Carolina political leaders a weapon which could be used to strengthen their power through appeals to the racial fears of the white public and pledges to maintain the "Southern way of life." That Clarendon County, with its 70 percent black population, was located in the heart of the rural, black belt area of South Carolina, where an excessive amount of the state's political power was concentrated, made the case seem even more important as a threat to the political status quo.[2] Actually, the Clarendon case began as an effort to secure better school facilities for ten-year-old Harry Briggs, Jr. and other black children in a poor, rural county where the existence of gross inequities in facilities was never denied by local officials, even in court. Reluctance of the officials to remedy matters led the black plaintiffs eventually to seek desegregation, just as did plaintiffs in Prince Edward County of Virginia, the scene of another of the 1954 "School Cases."[3]

When James F. Byrnes became governor of South Carolina in January, 1951, the state came under the leadership of one of its most illustrious citizens and one who was widely experienced in governmental matters. He had served earlier on a national level as a U. S. senator and member of the Supreme Court, and after World War II he was secretary of state. Several Greenville leaders, when interviewed by this investigator, stated that they believed that Byrnes as a southern leader was so influential that if he had urged compliance with the Supreme Court ruling, South Carolina and the South generally would have followed his lead. It has been suggested that Byrnes, "returned from Olympus to the governorship of South Carolina, must have then been well along with the plot to lead the South directly into the Republican fold."[4] By either chance

[2] V. O. Key Jr., *Southern Politics in State and Nation.*
[3] See Albert Blaustein and Clarence Ferguson, *Desegregation and the Law*, pp. 46–48; and J. W. Peltason, *Fifty-eight Lonely Men*, pp. 15–16, for background and discussion of this case.
[4] Harry Ashmore, *An Epitaph for Dixie*, p. 181.

or design, he took the traditional southern political viewpoint that there should be educational opportunities for all children, but clearly in the separate-but-equal manner. As he stated in his inaugural address in January, 1951, "It is our duty to provide for the races substantial equality in school facilities. We should do it because it is right." A few months later in discussing the Clarendon school case in a speech at the South Carolina Educational Association's convention, he said:

Should the Supreme Court decide this case against our position, we will face a serious problem. Of only one thing can we be certain. South Carolina will not now, nor for some years to come, mix white and colored children in our schools. . . . If the Court changes what is now the law of the land, we will, if it is possible, live within the law, preserve the public school system, and at the same time maintain segregation. If that is not possible, reluctantly we will abandon the public school system.[5]

Very early in his administration as governor, Byrnes began encouraging the legislature to adopt several "preparedness measures" in the event the federal courts should outlaw segregation. His first move was to urge adoption of a 3 percent state sales tax to raise funds for a $200 million "school equalization" program. He pointed out that "to meet this situation we are forced to do now what we should have been doing for the last fifty years. . . ."[6] The program was approved and went into effect July 1, 1951. By the time of the Court ruling in 1954, over $100 million had been raised for this program, about 65 percent of it being used to build or upgrade black schools.[7]

His second move was to prod the legislature into setting up a "committee to study and report on the advisable course to be pursued by the state in respect to its educational facilities in the event that the Federal Courts nullify the provisions of the

[5] Harry Ashmore, *The Negro and the Schools*, p. 96.
[6] Thomas Clark, *The Emerging South*, p. 173.
[7] *SSN*, September 1954, p. 12.

State Constitution requiring the establishment of separate schools for the children of white and colored races. . . ."[8] This fifteen-member committee, officially called the South Carolina School Committee, but popularly known as the "Segregation Committee" or the "Gressette Committee," was created in April, 1951. In January, 1952, the governor urged repeal of the state's constitutional provision requiring operation of "a liberal system of free public schools for all children between the ages of six and 21 years." After legislative repeal, this was submitted as an amendment to the state's voters in November, 1952. They approved it overwhelmingly by a two to one vote.[9]

REACTIONS TO 1954 SUPREME COURT RULING

Just a week before the Supreme Court's *Brown* v. *Board of Education of Topeka* ruling Governor Byrnes publicly reiterated his position. "If the Court changes what is now the law of the land . . . we will . . . maintain segregation" or "we will abandon the public school system."

When the federal decision actually came on May 17, Byrnes expressed himself as being "shocked to learn that the Court has reversed itself." However, he added, "I earnestly urge all of our people, white and colored, to exercise restraint and preserve order."[10]

Two days later at a White House press conference President Eisenhower helped to diminish the immediate effect of the ruling by praising the South Carolina governor for his "temperate approach" and "very fine statement." At the same time, the President "side-stepped giving any advice to the South on

---

[8] South Carolina School Committee, *First Interim Report to His Excellency the Governor and the Honorable Presiding Officers and Members of the General Assembly (July 28, 1954)*.

[9] *SSN*, September 1954, p. 12.

[10] *Greenville News* (hereafter referred to as *GN*), May 12 and 18, 1954.

how it should react to the Supreme Court's ban on segregated schools."[11] One former South Carolinian later took Eisenhower to task for this "flaccid inaction in the quiet time after the . . . decision when the moral weight of his office might well have headed off the polarization of public opinion."[12]

In Greenville, local political leaders indicated general disapproval of the Court ruling but most were cautious in their remarks. Of the five state legislators from Greenville, one declared himself as being "for separate but equal facilities four square,"[13] another said he "would oppose the abolishment of the public schools," a third expressed disappointment "that the decision was unanimous," and one had "no comment." Only one expressed strong opposition, and he did it in picturesque terms: "I'm Southern born and Southern bred. And when I die there'll be a Southerner dead."[14] He added that "these two gentlemen [referring to Supreme Court Justices Black, who was from Alabama, and Clark, who was from Texas] helped to stab the dagger into the back of the South. When they die, they could be placed next to Benedict Arnold and labeled the greatest traitors to all things the South has stood for."[15] Greenville's school superintendent, when queried by a news reporter on the day of the federal ruling, indicated that the local school officials would wait for the "full Court decision" before announcing action regarding desegregation. Superintendent W. F. Loggins pointed out that any local action would "depend on specific cases, action taken by the State Department of Education and any legislative action taken."[16]

The Greenville School Board held its regular monthly meeting on the evening of May 17. In contrast to the affirmative reaction and resolution of the Greensboro school officials, the

[11] *Greensboro Daily News* (*GDN*), May 20, 1954.
[12] Ashmore, *Epitaph for Dixie*, p. 182.
[13] *GN*, May 18, 1954.
[14] *Greenville Piedmont* (hereafter referred to as *GP*), May 17, 1954.
[15] *GN*, May 18, 1954.
[16] *GP*, May 17, 1954.

South Carolina group approved a cautiously worded statement that "the decision . . . by the Supreme Court cannot be adequately interpreted and understood until more facts are available," but added that the board would "in the future, as . . . in the past, continue to concentrate on the education of all the children of Greenville County. The schoolmen emphasized their efforts since 1951 "to equalize facilities between the two races," pointing out that "preference" had been "consistently given to applications for the construction of Negro schools." Even though "the Negro population . . . is about 20 percent . . . , approximately 60 percent of construction funds have gone to the building of Negro schools."[17]

The local press in Greenville was not as immediately outspoken in its editorial opposition to the Court ruling as it became later.[18] In its first reaction to the decision the *Greenville News* editorialized, "What the ruling does in effect is to put the states on notice that segregation is on the way out." It urged readers to "keep cool and don't start anything that may eventuate in disturbing the racial amity that has existed so long in this section."[19] The city's other newspaper, the *Greenville Piedmont,* also urged the public to "practice patience and forbearance." Even though "the decision . . . is momentous and far reaching and will be disturbing to many . . . the Court has deliberately refrained from issuing a sweeping order . . . it has asked for help from all parties in working out the details. The Court simply has enunciated the constitu-

[17] Greenville School Board, *Minutes,* May 17, 1954.

[18] Over a period of several years, beginning soon after the 1954 decision, the *Greenville News,* which was edited by a member of the "Segregation Committee," became one of the leading exponents of segregation in South Carolina. The larger of two papers in Greenville, it had a circulation of about 80,000 in several counties in the western part of the state during the period of this study. The city's other newspaper, the *Greenville Piedmont,* with a circulation of about 25,000, has been known more for its family and feature emphasis than for taking strong stands on political issues.

[19] *GN,* editorial, May 18, 1954.

tional principle that segregation is discriminatory and un-lawful. . . ."[20]

The bombastic headlines on numerous news stories in the May 18 edition of the *News* more nearly expressed the atti-tude toward desegregation which was to characterize the Greenville press for several years. These headlines included:

South Carolina Constitutionally Ready to Abandon Public Schools
    to Prevent Mixing Races
Court Reversal Shocks Byrnes
South Carolina Plans No Action on Decision Now: Could Take Years
Decision Stuns Clarendon Folk
Segregation Issue Expected to Flare in State Campaigning
County Candidates Assail U. S. Supreme Court Ruling
Russell Says Court Voids Ruling of "Real Lawyers"
Talmadge is Violent in his Reactions; Would Defy Court
Dangers of Great Consequence Seen by Byrd in Court's Ruling
NAACP Jubilant Over New Ruling

The *News* editor soon began his attacks on the federal ruling by attempting to cast doubt on its validity. He suggested that "the unanimity of the decision is surprising. We do not believe any great decision has ever come without a dissenting vote." However, he explained that "as the Court rendered a socio-logical rather than a judicial decision, it needed a solid front."[21]

A few days later he attacked two other subjects which were to become choice targets in relation to desegregation—the northern press and the National Association for the Advance-ment of Colored People (NAACP). A Chicago newspaper was chided for editorial remarks which evidently had been anti-southern. The *News* declared that "the South can meet the problems arising from the Court's ruling in its own way, and it won't need much aid or advice from outsiders who are not acquainted with conditions that must be met and are being met." As for the NAACP, the Greenville editor charged it with

[20] *GP*, editorial, May 17, 1954.
[21] *GN*, editorial, May 19, 1954.

being "more interested in the elimination of segregation than
. . . in the welfare of individual students. . . . NAACP leaders are pushing the South too fast and too hard."[22] The "vast
majority of South Carolina newspapers" shared the viewpoint
of the Greenville press "in their opposition to integrated
schools."[23]

As for other positive reactions in South Carolina to the federal ruling, they were almost nonexistent, except among black
leaders. The state president of the NAACP, James M. Hinton
of Columbia, "greeted the order joyfully," but "warned that
cooperation between the races is essential in meeting the
court's ruling."[24] A local black leader in Greenville said that he
had "expected the Supreme Court to rule in this manner. I
don't believe the ruling as such will change the custom of the
people. It will afford a greater area for discussion of the problem and bring about a solution."[25]

The state's two segregated teachers organizations took
opposing views on the ruling. The Palmetto Education Association (black) adopted a resolution "to work unceasingly to up-
hold" it.[26] The South Carolina Education Association (white)
voted to preserve separate schools "in the interest of both
races."[27]

Religious bodies varied in their reactions to the decision.
On a national and regional level most of them endorsed the
view that segregation was not in keeping with the Christian
tradition. The Southern Baptist Convention, representing the

---

[22] *Ibid.*, May 21 and 27, 1954.

[23] *SSN*, November 1954, p. 14. Only one paper in the state, *The Evening
Herald*, in Rock Hill, a small industrial Piedmont area city sixty miles
east of Greenville, is on record as favoring the Court ruling. Its editor
took a very pragmatic view about the matter suggesting editorially that
desegregation might be started on the first grade level. The Catholic
school in this community began desegregation in the fall of 1954, several
years before any other school in the state.

[24] *GN*, May 18, 1954.

[25] *GP*, May 17, 1954.

[26] *SSN*, December 1954, p. 13.

[27] *Ibid.*, November 1954, p. 14.

majority of white church members in the South and over 90 percent of those in South Carolina and Greenville, "overwhelmingly approved a report urging its members to adopt a Christian attitude toward the Supreme Court decision," declaring the ruling to be "in harmony with the Constitution and Christian teaching."[28] When the South Carolina Baptist Convention met in Greenville that fall, it approved a positive but more moderate report calling for "prayerful moderation in meeting the present school crisis, an attitude of friendliness in race relations, general strengthening of the public schools, and obedience of the laws."[29] No local Baptist leaders are on record as commenting on this issue in 1954. The General Assembly of the Southern Presbyterian Church, meeting shortly after the federal ruling, endorsed the *Brown* decision and urged all Presbyterian schools in the South to desegregate. The South Carolina Presbyterian Synod dissented, however, declaring that segregation was "in the best interests of harmonious relations between the white and Negro races in this section at this time." In Greenville, a local Presbyterian leader expressed the view that South Carolina Presbyterians were not likely to change their racial policies "anytime soon."[30]

South Carolina Methodists also held to a view differing from their national body. The state body voted "against mandatory mixing of the races."[31] In Greenville, however, the only white leader who is on record as publicly supporting the 1954 ruling was a prominent Methodist layman and retired local school superintendent, L. P. Hollis, who was still active in state and local civic and educational matters. He openly expressed approval of desegregation and called on white and black leaders to sit down together "to discuss and work out matters locally." And the United Church Women in South Carolina, which had a strong local chapter in Greenville, ex-

[28] Brooks Hays, *A Southern Moderate Speaks*, pp. 201–202.
[29] *SSN*, December 1954, p. 13.
[30] *GN*, June 3, 1954.
[31] *SSN*, November 1954, p. 14.

pressed approval of the federal decision in an open letter to Governor Byrnes.

The state's Catholic leaders generally remained silent on the desegregation issue. However, St. Anne's, a small white parochial school in Rock Hill, began accepting a few black students in September, 1954,[32] and the color bar began to disappear gradually in some urban churches, including those in Greenville.

STATE AND LOCAL ACTION FOLLOWING COURT RULING (1954–55)

Following the initial verbal reaction to the Court ruling, Governor Byrnes on May 20 temporarily halted all new school construction which was being financed by the state's multimillion dollar school equalization program until it could be determined whether tax funds could be spent legally for "schools which have been specifically designated . . . for 'white students' or for 'Negro students'." In the Greenville school district, this meant that three school projects, totalling about $1,500,000 in value were stopped.[33] Under the equalization program Greenville already had spent about six million dollars on new school construction,[34] nearly 65 percent of it being for black schools.

On June 1 the governor told South Carolina school officials to leave out any plans for "mixing the races during the 1954–55 school year. . . ." He also said that if blacks should attempt to enter white schools in Clarendon County, the trustees should deny admission unless or until they are ordered by the Court to admit them."

Shortly after this all school principals in Greenville received from the local school board a special directive which appears to have been prompted by the desegregation issue. The di-

[32] *Ibid.*, October 1954, p. 12.
[33] *GN*, May 22, 1954.
[34] *GP*, May 17, 1954.

rective advised them that if a pupil not ordinarily assigned to their school should seek admittance, he should be told that "he should attend the school in which he is enrolled or to which he has been assigned. . . . This should be done courteously and as privately as circumstances permit. All violence, threats of violence and controversy should be avoided."[35]

There was pressure on the governor to convene a special session of the legislature following the federal ruling. Upon the advice of the state's official "Segregation Committee" and legislative leaders, he decided against such a move.

The "Segregation Committee," set up by legislative action in 1951, played a passive role until after the 1954 Supreme Court ruling. Then it began to take a prominent part in state affairs, continuing to do so until it was dissolved by legislative action in 1966. The fifteen-member committee, included ten legislators and five gubernatorial appointees-at-large. One of the appointees-at-large was Wayne Freeman, editor of the *Greenville News*. The committee began a series of closed hearings soon after May 17. The group also conferred with various state officials and educational leaders and organizations. To show its "unbiased" approach, it conferred with leaders of both the National Association for the Advancement of Colored People and the newly created National Association for the Advancement of White People. The committee sent a delegation to Mississippi and Louisiana to learn what was being done in those states to maintain segregated schools.[36] By the end of July it issued an interim report pointing out that the Supreme Court had not ordered any specific desegregation action. In view of this, the committee recommended that public schools operate for 1954–55 on the same basis as in past years and that the legislature drop any plans for a special session.

The committee defined its own special assignment as

[35] Greenville School Board, *Minutes*, May 17, 1954. This special directive was attached to the 1954–55 enrollment procedures.

[36] *SSN*, September 1954, p. 12.

being the formulation and recommendation of courses of action whereby . . . South Carolina may continue its unsurpassed program of public education without unfortunate disruption by outside forces and influences which have no knowledge of recent progress and no understanding of the problems of the present and future; courses of action whereby the State . . . may offer to all children, regardless of race, color, creed or circumstances, equal educational opportunities in an atmosphere free of social conflicts and tensions which would tend to impede and inhibit the learning process.

The report included a warning that if disruption of "free public schools" should occur, "the Negro citizen, who has historically contributed the least to it, has the most to lose and may incur such a loss quite innocently." The committee pledged itself to maintain a public education system "in keeping with public opinion and established traditions and living patterns."[37]

This same warning note, often couched in terms of paternalistic "concern over the welfare of Negroes," was voiced by a number of white political, educational and religious leaders and groups in the months following the Court ruling. Typical of these statements was one by the South Carolina Methodist Conference:

It is apparent to us that an attempt to integrate the races in our public schools . . . would work grave injustice to many innocent persons, and . . . we fear the Negro would suffer most, as he has often when those far removed from his everyday problems have undertaken to speak in his name. Consideration must also be given to the large number of Negro teachers and administrators in our public schools, lest they be denied leadership among their people.[38]

Perhaps in the hope that the Court's follow-up decision would condone the old "separate but equal" concept in some form, the state's top political leaders used every opportunity

[37] South Carolina School Committee. *First Interim Report to His Excellency, the Governor, and the Honorable Presiding Officers and Members of the General Assembly, (July 28, 1954).*

[38] *SSN,* November 1954, p. 14.

possible to point to progress made in equalizing school facilities. Along with this went a call for voluntary segregation. As Governor Byrnes said in the fall of 1954, the state had spent nearly $125 million in public school construction or improvement since he had become governor four years earlier, and two-thirds of these funds had gone into black schools. "I believe the vast majority of Negroes in South Carolina would prefer to send their children to the splendid schools now being constructed for them, . . ." he stated, adding that "those who seek admission to white schools will do so only because they do not want to attend Negro schools with Negro teachers."[39]

Whereas in North Carolina very little legislation to counteract the Supreme Court's ruling was passed until after the supplemental decision of May 31, 1955, South Carolina leaders pushed ahead with a host of activities.

The state's "Segregation Committee," which had added six attorneys to its staff, was ready with its second report by the time the legislature opened its 1955 session. The report urged adoption of several new measures aimed at defending segregation. With the hearty endorsement of Governor George Bell Timmerman, whose segregation utterances were considerably stronger and harsher than those of his predecessor,[40] six new bills were passed with little or no opposition. Among these were bills to repeal the compulsory attendance law, to abolish teacher tenure, and to cut off state funds from any school involved in a desegregation court order.

Only the attendance law evoked any public response to the whole package of bills. The school superintendents in two cities, including Greenville, spoke against its repeal on grounds of administration. Several groups, such as the Greenville Young Women's Christian Association (YWCA) also opposed its repeal. As the YWCA president said in a public statement,

[39] *Ibid.*
[40] *Ibid.*, February 1955, p. 3, for extensive quotes from the inaugural address of George Bell Timmerman who succeeded Byrnes as governor in January, 1955.

"the repeal of the law will do nothing about solving our racial problems and will be detrimental to the welfare of South Carolina's children."[41]

In response to an appeal from the governor, two Greenville delegates to the state legislature sponsored a resolution asking the Congress to "curb the presently uncontrolled authority of the Supreme Court."[42] The legislature approved this without dissent and sent it to Washington where all of the South Carolina congressmen verbally endorsed it but expressed little hope for its approval by the national body. Typical of their comments was one made by Robert T. Ashmore, the representative from the Fourth Congressional District, which included Greenville, who said he was "in full accord" with the measure, but added that "the desire" in Congress "to control the Negro and foreign element vote in the big cities" gave him "very little hope of success" for favorable action on the resolution.

During the spring of 1955, attorneys representing South Carolina and Clarendon County in arguments before the Supreme Court on the school cases strongly defended segregation and, according to a *Greenville News* reporter, "in effect defied the unanimous decree" handed down the preceding year.

When the Court issued its supplementary decree, calling for "a prompt and reasonable start toward full compliance" with its 1954 desegregation decision, some South Carolina leaders vowed to "close the public schools rather than integrate."[43] South Carolina's Senator Strom Thurmond urged all southern states to "fight each case" of desegregation "with every legal weapon at their disposal."[44] Greenville political leaders, in contrast, reacted quite mildly. One remarked, "The Supreme Court was right in sending it [the desegregation

---

[41] *Ibid.*, March 1955, p. 14; April 1955, p. 13; and June 1955, p. 11.

[42] The sponsors, Frank Eppes and Rex Carter, were high school classmates of the author. Both of them had been known as being fairly liberal minded on racial matters prior to their entry into politics.

[43] *GN*, June 2, 1955.

[44] *Ibid.*, August 7, 1955.

decision] back to the district court. . . . I don't see any immediate effect."

The local school superintendent said he had no comment but that the Greenville schools would continue to provide public education "within the limits of the Supreme Court decision" for the county's "approximately 32,000 white students" and "over 8000 Negro students."[45]

The Greenville press reacted negatively to the 1955 ruling, stating that "if and when the majority of the public wants integrated schools, the change will come about. But that change in public opinion, which must come first, has not yet occurred, if ever it will."[46] In accord with this view, the editor took up Governor Byrnes's appeal for "voluntary segregation," which was becoming the slogan of North Carolina's Governor Hodges that summer. "Integration of the races in South Carolina is neither feasible nor desirable at this time," the editor declared. "Negro schools are being rapidly improved," and "the more responsible Negro parents will want their children to go to schools taught by members of their own race. Many will have the opportunity of attending better schools than some of the white children." He concluded that "voluntary segregation is the 'escape' from difficulties that will leave their marks on the children, and it is not illegal."[47]

RESISTANCE TO DESEGREGATION (1955–60)

By the fall of 1955 those white leaders who might have influenced and guided the state along a path of moderation and peaceful change regarding racial issues were too timid or too intimidated to speak or act. The few who did feel impelled to cast their weight openly against the prevailing forces during the next few years were often ridiculed, trampled upon, or forced to flee the state. The period from 1955 to 1960 was a

[45] *Ibid.*, June 1, 1955.
[46] *Ibid.*, editorial, August 9, 1955.
[47] *Ibid.*, editorial, June 1, 1955.

dark one indeed for the cause of racial justice, equality of opportunity, and brotherhood in South Carolina.

Even though Greenville had many economic, educational, religious, racial and political characteristics similar to North Carolina's Piedmont area cities, the forces of moderation in the South Carolina community were too weak to move. As one school official told this investigator, "Some of us in administrative positions were ready to begin desegregation in Greenville in 1954 or 1955, but we did not dare mention the subject openly."

There is little evidence of organized co-ordination between the various reactionary and racist groups and leaders in South Carolina during the late 1950s, but the acts and statements of each probably did much to nurture and encourage the other. There was a strong resurgence of the Ku Klux Klan throughout the South during this period even though almost no leading officials, especially in the Carolinas, voiced anything but harsh criticism for the organization. According to an Associated Press story on October 23, 1957, a Klan leader in Greenville stated at a public meeting on October 20 that Governor Timmerman of South Carolina had promised arms to the Ku Klux Klan if integration troubles developed in the state. The governor vigorously denied this in a press conference, labeling the Klan as "communist inspired to mislead Southern people and smear Southern officials like myself."

Marion A. Wright, a liberal white southern leader, stated, "Our political leaders . . . deplore violence. They have no truck with the Ku Klux Klan. But my contention is that they set in motion forces which bred the Klan and the very violence they now condemn. . . ."[48] It is easy to develop a case for this viewpoint. South Carolina's political leaders spent much of their time from 1955 to 1960 in criticizing the Supreme Court, the northern press, social scientists, integrationists, and communists for trying to "stir up racial conflict," "destroy the

[48] *Intimidation, Reprisal and Violence in the South's Racial Crisis*, p. 1.

South," "make the public schools into laboratories for solving social problems," and "mongrelize the races."

Among such statements were those made by former governor Byrnes;[49] Greenville's Representative Robert T. Ashmore, who called on the Court "to resign . . . and let nine new men . . . go in";[50] the current governor, who strongly criticized the Klan[51] but openly declared that "South Carolina will never be integrated in a thousand years"; and two state judges, who charged the Supreme Court with being "soft" on communism and determined to take away the lawful rights of the states.[52] One South Carolina congressman, L. Mendel Rivers, declared that "Nixon and Eisenhower . . . bow and scrape to the NAACP,"[53] Greenville legislator Burnet R. Maybank, Jr. charged that "federal leaders have sold America down the river for a small minority" and insisted that the NAACP was primarily interested in "social mixing,"[54] and Strom Thurmond and L. Mendel Rivers advocated publicly that the Supreme Court justices "be impeached."[55]

At the same time, every session of the South Carolina General Assembly from 1955 through 1958 was occupied with creating new laws to defend segregation and oppose desegregation. By the spring of 1958, there were twenty-eight such laws on the books, most of them dealing with some aspect of the school issue. Besides those mentioned earlier, there were bills to close any schools which might be ordered to begin desegregation, to sell or lease such school facilities to private groups, to ban from state or school employment any member of the NAACP, to investigate NAACP activities, to appro-

[49] James F. Byrnes, "The Supreme Court Must Be Curbed," *U. S. News and World Report*, May 18, 1956, pp. 50–58.
[50] *SSN*, December 1957, p. 6.
[51] *Ibid.*
[52] *Ibid.*, July 1957, p. 4. Quoted from a press interview on June 22, 1957.
[53] *Ibid.*, December 1957, p. 6.
[54] *Ibid.*, June 1956, p. 14.
[55] *Ibid.*, August 1957, p. 13.

priate funds only to racially separate schools and parks, and to strengthen antibarratry regulations—a law aimed at NAACP lawyers involved in desegregation cases. There were also resolutions to condemn the Supreme Court, to endorse the formation of White Citizens Council chapters, and to request the state's library officials to remove all books favoring integration from libraries it controlled. There was even a bill to require all blood banks to label blood as either "white" or "colored"! A 1956 resolution by the lawmakers endorsed the principles of the White Citizens Council and probably encouraged the formation of sixty or more local chapters of this prosegregationist organization within a year's time.[56] A Greenville chapter of the group included prominent local citizens among its officers and held its meetings in an official public building.[57]

In the spring of 1956, 101 southern congressmen, including the entire South Carolina delegation, signed the famous "Southern Manifesto," a public protest against the Supreme Court's 1954 and 1955 school desegregation rulings. This document charged that the Court had deserted the principles of the Constitution and "substituted naked power for established law," had "planted hatred and suspicion where there had been heretofore friendship and understanding," and had "substituted personal political and social ideas for the established law of the land." It commended the states which proposed to "resist forced integration by any lawful means."[58] That same year in a reaction against the civil rights platforms of both national

[56] *Ibid.*, April 1956, p. 12; May 1957, p. 3; and September 1957, p. 2. See also Southern Regional Council, *Special Report on Summary of Recent Segregation Laws Enacted in Southern States*, June 21, 1957; and U. S. Commission on Civil Rights, *Report on Education, 1961*. Washington, D. C.: U. S. Government Printing Office, 1961, pp. 76, 84, 86–87.

[57] *GN*, September 18, 1960. One of its leaders, Dr. Thomas Parker, a wealthy physician, has been identified with several "right wing" extremist groups by Arnold Forster and Benjamin Epstein in their book *Danger on the Right*. New York: Random House, 1964, p. 182.

[58] Clark, *The Emerging South*, pp. 235–36.

political parties, a third party of "South Carolinians for Independent Electors" was formed with the endorsement and support of such state leaders and groups as Senator Strom Thurmond, former governor Byrnes, and the Ku Klux Klan. In the 1956 presidential election the Democrats carried the state but made a very poor showing, the Republicans and Independents together winning over one half of the total votes.

A number of Protestant church groups throughout the state grew more and more critical of the Supreme Court ruling and any efforts at desegregation during the late 1950s. Some cut off their contributions or disaffiliated themselves from the National Council of Churches or their own denominational parent bodies. The widely-known "fundamentalist" evangelist Bob Jones, Sr., who was the president of Bob Jones University and the owner of WMUU, a radio station in Greenville, expressed the views of such segregationist church people when he declared that "the intermingling of races is not God's plan. . . . Every effort in the history of the world to create one world and one race outside the body of Christ has been of the devil. . . ."[59]

The South Carolina press contributed greatly to this spirit of opposition and defiance to the federal courts and desegregation. As John McCray, editor of the South Carolina edition of the *Baltimore Afro-American,* described the situation in 1959, the newspapers of South Carolina, with one or two exceptions, "have become propaganda sheets for intolerance. The effect has been to produce a climate of . . . reprisals and punitive

[59] *GN,* March 5, 1956. Bob Jones, Sr. was the founder and president of Bob Jones University, an ultraconservative school of about four thousand students which moved to Greenville in 1946. The school, whose chief goal is to train young "gospel evangelists," is reputed to have strong financial support from several politically conservative industrialists. It is not officially related to any religious denomination, but its graduates often begin in or become a part of various "independent" or "fundamentalist" groups which have broken away from the more orthodox Protestant bodies. The college's radio station is a combination "good music" and "gospel hour" station which regularly carries Carl McIntyre and Billy James Hargis.

action against those who may subscribe publicly or be suspected of favoring school desegregation."[60]

The *Greenville News,* especially in its editorial columns, became one of the strongest spokesmen for segregation in the state. One researcher described the *News* editor's views from 1955 to 1960 as follows:

He has consistently vindicated the Southern position of resistance to social change. . . . He stands staunchly for states rights and in 1956 advocated "resolutions of interposition.". . . He is intransigent in advocating the maintenance of separate white and Negro traditions as a sane and virtuous way of life, in denying civil rights legislation, and in distrust of the token integration policies of neighboring states. . . . [His] editorial policies defending the South reflect the current downtown Greenville point of view and are a powerful weapon for conservatism and the status quo.[61]

Stories of crimes by blacks were consistently played up. Terms such as "race-mixing," "forced integration," "federal oppression," "gestapo," "communist," "mongrelization," and "South-haters" were used frequently in referring to antisegregation views or actions. Both *White* and *Negro* were always capitalized as part of the paper's expressed belief in the separate-but-equal premise.

In this atmosphere, it is no surprise that the peddlers of violence, symbolized particularly by the Ku Klux Klan, found an open market for their wares. From an underground group holding only clandestine meetings in the early 1950s, the Klan became a public group, holding large open meetings throughout the state by 1955.[62] Several of these took place in the vicinity of Greenville, where James W. Bagwell, one of the top Klan leaders, lived. Audiences varied from one hundred to the several thousand people who would come to hear well-known

---

[60] *SSN,* May 1959, p. 3.

[61] Alfred S. Reid, "Literature in Greenville," *Furman University Bulletin,* 7:124–25, November 1960.

[62] *GP,* August 22, 1957. See also Southern Regional Council, *Intimidation, Reprisal and Violence,* pp. 2–3.

speakers, such as John Kasper, denounce the evils of "race-mixing" and all who advocated the same in any form or manner.[63]

At one such public meeting, attended by this investigator in August, 1957, five hundred or more spectators gathered during a warm, moonlit evening on the grounds of a small Baptist church on the outskirts of Greenville to hear several robed and hooded speakers denounce, in colorful language, varied advocates of "racial mongrelization." Included were the Supreme Court, President Eisenhower (who was "trying to become a dictator" by sending federal troops to Little Rock), Billy Graham (who had spoken at an integrated meeting somewhere), local "liberal preachers" and the "communistic" National Council of Churches, the NAACP and its "Jewish leaders," the mayor of Greenville (he had welcomed a black professional convention to the city a few days earlier), and the North Carolina school officials—the "traitors" who had desegregated the schools in Greensboro, Charlotte, and Winston-Salem. The Klan meeting included readings from the Old Testament about the Tower of Babel and "separation of the races," prayers to Jehovah who "made the races separate," and recorded gospel songs such as "The Old Rugged Cross." The evening's program concluded with the burning of two twenty-foot, kerosene-soaked wooden crosses. Memberships from the audience were solicited by thirty to forty hooded figures. Traffic to and from the church grounds was directed by several state highway patrolmen who seemed to be on friendly terms with the Klansmen.

It is impossible to know how much violence resulted from the Klan's activity, but from 1955 to 1959 there were at least thirty-four reported cases of intimidation, reprisal, and direct violence in South Carolina against blacks or whites who were in some way related to civil rights efforts. These included bombings, shootings, job losses, mortgage foreclosures, cross

[63] *SSN*, July 1957, p. 4. See also *GN*, September 15, 1957.

burnings, and threats. Three of these incidents occurred in or near Greenville. A black landowner and his wife were beaten severely by a group of Klan members for being too friendly with a nearby white family. Two news photographers were beaten and their cameras confiscated at a Klan public meeting,[64] and two of the city's leading white Protestant ministers were allegedly forced to leave their churches because their racial views were too liberal. One Methodist minister was "pushed" into an "early retirement" because he had been liberal and outspoken on race and peace issues, and a Presbyterian minister "found it expedient" to move to a less conservative area of the South. During the period 1955–60 job reprisals were also exerted in other parts of the state against several white ministers, college professors, and one editor, as well as against thirty or more black teachers because of views or actions opposing segregation.[65]

Many of the same political leaders, churchmen, and editors who openly advocated "legal" defiance and opposition to all efforts to change the racial status quo, were "shocked" at the acts of violence which occurred. They saw no connection between such acts and the views they had been espousing. Typical of such reactions was that by the *Greenville News* editor in an editorial about "four White men" who were charged with mutilating a black man. "It is hard to believe White men in any part of the South would stoop to . . . this act of wanton cruelty. This makes it increasingly difficult for the South to fight federal encroachment by legal means. . . . The South must . . . control its lawless elements."[66] The "respectable" defenders of the status quo were quick to castigate the Klan for any acts of violence. As the *News* editor wrote, "Wherever

[64] Southern Regional Council, *Intimidation, Reprisal and Violence*, pp. 3, 7, 13–14, 26–27.

[65] *Ibid.*, pp. 13–14, 26–27. See also unpublished address on "South Carolina and Civil Liberties," given by Marion A. Wright at the Unitarian-Universalist Fellowship in Columbia, South Carolina, March 22, 1964.

[66] *GN*, editorial, September 11, 1957.

the Klan exists, it is a readymade excuse for violence—it can always be laid at the door of the Klan and the Klan can't prove its innocence because of its clandestine nature."[67]

SUPPORT FOR MODERATION AND CHANGE (1955–60)

In this arena of screaming resistance to social change, the few voices calling for outright desegregation or even for moderation were almost lost.

As might be expected, a few black civil rights leaders spoke up for desegregation. They did so in moderate tones, asking that some beginning be made toward compliance with the Supreme Court's ruling on school desegregation. Immediately after the Court's 1955 supplementary ruling, the South Carolina NAACP chairman expressed approval of it, and within a few weeks petitions from groups of citizens in several communities were submitted to local school boards.[68] In Greenville "a petition with 209 signatures of Negro citizens" was presented to the school officials, requesting them to "take immediate steps with all deliberate speed to reorganize the public schools under your jurisdiction on a non-discriminatory basis."[69] As was the case in most of the other communities, the Greenville request was "received as information" without any discussion by the board.

A year later, after receiving no answer to the petition, an attorney for the Greenville black group sent a public letter to the school officials requesting "the dignity of a reply," pointing out that if the silence continued, "we will move the problem into a more formal stage."[70] A few weeks later, a public reply was released by the school officials in which they declared that "the Board is not aware that any of its actions are in

[67] *Ibid.*, February 24, 1957.
[68] *SSN*, June 1955, p. 6; and August 1955, p. 6.
[69] Greenville School Board, *Minutes*, August 2, 1955.
[70] *GP*, October 10, 1956.

conflict with any existing laws" and that it "does not intend to share its responsibilities in the operation of the schools with any group or organization."[71]

Earlier in 1956, NAACP leaders in Greenville publicly expressed opposition to a proposed local school tax increase because they had "no representation on the School Board."[72] An NAACP group obtained a hearing with the Greenville legislative delegation, at which they requested the legislators to use their influence "to get a Negro member on the school board" and to set up an interracial committee "to study the school situation."[73] The legislators "appeared to be sympathetic" to the requests but took no follow-up action so far as is indicated.

It appears likely that a number of school officials in South Carolina, including some in Greenville, would have begun to develop desegregation plans in 1954 or 1955 if state pressures had not been so strong against such action. This does not presume any enthusiasm on their part for desegregation, but rather a desire to be law-abiding and to do a good job of education. Such an attitude seems to be reflected in a resolution adopted in August, 1955, by the South Carolina School Boards Association at its annual meeting in Greenville. The schoolmen, including representatives from Greenville, acknowledged their responsibility to "play a major role in the policies and adjustment for the operation of our schools under the desegregation ruling of the U. S. Supreme Court" but pragmatically expressed the belief that "immediate desegregation . . . is impossible because of our inability to finance such schools under existing laws." The resolution ended with an appeal for "resolution of the legal conflict between state and

[71] *Ibid.*, November 9, 1956.

[72] *SSN*, June 1956, p. 14. The school board, made up of seventeen elected members representing various areas of the school district, has never had a black member. A black minister ran for election in the early 1950s but was defeated (from interviews with community leaders).

[73] Greenville Chapter of NAACP, *Minutes*, March 15, 1956.

federal authority" so that the school people could "go on about the job of education."[74]

Except for this resolution, most school officials throughout the state remained silent on the desegregation issue unless they were compelled to speak or were staunch supporters of the status quo. A few, including the Greenville superintendent, spoke out against certain legislative acts which they felt would hamper school administration. A small number of South Carolina educators spoke openly against segregation and for compliance with the Supreme Court ruling, but almost without exception they lost their jobs as a result. Among the reported cases were thirty or more black public school teachers and at least six white college professors, including Dean Chester C. Travelstead of the School of Education at the University of South Carolina.[75] There are no reports on record that Greenville teachers or school officials suffered any such reprisals. This investigator recalls, however, a personal conversation in 1957 with a top public school official in Greenville in which the schoolman stated that he and "two or three other officials" would like "to begin experimenting with some desegregation plans," but that in the existing social and political climate, none of them "would dare to mention the subject openly" for fear of losing their jobs or being subjected to other reprisals. This official moved to another state within a year or so, presumably to accept a better job.

The only reported incidents in which school-related people spoke against segregation in Greenville during the 1950s occurred at one of the local colleges. At least one Furman University professor publicly criticized the state's resistance to desegregation as embodying "the very principles of persecution which we resent as being so very characteristic of com-

---

[74] *GN*, August 7, 1955. The resolution was adopted by 126 school trustees representing thirty of the state's forty-six counties.

[75] Southern Regional Council, *Intimidation, Reprisal and Violence*, pp. 13–14. See also *SSN*, January 1956, p. 5; February 1958, p. 7; and August 1958, p. 5.

munism."[76] At another time, the college's student magazine, *The Echo*, carried a pro-integration article which stated that many students were ready for change and wanted "the leaders of the day to lead the way . . . forward, not backward."[77] That issue of the magazine was banned at once and all 1,500 copies of it were seized by the college officials.[78]

One retired school administrator, L. P. Hollis, who had spoken in favor of desegregation before and immediately after the 1954 ruling, continued to call for co-operation between the races. He criticized political leaders for their failures along these lines, pointing out that blacks should be encouraged to vote and should have representation on "the city council, school board and the legislature."[79]

The leaders in several local civic and religious organizations spoke up for racial moderation during the years 1955–60. Among these were the Young Women's Christian Association, the League of Women Voters, the American Association of University Women, and the Council of Church Women. In 1958 these four groups issued statements urging political candidates "to deal with the race issue in a dignified manner."[80] The YWCA, which had carried on a few interracial program activities for several years, provided one of the very few places in Greenville where blacks and whites could meet together and probably the only place in the white community where meal facilities for interracial meetings were available until the 1960s.

The local chapter of the National Conference of Christians and Jews, which was made up of leading Protestant, Catholic, and Jewish layman, sponsored a number of human relations programs in the community during these years. However, since it excluded blacks from membership and activities on

[76] *GN*, March 20, 1956.
[77] *GP*, May 19, 1955.
[78] *SSN*, June 1955, p. 11.
[79] *GN*, May 15, 1958.
[80] *SSN*, June 1958, p. 15.

the premise that the time had not come when such would be acceptable in the community, it is doubtful that this organization had any effect on local race relations. The same can be said of local white and black ministers. A few were involved individually in human relations activities, but their segregated white and black ministerial organizations took little or no part in local racial matters, except to meet together on a biracial basis once or twice a year for "brotherhood and fellowship." Among the local white churches, the Unitarians and Catholics were the only ones open to all races.[81]

In 1956 the Greenville Council on Human Relations, a biracial citizens group "to promote understanding and good will between the white and Negro races" was formed. Initiated by leaders in several of the civic and religious groups just mentioned, the council grew to seventy-five members within a few months.[82] Even though Carll Ladd's study of Greenville's leadership patterns in the early 1960s, *Negro Political Leadership in the South,* labeled the council's work as "very limited," he added that "it has provided a forum for bi-racial discussion." He justifies this evaluation by stating that the only whites participating in it "tend to be the 'town radicals,' generally in sympathy with Negro welfare if not status demands." This results, he explains, from the structure of race relations in Greenville which makes "the association of whites even with this kind of race-advancement organization . . . not wholly respectable."[83] Several community leaders who were inter-

---

[81] The Unitarian Fellowship had no black members but occasionally had black visitors and fairly often had programs related to racial and other human relations issues. The Catholic churches in the community were located in predominately all-white or all-black neighborhoods, but were officially open on a nonracial basis.

[82] From files of the Greenville Council on Human Relations, *Newsletter,* 1956–65, and from interviews with community leaders.

[83] Carll Ladd, *Negro Political Leadership in the South,* pp. 251–52. In the 1950s most of the council's meetings were only semipublic. There was great difficulty in finding a regular meeting place aside from private homes and black churches. The YWCA and Catholic Church

viewed for this study agreed that the council had been ineffective in many ways, but as one commented, "It provided the only significant interracial communication which we had for several years in Greenville and it probably did much to prepare leadership for the later desegregation of schools and other facilities."

Greenville's black citizens were encouraged to take more part in politics by the formation of a local chapter of the Palmetto State Voters Association in July, 1957. The next year the Greenville Committee on Social and Political Action was established to expand the number of black voters.[84]

On the state level, one of the most positive calls for racial moderation during that period came with the publication in 1957 of a small book, *South Carolinians Speak*. The volume, containing statements by twelve white "moderate" leaders, was sponsored by several young Protestant ministers to counteract "the extreme positions that have dominated the picture in our state."[85] It provoked at least twenty-five newspaper editorials and several hundred letters "mostly favorable to it." In one community near Greenville, however, the home of one of the authors was badly damaged by bombing, and two or perhaps three of the sponsoring ministers lost their parishes because of the book.[86]

Finally, in the last days of 1959, South Carolina became the last state to set up an advisory committee to the United States Civil Rights Commission. The governor, who had earlier

---

were the only two downtown predominantly white institutions in which the council was able to meet prior to the 1960s.

[84] *Ibid.*, p. 100.

[85] From a statement by the compilers of the book, as quoted in *SSN*, August 1957, p. 15. The ninety-page book, entitled *South Carolinians Speak: A Moderate Approach to Race Relations*, was compiled by five young ministers and was privately printed. One of the ministers, John B. Morris, later helped to found and became National director of the Episcopal Society for Racial and Cultural Unity (ESCRU).

[86] Ed Cony, "Religion and Race: More Southern Pastors Plead for 'Moderation'; Many Fight Segregation," *The Wall Street Journal*, February 14, 1958. See also *SSN*, December 1957, p. 6.

called the idea of such a group "a very dangerous move in government," finally agreed to its being set up in South Carolina, but reiterated his refusal to co-operate with any of its activities.[87]

Overall, the racial scene in South Carolina during the 1950s was a gloomy one. As the decade ended, a panel of fifteen social science scholars and human relations specialists took a hard look at the state and labeled it as "most firmly resisting" any racial changes. As they described it, "This is one of our states with no desegregation of public educational facilities at the elementary, secondary, or college level. The channels of political expression are firmly under the control of bitter-end segregationists. The laws erected to preserve segregation are as strict and extreme as any in the South." They made the dire prediction that "if any state abandons its entire system of public education to evade compliance with the Constitution of the United States, that state may be South Carolina."[88]

Howard Quint summed up the situation in extremely negative terms:

> South Carolina has not yet embraced democracy as the term is generally defined by Americans outside the South.
>
> Many white South Carolinians still accept a racism which in its extreme form approaches that of Hitler and the Nazis.
>
> Not a few of the arguments and defenses advanced by segregationists against the Court decision are so illogical and so riddled with inconsistencies that sometimes one is obliged to question not only the sincerity but also the intelligence of the spokesman.[89]

[87] *SSN*, April 1959, p. 13; and February 1960, p. 11.

[88] Human Relations Programming in South Carolina, p. 1. The conclusions of the group were described in this unpublished report circulated privately by Penn Community Services, St. Helena Island, Frogmore, South Carolina, October 1, 1960. Among the panelists were Lee Coleman, C. G. Gomillion, Harold Fleming, Marion Wright, the late James McBride Dabbs, Jean Fairfax, and the late Ira De Reid.

[89] Howard H. Quint, *Profile in Black and White: A Frank Portrait of South Carolina*, p. 183. Quint, a professor of history at the University of South Carolina from 1947–58, left the state to accept a position at the University of Colorado just as his book was being published.

A psychologist observing the scene at that time labeled the resistance of South Carolinians as being "not wholehearted resistance . . . but the enactment of a role" related to "the lost cause" of the South, a role in which "the South sees that it has left to itself only the exhibition of loyalty in defeat." He blamed this, plus a sense of "moral embarrassment," as being the cause of so much violence and defiance of all that represents change of status quo.[90]

PRESSURES FOR CHANGE INCREASE (1960–63)

With the 1960s, a fresh and vigorous push was given to the whole civil rights effort with the spontaneous eruption of the "sit-in" or "student demonstration" movement which swept the South and eventually the nation. This, together with a steadily increasing firmness by federal courts in dealing with desegregation cases, a federal administration committed to a strong civil rights program, and the growing pressures from economic leaders for peaceful accommodation to the racial revolution, brought major changes to the southern racial scene and especially to South Carolina by 1963.

The student movement, originating in Greensboro on February 1, 1960, as a protest against segregated lunch counters, spread within a few months to one hundred or more southern communities and involved an estimated 70,000 or more students and supporters who participated in one or more of the "sit-ins" or other direct action projects. Its emphasis soon broadened to include parks, swimming pools, theaters, restaurants, churches, interstate transportation, voting registration, libraries, museums, art galleries, laundromats, employment, beaches, and courtrooms.[91] The movement encountered much

[90] Joseph Margolis, "The Role of the Segregationist," *New South*, January 1958, pp. 8–10. Margolis, a psychology professor at the University of South Carolina at the time the article appeared, left the state at the end of the school year, reputedly under pressure, although college officials refused to comment on his leaving (*SSN*, May 1958, p. 11).

[91] Southern Regional Council, *Special Report on the Student Protest Movement, a Recapitulation, September 1961*, p. 3.

opposition in the form of students and supporters being arrested, state legislators passing a host of antidemonstration laws, public officials making inflamatory remarks, and groups such as the Ku Klux Klan harassing and assaulting demonstrators. But it provoked amazing progress in many areas. It helped to create a new spirit among blacks, giving vigor and cohesion to the civil rights effort. It brought desegregation of public facilities in a number of places, touching off a wave of support which led eventually to the passage of major national civil rights legislation.

Actually, protest began in Greenville several months before the student movement began. In the fall of 1959, at a statewide NAACP meeting in Greenville, the 1,700 participants were encouraged to "work untiringly to eliminate racial discrimination and segregation from all aspects of public life." One local leader predicted that school desegregation would soon become an active issue in Greenville. To add challenge to the conference participants, the chief visiting speaker, Jackie Robinson, was insulted at the local airport by being ordered out of the main waiting room and told that he would have to wait in a small side room reserved for blacks.[92]

The local press reacted to the conference and the airport incident by deploring the "overtones of belligerency" of the blacks, the "talk of demanding and asserting 'rights'," and the emphasis on "efforts to bring about integration of the races at all levels and in all places by force."[93]

The airport incident prompted probably the first public demonstration ever held by Greenville blacks to protest segregation. This took the form of an Emancipation Day "prayer pilgrimage" to the local airport by about three hundred black citizens on January 1, 1960. The peaceful march, led by a local

[92] *GN*, October 25 and 26, 1959. Actually a federal court case had been filed against the airport's segregated facilities in February, 1959, by a Michigan black who had visited Greenville on a business trip. The case remained in the courts for more than a year before finally being settled on technical grounds which did not clarify the basic issue.

[93] *Ibid.*, editorial, October 27, 1959.

clergyman, was closely observed by several hundred whites and an estimated seventy or more policemen.[94]

By early March the first student desegregation effort appeared in Greenville when eight black high school students entered the downtown "white only" public library to try to borrow books.[95] They were refused service and were arrested after declining to leave. When faced with a federal court suit, the city's officials responded by announcing that the public library would be closed to everyone.[96] Actually, there was some public support for desegregating the library as shown by several letters to the local newspapers.[97] But the city's official reaction, as expressed by the mayor, was that these "few Negroes . . . if allowed to continue their self-centered purposes, may conceivably bring about a closing of all schools, parks, swimming pools and other facilities." He added that he could not understand what prompted such action, especially since "the library board has, at considerable expense, built up an excellent Negro [branch] library" which "contains an excellent collection of books, pamphlets and magazines of particular interest to the Negro race."[98]

[94] *Ibid.*, January 2, 1960. The minister, the Rev. James S. Hall, pastor of Springfield Baptist Church, one of Greenville's largest black churches, was harassed so much for this and other civil rights activities that he left the state in 1963.

[95] *Ibid.*, March 17, 1960.

[96] *Ibid.*, July 29, September 3 and 4, 1960.

[97] *GN*, September 7 and 18, 1960. During the library crisis one of Greenville's top elected officials, who had devoted much time and effort to obtaining support for an enlarged library system, was asked if he could do anything to resolve the crisis situation. "It's like this," he replied. "I know that integration is the right thing. After all, I teach a Sunday school class in my church. However, I am in politics, the Negro vote in Greenville is very slight, and I do not feel that my white constituency is ready for integration. So, for the present I feel that I must remain quiet about racial matters. However, if and when the time comes that I feel that I can speak out on such matters, I will gladly do so." Several years later when the Greenville schools were ordered to desegregate, this same official was one of the chief local spokesmen for "law and order" and "compliance" with the court order. (From the American Friends Service Committee's *Staff Report*, April 1960.)

[98] *GN*, September 3, 1960.

One local editor, who was also a member of the public library board, blamed the "handful of Negroes" for having "seriously impaired if not destroyed" a library system "intended to serve upwards of 200,000 Negro and white citizens. . . . " The board had "acted reluctantly, perhaps loathfully," he explained, to avert "an influx of mixed races."[90]

After a few weeks the library, with little or no publicity, was reopened, still on a "segregated" basis, but this time by sex instead of by race. This arrangement lasted only a short time.

The official response to the library crisis was typical of Greenville's reaction as well as that of the rest of South Carolina to the forty or more protests in the state against segregation during the spring of 1960 and the numerous others which occurred during the next two years. State political leaders generally condemned the protests. One of them, the lieutenant governor, a Greenville resident, blamed the "racial unrest" on "outsiders," and called the "demonstrations by Negroes a shame and a black eye to our history of sound, reasonable race relations in South Carolina."[100] The governor pledged to Greenville and other communities the support of "any help desired" from state law enforcement officials in quelling disturbances.[101] In the legislature there was a flurry of bills and resolutions to strengthen trespass laws, to curb demonstrations, to impeach the Supreme Court, and to curtail the power of the federal government. One resolution condemned the federal government for interfering in the internal apartheid affairs of South Africa,[102] and another censured Frank Graham, prominent North Carolinian and United Nations mediator, for a speech he made at a South Carolina college in which he casually commended the idea that public facilities should be desegregated.[103]

[99] *Ibid.*, editorial, September 7, 1960.
[100] *SSN*, April 1960, p. 4; June 1960, p. 10.
[101] *New York Times*, July 27, 1960.
[102] *SSN*, March, April, and May 1960.
[103] *Ibid.*, June 1961, p. 15.

In Greenville, demonstrators at lunch counters and other facilities were arrested on numerous occasions during the summer of 1960 and later,[104] and, as a result of several clashes between groups of teen-agers, a nighttime curfew was imposed for several weeks on all persons under twenty-one years of age.[105] The city's roller skating rink was closed permanently when a black group tried to use it, and the city's two segregated public swimming pools were closed in the face of integration threats.[106] The "Negro" pool was sold to a private group. In the case of the "white" one, city officials imported several sea lions and Greenville became perhaps "the only city in the United States that provides swimming facilities for sea lions but not for its citizens."[107] This situation existed for several years. Then in the late 1960s, after a "reported leak" in the pool, city officials had it drained, filled with dirt, and made into a flower garden.

The local press spent much time during these years lamenting the "violence, threats of violence . . . and flouting of the law" by the demonstrators. The mayor continued to declare that peace would be maintained at all costs, for " 'colored' and 'white' alike and . . . demonstrator and spectator alike,"[108] although on one occasion a prominent local business leader predicted that "bloodshed appears to be inevitable if something is not done."[109] At another time the Greenville Kiwanis Club cancelled a luncheon speech by Harry Golden because they feared that his visit might provoke violence.[110] Golden, the liberal but popular editor of the *Carolina Israelite*, author of several best selling books, and noted satirist regarding racial issues, commented, "I wouldn't be rude, but I would talk about integration. . . . I would tell them to integrate their schools. . . . I told them [the Greenville Kiwanis Club leaders] that

[104] *GN*, August 10 and 25, 1960.
[105] *Ibid.*, July 26 and August 24, 1960.
[106] *Ibid.*, September 29, 1965.
[107] Ladd, *Negro Political Leadership*, p. 80.
[108] *GN*, editorial, August 24, 1960.
[109] *New York Times*, July 29, 1960.
[110] *SSN*, July 1960, p. 10.

it's silly for a state that produced a great general like Francis Marion, the 'Swamp Fox,' to be worried about a little fat guy making a speech."

Despite the numerous sit-in demonstrations of 1960 and the "Freedom Rides" of the following year, almost no racial barriers dropped in Greenville or other South Carolina communities until 1963.[111] In contrast, a number of lunch counters and restaurants, a few theaters, and some other facilities in North Carolina, particularly in Greensboro and other Piedmont area cities, desegregated in 1960 and 1961.[112]

Ladd accounts for this difference in reaction by pointing out one factor already noted in this study, namely that the Piedmont areas of the two states have many characteristics in common, but politically they have been in very different categories, both being strongly bound to the politics of their respective states. The North Carolina Piedmont industrial area, with its trend toward accommodating to moderate racial changes so as not to upset industrial growth, has strongly influenced that state's political stance. In South Carolina, however, the "low-country" rural and small town area, suffering from a "Reconstruction era" hangover, still dominated state politics in the early 1960s. Ladd credits this difference in action in the two areas to the difference in strength of the blacks (politically, economically, educationally, etc.) in each place. In Greenville, he cites "the relative weakness of the Negro community" as being responsible for "little pressure" being "exerted on the city's white population to take a new posture toward Negroes." In the North Carolina Piedmont blacks developed enough strength to exert some power for change by the late 1950s and early 1960s. By 1963, however, the "massive" racial demonstrations which were then sweeping much of the South, but not Greenville, "convinced many Greenville whites that their turn would soon come." This

---

[111] Ladd, *Negro Political Leadership*, pp. 77, 83.
[112] Southern Regional Council, *Special Report*, p. 3.

accounts for the fact that suddenly the city moved from having no biracial forum for its leaders to having two such groups in 1963, a semiofficial one and an unofficial one.[113]

Certainly there was little publicly displayed moderate leadership regarding racial matters in Greenville prior to 1963. On one occasion in 1960 a Chamber of Commerce official made a plea for creation of a city biracial committee,[114] but neither he nor other top leaders seem to have done anything to further the idea at that time.

There are several versions as to how the two 1963 committees came into existence.[115] Undoubtedly, much credit for beginning the unofficial group, which began to meet in 1962, must go to L. P. Hollis, who spoke out for school desegregation even before 1954 and who was able, despite his liberal views, to maintain a leadership position in the city and use his influence for human relations. The biracial group which he convened soon prompted the Greenville Chamber of Commerce to set up a semiofficial race relations committee of top business, industrial, religious, and civic leaders.

In the summer and fall of 1963, without any fanfare or demonstrations, these committees brought about desegregation of the city's lunch counters, some restaurants, and a few other facilities.[116] Most other facilities, however, did not desegregate until the Civil Rights Act of 1964 became law.[117]

A second major factor in bringing racial change to Green-

---

[113] Ladd, *Negro Political Leadership*, pp. 73–77, 83.

[114] *New York Times*, July 29, 1960. A local black leader responded publicly very favorably to this idea (*SSN*, September 1960, p. 11), and the State Advisory Committee to the U. S. Civil Rights Commission made a similar recommendation to all South Carolina communities (*SSN*, August 1960, p. 2). In Greenville an unsuccessful follow-up effort was made in the fall of 1960 by members of the local Human Relations Council to promote this idea of an official biracial committee (from American Friends Service Committee, *Field Reports*, unpublished, October 1960).

[115] Ladd, *Negro Political Leadership*, pp. 77, 83.

[116] *GP*, September 30, 1965.

[117] Ladd, *Negro Political Leadership*, p. 83.

ville and the entire South after 1960 was the increasing federal government pressure regarding civil rights. This included the strong commitment on the part of the Kennedy administration to "equality of opportunity for all citizens" and the growing firmness with which federal courts dealt with desegregation cases.

Both national political parties included firm civil rights planks in their 1960 platforms, but Democrat John F. Kennedy pledged to put this item at the top of his list of proposed legislation if elected. When the votes were counted, he was the new President, and he had received almost 90 percent of the nation's black vote.

The Democrats lost six southern states, but South Carolina, along with its state administration, remained in the Kennedy fold despite a strong "Democrats for Nixon" drive led by Senator Thurmond and other conservatives.

Under the Kennedy administration there was a slow but steadily increasing drive to encourage local compliance with existing civil rights laws, to provide supportive action for enforcing court orders, and to increase in various ways the amount of desegregation in federal agencies, schools, employment, and other areas of life.[118]

As more and more school cases reached the federal courts, the rulings on them became clearer and firmer regarding the necessity for southern school systems to give some evidence of complying with the 1954 Supreme Court ruling. In the fall of 1960 New Orleans began desegregation under court order. In January, 1961, the University of Georgia was ordered to accept its first black students, and that fall Atlanta's public schools acceded to a court order to desegregate. That same fall, Memphis and Dallas also began court-ordered desegregation.[119] This left only three states in the nation with no desegregation

[118] *SSN*, October, November, and December 1960; March and May 1961; January and November 1962.

[119] *Ibid.* See ten-year summary of school desegregation highlights, May 1964, pp. 12–13B.

at any level in their public education systems—Mississippi, Alabama, and South Carolina.

The University of Mississippi was ordered in 1962 to accept its first Negro student. Mississippi's state officials had vowed never to permit desegregation in their state. However, with firm federal support from President Kennedy and the Justice Department, the court order was carried out in the fall of 1962. Riots, bloodshed, and major destruction of property ensued, but it became very clear to the nation that desegregation orders by federal courts would be obeyed, even if force were required.[120]

The Mississippi violence had a strong impact on South Carolinians, for they realized that their turn to face the reality of desegregation could not be far away. Even as the Mississippi crisis occurred, four federal court cases to desegregate public schools in South Carolina were awaiting trial,[121] and similar suits against three of the state's public colleges—the University of South Carolina, Clemson, and Winthrop—had been or were in process of being filed.

There was considerable sympathy expressed that fall by South Carolina's political leaders and editors for the plight of their fellow Southerners upon whom "integration" had been forced so violently, and there was strong criticism of the federal government. However, there was a noticeable lack of the rigid segregation attitude which had prevailed earlier in the state. As one Greenville editor expressed it, "With a feeling of horror the thinking South Carolinian realizes full well that what has happened in Mississippi can happen" here. "Even as they sorrow with Mississippi in her suffering, thinking South Carolinians hope the lesson is being impressed upon

[120] For an excellent analysis of conditions and factors involved in this crisis situation, see James W. Silver, *Mississippi: The Closed Society.*

[121] Desegregation suits had been filed in Charleston, Darlington, Marion, and Sumter by the fall of 1962. The Clarendon County case was still in the courts but was not being pressed. Actually, only the Charleston case was being given any high priority at that time (see *SSN*, May 1964, June 1962, February 1961, and October 1960).

the leaders of this state and upon all the people of this state."[122]

A Carolina social scientist, in commenting on the situation, pointed out that "aggression—and that is what you must term the Mississippi riots—is the result of frustration. . . . The best way to prevent aggression is either to reduce the frustration or eliminate the gains made by it. . . . I'm not saying there won't be some violence in South Carolina" when desegregation comes, for "some [people] react to how they feel instead of analyzing the results of what happened somewhere else. . . ." He predicted, however, that "organized violence" would not occur because, as he viewed the scene, the tragedies of Oxford, Mississippi, eliminated from the minds of most Carolinians the thought that any benefit could result from such violence.[123]

This prediction proved to be remarkably valid. When South Carolina's first school desegregation came just four months later with the court-ordered admission of Harvey Gantt to Clemson University in January, 1963, "there was no violence, no demonstrations occurred and regular educational processes were not interrupted. . . ." In fact, the biggest problem on the scene appears to have been a logistical one—what to do with the 160 newsmen from over the nation who showed up and insisted on accompanying the lone black student around the campus and to classes.

In the days and weeks before Gantt's admission, many of the state's leaders and groups publicly called for peaceful and orderly compliance with the court order. This included many state officials, most of whom, as one newsman reported, were "staunch segregationists," but most of whom "had spoken softly, some bitterly, some resignedly" but "all firmly" appealing for "peace and order," though many reiterated their opposition to desegregation. Such appeals came from across

---

[122] *GP*, editorial, October 2, 1962.

[123] From a speech in November, 1962, by a Winthrop College psychology professor, Rondeau G. Laffitte, Jr., as reported in *SSN*, December 1962, p. 8.

the state, from both the outgoing governor and his successor, from the chairman of the state's "Segregation Committee," from former governor James Byrnes, from the Clemson University president, from the state's Republican party officials, from numerous church, professional, and business leaders and organizations.[124] Most of the state's major newspapers joined in this plea.

The state's outgoing governor, Ernest F. Hollings, epitomized this revised racial stance on the part of many Carolina leaders in one of his final official speeches in January, 1963:

> South Carolina is running out of courts. If and when every legal remedy has been exhausted . . . [we] must make clear [our] choice, a government of laws rather than a government of men. As determined as we are, we must realize the lesson of 100 years ago and move on for the good of South Carolina and our United States. This should be done with dignity. It must be done with law and order.[125]

A third major factor in bringing this official change in South Carolina's racial policies was the growing pressure from business and industrial leaders who had come to realize that racial unrest was a threat to economic growth and prosperity.[126] A. W. Bethea, an ardent segregationist, in criticizing Clemson University's "downfall," pinpointed the economic issue. He accused state leaders of having "sold their way of life for a few measly industries."[127] He referred particularly to one of the state's leading contractors, the late Charles E. Daniel of

[124] *SSN*, February 1963, pp. 1, 8–9.
[125] *SSN*, February 1963, p. 8.
[126] The significance of economic influences in altering desegregation policies of various southern states is documented in William H. Nicholls' *Southern Tradition and Regional Progress*. His discussion of "Economic Aspects of the School Integration Issue," pp. 114–23, is especially helpful. Harry Ashmore's *An Epitaph for Dixie*, pp. 113–32, includes an excellent discussion of this issue. Cal Brumley's "Segregation Costs," *Wall Street Journal*, December 17, 1957, contains several pertinent illustrations and quotes from specific situations.
[127] From a speech in the state legislature on March, 1963, as reported by *SSN*, April 1963, p. 15.

Greenville, a Clemson trustee and a former United States senator,[128] who had been mentioned in a national magazine as being a key figure among a group of "business and political leaders" who worked together, "often behind the scenes," to insure that no violence would accompany the college's desegregation.[129] As early as July, 1961, Daniel had begun to express for himself and undoubtedly for other business and industrial leaders in the state dissatisfaction with the way racial matters were being handled. In what came to be known and quoted as "Daniel's watermelon speech"—it was delivered at the annual Watermelon Festival at Hampton, South Carolina—he made a pointed appeal for a more realistic approach to desegregation, particularly in improved training and use of "all" labor resources, black and white.

The desegregation issue cannot continue to be hidden behind the door. This situation cannot be satisfactorily settled at the lunch counter and bus station levels. We must handle this ourselves more realistically than heretofore, or it will be forced upon us in the harshest way. Either we act on our own terms or we forfeit the right to act.

The Negro population represents a large working force in South Carolina relatively untrained. It is an important potential to industry. We have a definite obligation to increase the productivity of our Negro citizens, to provide them with good jobs at good wages and to continue to assure them of fair treatment. By raising their educational and economic status, we would raise the whole economy of the state. . . .

[128] Almost every Greenville leader who was interviewed for this study listed Daniel as one of the key power figures in city and state affairs. As head of one of the nation's largest construction firms (listed in 1960 as the second largest industrial builder in the nation), Daniel was not noted for liberal views on race or labor, but he was a determined advocate of industrial development for South Carolina and the South. He is credited personally with having recruited scores of northern industries to move South and with having built several hundred industrial plants, hospitals, college buildings, and commercial establishments, many of them in South Carolina and Greenville.
[129] George McMillan, "Integration with Dignity," *Saturday Evening Post*, March 9, 1963.

We rank at, or near the bottom [in the nation] in per capita income; in standards of education; indeed, in too many areas of life. . . . To catch up, our state must forsake some of our old ways and aggressively outdo other states in selling South Carolina to the nation. . . .[130]

There was little enthusiasm for Daniel's speech at first. The governor reacted by declaring that "under my administration we will not have a policy of integrating any industry."[131] Within a few months, however, he was speaking more moderately, saying that the state had "a firm policy of flexibility" regarding school desegregation and that this policy received "a new look" daily. He added that there was nothing in state law to prevent voluntary desegregation, but that he had seen no indication of interest in such a movement.[132]

About this same time, at least two other state officials, Robert E. McNair and Frances B. Nicholson, expressed similar views regarding school desegregation, one proposing that "the people in the areas affected will have to determine their own course of action."[133] Probably these officials had heard of or read the remarks made by Virginia's Governor J. Lindsay Almond a few days earlier. The governor declared that his administration had acceded to desegregation rather than have a widespread closing of schools because the latter would have destroyed the state's industrial growth. Certainly they must have been aware of Arkansas' major loss of new industry during and after the Little Rock school crisis,[134] of Virginia's poor

---

[130] *GN*, July 2, 1961.

[131] *SSN*, August 1961, p. 13.

[132] *Ibid.*, January 1962, p. 15.

[133] *Ibid.*, December 1961, p. 16.

[134] From a luncheon talk in Richmond on December 4, 1961, as reported in *SSN*, January 1962, p. 9. The economics of the Little Rock story are reported in numerous places, including: Jim Montgomery, "Challenge from Little Rock," *Atlanta Constitution*, November 5, 1959; Nicholls, *Southern Tradition*, pp. 118–19: Erwin McDonald, "Arkansas Cannot Afford Issue of Racial Strife," *New South*, March 1959, pp. 11–12; and the *Wall Street Journal*, October 1, 1962.

record of attracting industry during its "massive resistance" era,[135] and of North Carolina's significant success in industrial growth, the result of the state's moderate approach to racial problems.[136] Undoubtedly, they had heard such stories as that of the northern firm which planned to move South, and after narrowing the choice to Alabama or North Carolina, visited both states to inquire about schools. Alabama's Governor Patterson supposedly told the firm's officials that he would close every school before permitting any desegregation. In contrast, North Carolina's Governor Hodges assured them that not only would his state's schools remain open, but they would receive increased financial support. The firm moved to North Carolina.[137]

The economic consequence of adhering to a rigid segregation policy was dramatically expressed by one official of South Carolina's State Development Board just after the Mississippi crisis. He predicted that if South Carolina should permit such a situation to develop, the state's industrial development program would have to "fold up its tent and go to bed."[138]

These major changes in the state's racial policies did not come without opposition. There was loudspoken criticism from Citizens Council and Ku Klux Klan groups and from those politicians who continued to find support from such segregationist quarters. In the fall of 1962 and early 1963, this opposition became focused on the Clemson University desegregation. Several political leaders, primarily from rural areas,

[135] Nicholls, *Southern Tradition*, pp. 115–18. See also Benjamin Muse's "Bring New Industry to Virginia," *New South*, May 1959, pp. 13–14, and *Virginia's Massive Resistance*, pp. 106-110, 120–21.

[136] Macolm Seawell, "North Carolina at the Crossroad," *New South*, January 1959, pp. 3–5; *SSN*, December 1959, p. 9.

[137] From a column by Ralph McGill in the *Nashville Tennessean*, March 10, 1959, as referred to in Nicholls, *Southern Tradition*, pp. 117–18. Nicholls cites quotes from Alabama business leaders in the *Birmingham Post–Herald*, February 6, 1957, in support of the McGill story.

[138] As quoted in an editorial in the *Florence Morning News*, October 6, 1962.

made speeches attacking the federal courts and the "sellout" by state leaders. A number of segregation bills were introduced in the legislature. These included measures to close Clemson, to ban "class action" in court cases, to require segregation by sex in public schools, to establish a state tuition grant program for developing private schools if desegregation should come to public schools, and a bill designed to thwart the federal government's desegregation pressures on affected schools near military bases.

The tuition grant bill was the only one which passed both houses. It was opposed by many professional educators and various leaders and groups, especially in Greenville and other major cities, but it had the backing of the "Segregation Committee," the White Citizens Association, and the governor.[139] A drive to set up private schools, similar to the one in Prince Edward County, Virginia, was started by a small South Carolina group as early as 1961, but even after the tuition grant bill was passed, very few private schools were opened.[140]

By the spring of 1963, "a very significant change of mood" had occurred in South Carolina's racial climate, as Howard G. McClain, a human relations worker, interpreted the scene. "Racism as a political issue" had "died," he observed, and the Mississippi crisis had convinced South Carolinians that the violence of Oxford "must not occur in South Carolina." He gave much credit for the change to "the state's political and

---

[139] *SSN*, February, March, April, May, June, and July 1963. Officials of the State Department of Education remained very cool toward it however, and various professional groups such as the State Parent-Teacher Association Congress, State Education Association (white) and State chapter of the American Association of University Professors opposed it.

[140] *Ibid.*, April 1961, p. 14; September 1964, p. 13. The group was chartered as the Foundation for Independent Schools, Inc. Its chief supporters were in the Charleston area. As late as September, 1964, only five private schools, enrolling about seven hundred students, were operating in three coastal area communities. There were none in the Greenville area except two church-related ones until 1970 when the creation of a "unitary" public school system prompted the opening of "at least a half dozen" segregated white private schools.

economic leaders," but added that "many churches and Christians—lay and clergy," had helped to prepare public opinion for the change.[141]

Certainly religious leaders and groups had begun to act and speak with less timidity in support of racial change than they had in the 1950s. As early as 1961 a move was made by Greenville's white and black ministerial groups to have some exploratory meetings together "in the hope of opening lines of communication between the races."[142] That same year the state's Roman Catholic prelate publicly declared that all parochial schools in the state would desegregate "not later than the public schools," and in 1962 the South Carolina Council of Churches organized itself on an interracial basis. In 1963 the South Carolina Methodist Conference approved the idea of its colleges being desegregated, and a joint ministerial group was finally formed in Greenville.

Other indications of the changes that had been going on included the general de-emphasis of racism in the state's 1962 political campaigns by all major candidates,[143] the lack of segregation bills or resolutions in the state legislature after 1961 (except for a flurry in 1963 as noted earlier),[144] and the legislative deletion in 1961–62 from the annual state appropriation bill of a school segregation requirement which had been a regular part of such bills since 1956. The removal of the "segregation" phrase from the appropriations bill was interpreted in at least two ways. Some observers thought that it was done to make it less difficult to adjust to desegregation. Officials who advocated that the phrase be dropped, however,

[141] From the director's report to the South Carolina Christian Action Council, April 18, 1963 (as reported in SSN, May 1963, p. 14).

[142] GN, February 7, 1961.

[143] SSN, March 1961, p. 16; June 1962, p. 5; and July 1963, p. 7. One factor contributing to this lack of racism may have been the upsurge in black voter registration in 1961–62. The total state registration was up from 606,886 in 1960 to over 650,000 in 1962, and it was estimated that over 90,000 Negroes were registered by 1962.

[144] Ibid., March 1962, p. 2.

argued that the action would fortify the state's segregation stand legally by strengthening another law which required that a tedious, complicated set of administrative procedures be exhausted by every transfer applicant before going to court.[145]

By the summer of 1963, two other court rulings had been handed down against South Carolina schools. The University of South Carolina was ordered to accept its first black students since the Reconstruction era, and the Charleston City Schools, the second largest public school system in the state, was ordered to desegregate. Both orders were carried out peacefully in September, four blacks being admitted to the university, and eleven black students being transferred into four previously all-white schools in Charleston.

In contrast to the one public school system and two state colleges desegregated in South Carolina by the fall of 1963, North Carolina had thirty-nine public school districts, all state colleges and all major private colleges desegregated to some extent by that time. However, most of the desegregation in both states was still "token."[146]

GREENVILLE COURT CASE (1963–64)

Greenville's first real confrontation with the school desegregation issue came in August, 1963, nine years after the Supreme Court's historic decision, but only six months after South Carolina's first compliance with it.[147] Just as Charleston was being ordered by a federal judge to begin desegregation in its public schools,[148] the parents of six Greenville black

[145] For discussions of both views, see *SSN*, June 1960, February 1961, and February 1962.

[146] *SSN*, September 1963, pp. 1, 22; October 1963, p. 16.

[147] Clemson University accepted one black student by court order in January, 1963, the first state supported school on any level in South Carolina to begin desegregation (*SSN*, February 1963, p. 1).

[148] On August 22, 1963, Charleston was ordered by a federal judge to begin desegregation in September by transferring eleven black students

students requested that their children be transferred into all-white schools.

At a Greenville School Board meeting in August, 1963, the school superintendent reported that he had received the applications and that they were "being given careful attention," but no discussion ensued. Several parents attended the meeting, hoping to be able to discuss the requests with the board, but they "were not given an opportunity to speak."[149]

All the requests were denied in writing a few days later by the superintendent. The reasons given, if any, were technical ones having little or no relationship to the issue of desegregation. At least two of the parents still seemed to think that the school officials might quietly begin desegregation that fall, for they sought to enroll their children at all-white schools at the beginning of the fall term. One parent said, "We had all hoped that integration in the Greenville public schools would come without any trouble and we still hope so." Their hopes were temporarily denied, so they turned to the use of litigation. The parents of five students joined in a desegregation suit against the school board.[150]

While this court case was being filed, desegregation began quietly, without any publicity, at the city's new adult technical training center which was financed with local, state, and federal funds and administered by Greenville's school officials. Elsewhere in the state that fall, desegregation began peacefully in the Charleston public schools and began, or continued, on three state college campuses.

In contrast, Alabama, which was under a court order to

---

into previously all-white schools. The case of *Millicent F. Brown, et al.,* v. *School District 20 of Charleston County,* had been filed May 28, 1962 (*SSN,* September 1963, p. 1, and May 1964, p. 16B).

[149] Greenville School Board, *Minutes,* August 13, 1963. See *GN,* August 14, 1963.

[150] *GN,* August 16 and 20; September 4, 1963. On August 19 one of the parents, A. J. Whittenburg, a local black businessman and NAACP president, filed suit on behalf of his eleven-year-old daughter, Elaine. The parents of four other students joined the suit by early September.

begin public school desegregation for the first time that fall, was the scene of riots, bombings, and bitter conflict between state and federal officials.[151] To show that there was some change of mood in South Carolina from earlier years, one Greenville editor stated, "Governor Wallace invites bloodshed" by "stirring up the rabble" and creating a situation in which "innocent people are suffering." He added that "the people of South Carolina do not want integration, and they will oppose it as long as they can . . . but it is obvious" that they "intend to preserve their public schools" and that "they will preserve peace and good order."[152]

Even though there appeared to be a new mood of peaceful acceptance of change as the only alternative to violent change in the South Carolina community, racism was not dead. Only a few days earlier, the same editor, in a long diatribe on the "March on Washington" of August, 1963, labeled it as that "long planned and widely publicized 'Freedom March' . . . by 200,000 Negroes, mulattoes and white sympathizers" whose "months long emotional binge has passed its climax."[153] Even a year later, after the passage of the 1964 Civil Rights Act, he was still militantly espousing segregation, calling the bill "shameful, vengeant," and "compounded of misguided altruism, harsh political pressure and militant minority threats of violence in the streets. . . ." He declared that it would "produce not equality but federal harassment or worse and a form of civil chaos." At the same time, he emphasized, "just as we opposed by all lawful means the integration efforts . . . in public school cases . . . and implementation of that erroneous legal folly [the 1954 Supreme Court ruling], so we have opposed the civil rights bill—by lawful means." He added that "we do not intend to disobey the laws. . . ."[154]

There were overt tones of racism also in the Greenville

---

[151] See *SSN*, September, October, and December 1963.
[152] *GN*, editorial, September 7, 1963.
[153] *Ibid.*, August 30, 1963.
[154] *Ibid.*, July 5, 1964.

School Board's reply to its desegregation suit. The board's attorney, in seeking to have the case dismissed, spoke of "the distinctly, . . . ethnological, . . . biological, . . . mental and behavioral" differences between the races as being valid grounds for the longstanding policy of "voluntary segregation" used in the school system.[155] Much of the statement seems to have been borrowed from the argument used a few weeks earlier by the Charleston School Board, arguments based on testimony by two "scholars," William E. Hoy, a University of South Carolina biologist, and Ernest van den Haag, a New York University psychologist.[156] The statement pointed out that "existing ethnic and group differences in educational achievement and psychometric intelligence are of such a magnitude" that desegregation would "seriously impair the academic standards and educational opportunities for the white children of Greenville." It added that "the mean mental age of white children in the . . . district . . . ranges from two to four years ahead of the mean mental age of Negro school children in the same district. . . ." It referred also to "modern social science" which "recognizes physically observable racial differences," and forms "a basis for preferential association and social distance." "Compulsory association of two diverse and physically distinct racial groups" would "lead to an increase in tension and promote social disharmony" which would prevent "the members of each race" from developing "the unique combination of different abilities and traits each has. . . ." The statement went on to say:

The board is informed and believes that there are such differences and disparities between ethnic groups attending schools in the School District of Greenville County as to form a rational basis for separation of such ethnic groups in the schools. . . .
Defendents further allege that the origins and formation of the various races of mankind have resulted from differential and adap-

[155] From the school board attorney's statement as printed in the *GN*, September 10, 1963.
[156] *SSN*, September 1963, p. 22.

tive selection of heredity variation (arising from mutations and genetic drift) in reproductively isolated populations. The differences have been perpetuated and stabilized through continued isolation and inbreeding of the major races over long periods of time. There are significant differences in cerebral morphology and physical constitutions which are structurally related to racial differences in mental, physical and behavioral traits. Such differences constitute a rational basis for segregation of races in schools, particularly among the young and immature. . . .[157]

At a preliminary hearing in March, 1964, Federal District Judge Robert Martin refused to dismiss the Greenville case, but, at the request of the school board attorney, he granted the board thirty days to reconsider the black students' transfer applications and "to outline a broad policy" on what it planned "to do about future transfer applications or initial assignments."[158]

On April 14, the board held a special meeting and voted to transfer the five students as of that fall. It also adopted a new five-point policy regarding "the enrollment, assignment and transfer of pupils," such to be done "without regard to race, color or creed."[159] Two weeks later, in a second court hearing, the board's "voluntary" actions were accepted by the judge and the case was settled without a formal trial, but with the court issuing a "consent order" on April 27.[160]

The board's actions in going to court and then pursuing the litigation in the manner as described were "purely a matter of strategy" as interpreted by at least four interviewees, who were either school officials or persons closely related to the

[157] *GN*, September 10, 1963.

[158] *Ibid.*, March 20, 1964.

[159] Greenville School Board, *Minutes*, April 14, 1964. The new policy provided that initial assignment and transfer of each pupil would be governed by such factors as the preference expressed by the child, whether the school offered the educational program needed by the child, physical capacity of the school, and distance the child lived from the specific school.

[160] *GN*, April 28, 1964. See also *Race Relations Law Reporter*, 9:719–23, and *SSN*, May 1964, p. 8-A.

operation of the schools. One commented, "We knew we had to desegregate, whether we liked it or not. It was just better public relations in our area to have it appear that we were forced to take such an action. Then the federal courts would have to bear the brunt of public criticism." In the words of another official, "We could have desegregated earlier voluntarily, but we were bound by tradition, there was state pressure on us to conform to the state pattern, and there was a reluctance on the part of most board members to raise controversial issues." This official added, however, that "expedience was more important to most of the board than any belief in segregation." As to why the board took its "voluntary" step at the last moment rather than go through a trial, it appears that expediency was again involved. One interviewee explained it by saying that "the board volunteered to accept what it knew would be the judge's minimum order" in view of his earlier Charleston decision. "It feared that a trial might result in a much stronger order," he added. The board's official statement was that "from a legal standpoint, no useful purpose could be served by prolonging the litigation."[161]

Under the court-approved policy, any child in the system could seek transfer from one school to another during a designated thirty-day period. The request would be acted upon within another thirty days by the board "without regard to race, color or creed."[162] During the reassignment period, set for the month of May, the school officials received requests from seventy-five black students for transfer to previously all-white schools.[163]

In July the school superintendent announced that fifty-five of these, including the five in the court case, would be transferred in September to sixteen schools scattered throughout

---

[161] From a "Public Statement by the Greenville County School Board," as it appeared in *GN*, April 28, 1964.
[162] Greenville School Board, *Minutes*, April 14, 1964.
[163] *Ibid.*, June 9, 1964.

the school district. The group included eighteen elementary and thirty-seven high school students.[164]

PREPARATION FOR DESEGREGATION (1964)

Most of the general efforts at community preparation for accepting school desegregation in Greenville had strong negative overtones. It was as if the community was faced with an unpleasant but inevitable change which it must accept peacefully or at the risk of untold violence and disaster.

One local editor expressed this view in blunt terms: "We are opposed to integration of the schools, now or in the foreseeable future," and "we are certain . . . that the overwhelming majority of the citizens of Greenville County . . . object" because "it is detrimental to the cause of education of both races . . . , it is being forced on them by the federal government" on the basis of a "Supreme Court decision which we are sure . . . is unconstitutional," and "almost everywhere it [integration] had been tried . . . it has resulted in increased racial tension, more bitterness and sometimes strife and violence." However, the school board "has exhausted every legal resource," and it is "a choice between coercive federal enforcement of this decree, or a more harsh one, and reluctant but good faith compliance." He concluded, "For now we can only make the best of this inevitable situation . . . ," but "agitators and troublemakers of whatever race or opinion should be advised that . . . disruption of the schools or the public peace and good order will not be tolerated."[165]

"Law and order" was emphasized in the local press during the next few months prior to and after the fall opening of school. Local law enforcement officials took up this theme also,

---

[164] *Ibid.*, July 14, 1964. See also *GN*, July 15, 1964.

[165] From a lengthy editorial in the *GN*, April 28, 1964, on the day following the court's "consent order" against the local school board to desegregate.

some of them reluctantly but with the determination that no violence would occur.[166] The county solicitor made several public speeches, emphasizing that "whether we like it or not, we are going to support law and order, and anyone who causes trouble will be prosecuted."

Greenville's two semiofficial, biracial committees, which had been organized the year before, were not directly involved with the school issue. However, their behind-the-scenes efforts in bringing about the peaceful desegregation of lunch counters, theaters, hotels, and restaurants undoubtedly helped to lay the groundwork for community acceptance of other racial changes.[167] Some white church leaders and groups carried on programs to prepare their constituencies, but these activities were few and widely scattered. One church sponsored several Sunday evening discussions about desegregation and included a few local black leaders, another church's official board sent letters to all its high school students to urge their "Christian response" to any black fellow students who might be in school with them that fall, and several individual ministers, religious education directors, and Sunday school workers are reported to have made appeals through sermons, discussions, or various human relations materials for the peaceful acceptance of desegregation. The Greenville Ministerial Association, which became interracial in 1962, kept aware of desegregation moves in the city and heard pleas from several individuals for support of peaceful change, but it took no official action.

One group which had considerable influence in preparing the black community for desegregation, particularly the students who were to be transferred, was the Greenville Education Committee. Begun in early 1964 by the parents of the five

[166] Two members of the city's semiofficial biracial committee reported that "numerous conferences" between members of the committee and city and county law enforcement officials had been held, and "much persuasion" had been needed to convince the law enforcement representatives that they should support peaceful desegregation.

[167] See *GN*, September 29, 1965; Ladd, *Negro Political Leadership*, pp. 77, 83; and *GP*, September 30, 1965.

students in the court suit, plus a few other black leaders, the committee organized a county-wide effort during the spring to encourage support for desegregation. Most of the seventy other students who sought desegregation in May of that year were recruited through the work of this group.[168] To aid the transferees "both academically and psychologically" in making "the adjustment to all-white schools," the committee sponsored a six-week "tutorial program" for them. Held in a local black church, the project had an interracial volunteer staff of eighteen teachers headed by Sarah Lowrey, a retired Furman University speech professor. Local school officials loaned textbooks for the program.[169] There was considerable praise from schoolmen and others for the project's effectiveness in orienting the transferees to the new experiences ahead for them.

There was little or no obvious desegregation preparation carried on by Greenville school officials among teachers, students and parents, or in the general community, except in their call for "law and order."

The school board's public statement, just after agreeing in court to a plan of desegregation, was that it was "not pleased with the prospect of integration of the schools" but that it had no alternative. The board appealed for "the best efforts and calm judgement of all our citizens . . . to assure the continued growth, improvement and harmony of our schools."[170] Privately, some school leaders met with local press and police officials to gain their co-operation in setting the stage for the peaceful desegregation of schools. There were three meetings of all school principals to map out plans for handling administrative or disciplinary problems which might arise in the schools which were to be desegregated. Responsibility for preparing teachers and students in each school was left apparently to the principal of each school, so the results varied.

[168] From *Minutes* of the Greenville Education Committee, 1964–65, and from interviews with its leaders.
[169] *GP*, August 14, 1964. See also *SSN*, September 1964, p. 16.
[170] *GN*, April 28, 1964.

There were reports that some teachers talked with their classes during the spring about the impending change and made good use of human relations resources. Others ignored the subject. One teacher was reported as making derogatory remarks to her pupils about "those stupid Negroes."

One schoolman commented, "The whole matter of preparation was poorly handled from an educator's viewpoint. If any other kind of major change had been involved, we would have had a series of professional workshops. Since desegregation was the issue, however, and no officials wanted to give it open approval, we had little or no organized preparation."

According to one interviewee, some effort was made by school officials to assign the black transferees to teachers known to be tolerant or sympathetic to desegregation. P.T.A. officials urged all members to remain calm and law-abiding in the face of the approaching change. At the same time, when several white high school student leaders arranged an informal meeting to get acquainted with some of the black students who were to be in school with them, there was strong criticism from school officials.

On the state level, the public acquiescence to the concept of desegregation as expressed by top officials that summer helped to prepare public opinion in the state and local area for change. Governor Donald Russell, for example, in a national speech in June, conceded that "though many disagree with the U. S. Supreme Court decision, it has established the rights of all with respect to school admission." He added that South Carolina was a law-abiding state and had conformed peacefully with "every federal court order" regarding desegregation.[171]

DESEGREGATION BEGINS (1964)

When desegregation actually began in Greenville's public schools on September 1, 1964, there was little or no accompanying fanfare. The schools opened "quietly, calmly and

[171] SSN, July 1964, p. 7.

peacefully," even though there were forty-nine black students attending classes with white students for the first time at fifteen schools.

At the end of the first day, the school superintendent said that he had "not heard of a single incident" and that so far as he could ascertain, the new students were "received courteously and with respect." He expressed the view that this change had come peacefully because it "had been planned and announced ahead of time" and this "made for possible better acceptance."[172] He commended the "news media for their fine pre-school coverage" and thanked publicly "all the other people who had a role in our success." The school board chairman gave credit for much of this success to "the caliber of leadership" shown by the superintendent.[173]

The local press commented that "school officials, law enforcement officers, and above all, citizens of both races, can take honest pride in the fact that . . . an atmosphere of peace and good order" prevailed as desegregation began.[174]

Actually, a close watch was kept on the situation by the press and by law enforcement officials for several days. On the opening day of school the local newspapers had an observer at each desegregated school and they reported seeing two to three carloads of law enforcement officers, uniformed or otherwise, in the vicinity of each school. There were also a few state and federal law officials on hand, just in case their aid should be needed. No incidents were reported by the press observers other than one or two cases of name calling. In contrast, their reports indicated that the black students were received rather well.

That same month Greenville's Catholic parochial school began desegregation without difficulty.[175] Another private school, an Episcopal elementary school, which had been established

---

[172] *GN*, September 2, 1964.
[173] Greenville School Board, *Minutes*, September 8, 1964.
[174] *GN*, editorial, September 6, 1964.
[175] See statement on June 24, 1963, by Catholic bishop of South Carolina (*SSN*, July 1963, p. 7).

earlier in the 1960s, remained all-white, however, despite criticism by several church leaders. The three local colleges, all private institutions, also remained segregated, for whites only, as of the fall of 1964. One of them, Furman University, accepted its first black student in January, 1965.[176]

In all of South Carolina there had been only one public school system with any desegregation the year before. However, as Greenville began its move in the fall of 1964, it was joined by fourteen other communities in various parts of the state, most of them making the change voluntarily and all of them doing it peacefully.[177]

As one Greenville leader commented, "After Charleston's peaceful integration last year, and after our district, the largest in the state, voluntarily worked out the matter with the courts, it seemed useless to a lot of other communities to continue to fight the issue." Another interviewee may have been nearer to the truth when he said that "it's purely a pragmatic matter. The time has come when a school system either desegregates voluntarily and sets its own controls, or waits for a court to set all the controls, and most of us prefer to do this thing our own way, if we have to do it at all."

While Greenville was beginning its first desegregation in 1964, Greensboro was beginning its eighth year of desegregation, having by that time an estimated five hundred black students in sixteen biracial schools. The desegregation percentages were hardly significant in either community, however. In Greenville, less than one-half of one percent of the school system's 11,500 black students were involved; in Greensboro, about six percent of the 7,600 black students were in desegregated schools,[178] although until the year before it had been less than one-fifth of one percent.[179]

[176] GN, January 30, 1965.
[177] SSN, September 1964, pp. 12–13.
[178] Southern Education Reporting Service, Statistical Summary . . . (1964–65).
[179] Ibid., (1962), p. 33.

LATER DEVELOPMENTS (1964–65)

During the first year of desegregation in Greenville's schools the situation remained generally peaceful. As one schoolman said, "The Negroes are tolerated in my school, but they are not really a part of the student body. They seem to prefer to eat together and to be together in any kind of a gathering, and the whites seem to want it that way, too."

In the desegregated schools one black high school student was accepted into the glee club and another won a place in the band, but none were permitted on athletic teams. Most social events, such as dances and parties, were suspended. All students and parents were encouraged to attend football games, musical and dramatic events and P.T.A. meetings, but almost no blacks attended. There were several incidents of harassment, although none were reported by the local press. Most of these involved name-calling, pushing or shoving, or being ostracized from student clubs or activities. One student reported being slapped by a teacher, and in one school there was a report of a "small bomb" being exploded just outside a desegregated classroom.

The social and political climate remained quite conservative in Greenville and South Carolina, even though some desegregation was accepted. In the 1964 political elections, several blacks ran for legislative or other offices for the first time in various parts of the state. One of them was Donald Sampson, a Greenville attorney. However, all were defeated.[180] In the national presidential race much of South Carolina, including Greenville, voted for Barry Goldwater, although the state as a whole remained in the Democratic fold.

Several Greenville leaders reported that local support appeared to be growing for the John Birch Society, which reputedly had several local influential citizens in it.

The local press de-emphasized its anti-integration views

[180] *SSN*, July 1964, p. 7.

and promoted "law and order" in strong terms for a short time before and after the opening of schools in 1964. Within a few months, however, its anti-federal government, anti-Supreme Court, anti-integration views again were being expressed almost daily. Only a few days following the fall opening of schools, one local editor expounded his view that "the schools are institutions for imparting knowledge, not for experiments in social science or amalgamation of different races, cultures and backgrounds. . . . Our educators do not have time to conduct a large-scale laboratory in race relations, nor . . . to be bothered with a continuing problem of discipline and law enforcement."[181] By the end of the first year of school desegregation in Greenville, all of the black students who had been in desegregated schools that year were ready to remain there. An additional 226 black students asked for transfer to desegregated schools for the next year.[182] Only 100 of these were transferred, however, and when the second year of desegregation began in September, 1965, there were still only 146 black students in school with whites. From interviews that fall with school and community leaders, it appeared that most of the harassment of the year before had disappeared, and there was some evidence that the black students were gradually being accepted into various school and student affairs.

[181] GN, editorial, September 6, 1964. See also Alfred S. Reid, "Recent Literary Developments in Greenville," Furman University Bulletin, 12:24–30, November 1964.
[182] Greenville Education Committee, Minutes, May and June 1965.

Chapter IV

ASSESSMENT OF DESEGREGATION PROCESS

TECHNIQUES

In the previous two chapters, a description of the events leading up to and including the beginning of school desegregation in Greensboro, North Carolina, and Greenville, South Carolina, has been presented. In this analysis, a number of intergroup relations principles or factors have been mentioned or discussed in one way or another. To understand more clearly their relative roles in these situations, it is necessary to define these factors more closely as to their presence, their relationship to each other, and their importance in the ongoing school desegregation process.

To do this from as much of a nonfragmented view as possible, it is important to consider data from all of the major sources used in making this study. This includes information collected from interviews with twenty selected leaders in each community, from various local and regional mass media, from records of school boards and other official bodies in each place, from public statements by community and state leaders, from other research studies dealing with the two communities, and from the participant-observer experience of this researcher in the two places.

A good focal point for such an examination is provided by the questionnaire used in the two communities to test for the presence and importance, if any, of the following twenty-five intergroup relations principles or factors which a national panel of social scientists indicated should be important in any local school desegregation situation:

ITEM NO.   BRIEF DESCRIPTION OF ITEM

1.   leadership from school board
2.   leadership from school superintendent
3.   clear policy statement from school board
4.   clear policy statement by law enforcement officials
5.   firm support from press
6.   firm support from religious and civic leaders
7.   firm support from business and industry leaders
8.   firm support from power structure leaders
9.   firm support from political leaders
10.   firm support from black leaders
11.   federal funds requiring nondiscrimination
12.   threat of legal action
13.   federal court order
14.   pressure from federal agencies
15.   pressure from civil rights groups
16.   community preparation by human relations groups
17.   community preparation by press
18.   other existing desegregation in community
19.   high educational level of white community
20.   high educational level of black community
21.   good communication between races
22.   moderate or liberal social climate
23.   black population ratio low
24.   moderate or liberal political climate
25.   legislation favorable to desegregation

The questionnaire involving these twenty-five principles or factors was tested with forty key persons who had some significant role in the school desegregation situation in either Greensboro or Greenville.[1] Among these were subgroups including white and black leaders, school leaders, religious and civic leaders, and business and industrial leaders.

The data obtained from forty questionnaires was analyzed first by selected statistical techniques. Then it was checked against and compared with the data obtained from all other

[1] A copy of the questionnaire is included in Appendix B. Responses were obtained from twenty selected leaders in each community during a lengthy three-part interview with each person.

major sources used in this study, in order to corroborate, supplement or, in some instances, to refute the questionnaire findings. The results of this analysis are shown in the following pages. First, the findings relating to each community are presented separately.[2] Then they are compared and analyzed jointly for the two places to determine the presence and importance, if any, of the selected principles or factors in the two communities and any correlation in how comparable interviewee groups in each place viewed the various items.

GREENSBORO—MOST IMPORTANT ITEMS

All of the factors judged by most leaders and groups in Greensboro as of great importance in bringing about school desegregation locally are shown in Table A. Thirteen of these items are rated and ranked rather consistently as "most important" by most individual leaders, by the total group of leaders, and by most subgroups of leaders[3] (see last column on right in Table A). These items include:

2. leadership from school superintendent to desegregate.
3. clear and firm policy statement from school board to support desegregation.
4. clear and firm policy statement by law enforcement agencies and officials to support law and order.
5. firm support for desegregation from the press.

[2] For a discussion of these techniques and a more detailed analysis of these findings in each community see Appendix E.
[3] "Most important" refers to items which meet three or more of the following criteria:

a) rated high by interviewee group of twenty persons.
b) rated high by 60 percent or more of interviewee subgroups.
c) rated high by 60 percent or more of individual interviewees.
d) ranked high by total interviewee group.
e) ranked high by 60 percent or more of interviewee subgroups.

Actually, ten of the thirteen items conform to all of the five criteria. Three (items nos. 3, 16, and 21) conform to four of the criteria.

6. firm support for desegregation from civic and religious groups and leaders.
10. firm support for desegregation from black leaders.
12. threat of court suit to seek desegregation.
15. pressure from local civil rights or social action groups to desegregate.
16. efforts to prepare community for desegregation by human relations groups.
19. educational level of white community is high.
20. educational level of black community is high.
21. communications and race relations between white and black leaders are good.
22. social climate and public opinion in community is moderate or liberal on racial matters.

Not only do these principles or factors appear as "most important" from the interviewee questionnaire data, but on most of the items there is agreement by other sources as to their importance in the local school desegregation process.

The leadership of the Greensboro school superintendent in calling for desegregation (item no. 2) on both moral and legal grounds from May, 1954, until the local school policy was changed in 1957 is amply documented. His own statements to the press and in public speeches, his report at a public hearing of a civil rights commission,[4] editorial comments about him in the local press, and comments about him by other school and community leaders attest to the important role he played in bringing about desegregation in his school system.

The clear and firm policy of the Greensboro School Board in support of desegregation (item no. 3) is best set forth in two resolutions adopted by that group of officials and reported in their *Minutes*.[5] One statement, adopted in May, 1954, endorsed the Supreme Court ruling on desegregation, and the other, adopted in the summer of 1957, announced procedures

[4] U. S. Commission on Civil Rights. *Conference on Education* (*Nashville, 1959*), pp. 103–115.

[5] Greensboro School Board, *Minutes*, May 18, 1954; July 23, 1957; and August 21, 1957.

for beginning desegregation locally that fall. Both statements received widespread news and editorial coverage in the press because of their positive nature and particularly because both announcements were "firsts" of their kind to be adopted by any southern school board. Both were often mentioned by community leaders when interviewed for this study.

Support for law and order by local law enforcement officials in connection with school desegregation (item no. 4) in Greensboro does not appear in any public statement by such officials. However, evidence that they adopted and implemented such a policy with carefulness and firmness is found from several sources. Such a policy was mentioned by local school officials as one of the major factors in the successful beginning of desegregation. To support this view, at least one other research study reports in detail that Greensboro's law enforcement during the beginning of desegregation was an outstanding example of such policy and action.[6] News stories in the local press[7] and background interviews with local leaders help to corroborate this.

Support for school desegregation by the local press in Greensboro (item no. 5) is best shown from its own pages. The two local newspapers announced their support for desegregation almost as soon as the Court ruling occurred. Even though both local newspapers later backed North Carolina's slow, token approach to change, their editorial policy supported desegregation as being legally, morally, economically, and educationally right and sound. They were quite critical of state and local leaders who openly opposed desegregation. The importance of the local press in supporting desegregation and in helping to prepare the local community's public opinion for this social change is supported by numerous editorials in the local newspapers, by a report of local school officials to the

[6] Herbert Wey and John Corey, *Action Patterns in School Desegregation*, pp. 6, 40, 192–95, 201.
[7] *GDN*, September 4, 1957.

above-mentioned civil rights commission, by Wey and Corey's study, and by comments from local leaders.

The backing of local religious and civic forces in Greensboro (item no. 6), especially from several specific leaders and groups, can be verified from various sources. Some of this support appears in the form of public statements, but much of it is referred to informally or in off-the-record comments. There are a number of references to this support in local news stories, a civil rights commission report,[8] Wey and Corey's study, local school board records, reports from local human relations groups, and in background data obtained from local interviewees.

The view that support from Greensboro's black leaders helped to bring about desegregation (item no. 10) is borne out by several sources. The strength of any such support from the community's black leadership can be defended on the basis of Carll Ladd's study of black leadership in southern cities, and from the general role of such leadership in Greensboro in the 1950s.

The threat of legal action (item no. 12) as a factor in bringing about school desegregation in Greensboro is given considerable importance by several sources, although some of them do so more by implication than by direct statement. The best supporting discussion for this is found in *Southern School News* and in the 1962 civil rights commission study of North Carolina school desegregation.[9] Several local newspaper editorials refer to this factor, praising the school board for making a "voluntary" move to prevent court action against it. Background information obtained from local interviewees supports this view.

Local civil rights pressure as a major factor in bringing about school desegregation (item no. 15) in Greensboro is

---

[8] U. S. Commission, *Conference on Education* (*Nashville, 1959*), pp. 113–14.

[9] U. S. Commission on Civil Rights, *Civil Rights U. S. A., Public Schools Southern States* (*1962*), pp. 72–73.

strongly supported by the local press, school board records, background data obtained from local interviewees,[10] and by the civil rights commission study mentioned above.

The active role of local human relations groups in preparing the Greensboro community for desegregation (item no. 16) is well documented and is given a fair amount of significance by local interviewees in background discussions. Specifically, the efforts of these groups in conducting human relations workshops and discussions, issuing supportive statements, and promoting acceptance of desegregation are referred to in a civil rights commission report,[11] school board records, and reports from human relations groups.[12]

The important role played in Greensboro by a high educational level among both whites and blacks in the local desegregation process (items nos. 19 and 20) is borne out by the local press, interviews, and the above-mentioned civil rights commission report. The fact that the community is home for six colleges, that its public school system rates high in the state, and that its citizens, both white and black, rank about 30 percent higher educationally than the state average, are credited by several sources as helping to prepare the community for desegregation and to provide leadership for it. Carll Ladd's study points to Greensboro for an outstanding example of the role played by education in preparing black leaders for social action.[13]

The presence in Greensboro of good relations and communication between the races as factors in bringing about local

[10] At least 60 percent of the local interviewees, in open-ended discussions, referred to this factor as of major importance in the local school desegregation situation.

[11] U. S. Commission, *Conference on Education* (*Nashville, 1959*), p. 113.

[12] Referred to in *Minutes* of the Greensboro Interracial Commission, January to September 1957; American Friends Service Committee, *Staff Reports* (unpublished) ; Southern Regional Council, *Special Report on Charlotte, Greensboro and Winston-Salem, N. C.*, September 1957, pp. 7–9.

[13] Carll Ladd, *Negro Political Leadership in the South*, pp. 68, 195.

school desegregation (item no. 21) is supported by editorials in the local press, public statements by white and black leaders, the civil rights commission report *Conference on Education (Nashville, 1959)*, and Ladd's study.

The importance of a moderate to liberal social climate and public opinion regarding racial matters in the local desegregation process (item no. 22) is supported by sources other than the interviews. These include numerous editorials in the local press, the civil rights commission report cited earlier, and scholarly studies by Melvin Tumin and V. O. Key.[14] Key describes this social situation as typical of the Piedmont industrial area of North Carolina, where moderation in racial matters is closely interwoven with the economic, political, and educational development of the area.

GREENSBORO—LEAST IMPORTANT ITEMS

The factors given little or no importance in the Greensboro school desegregation process by most leaders and groups are shown on Table B. The following eight items were rated and ranked as "least important" by most individual leaders, by the total group of leaders, and by most subgroups of leaders[15] (see last column on right on Table B). They include:

7. firm support for desegregation from business and industrial leaders and groups.
8. firm support for desegregation from power structure leaders and groups.

[14] Tumin, *Desegregation: Readiness and Resistance*, pp. 4–6, 203–204; Key, *Southern Politics*, pp. 205–210.

[15] The category refers to items which meet three or more of the following criteria:
a) rated low by total interviewee group.
b) rated low by 60 percent or more of interviewee subgroups.
c) rated low by 60 percent or more of individual interviewees.
d) ranked low by total interviewee group.
e) ranked low by 60 percent or more of interviewee subgroups.

Actually, six of the items conform to all of the five criteria. The other two (items nos. 7 and 23) conform to three of the criteria.

9. firm support for desegregation from state political leaders.
11. school system receives federal funds requiring nondiscrimination in their usage.
13. court order to desegregate.
14. pressure from federal agencies to desegregate.
18. other facilities were desegregated prior to or at same time as schools.
23. black population is smaller than white population.

Not only does the interviewee questionnaire data show these eight principles or factors to be of little or no importance in the local desegregation situation, but other sources help to confirm this view about several of the items.

The majority opinion of Greensboro interviewees regarding the lack of importance of any support for school desegregation from local business, industrial, and power structure leaders and groups (items nos. 7 and 8) is not supported by other sources. In fact, the business and industrial leadership, which is often equated with the power structure in Greensboro and North Carolina, is credited by others as being very important —behind-the-scenes if not publicly—in the decision-making processes regarding racial policies locally and statewide. Editorials in the local press, studies of leadership and economic patterns in the area and community,[16] and data obtained from many of the Greensboro leaders in open-ended interviews confirm the impression that "business and industry" represent the major local power, even though it may not always function cohesively, as one editor pointed out. Among the reasons for these two factors being given such low ratings and rankings by interviewees on the questionnaire may be the lack of any visible support given to desegregation locally by "business and industry" and "power structure" forces, lack of understanding of the meaning of these two items on the questionnaire, or lack of understanding on the part of interviewees as

---

[16] See Key, *Southern Politics*, pp. 205–206; Tumin, *Desegregation*, pp. 149–70; and William Nicholls, *Southern Tradition and Regional Progress*, pp. 117–19.

to the nature of community decision-making and the forces involved in it. Also, the fact that three of the twenty interviewees omitted these two items on their questionnaires probably causes the statistical results to be lower than they should be in comparison to other items.

The lack of support for Greensboro's school desegregation by North Carolina political leaders (item no. 9) is borne out strongly by several sources other than the interviewee questionnaires. The general opposition to desegregation by various top state leaders may be found in numerous news stories and editorials in the local press, a civil rights commission report, a report by the North Carolina Advisory Committee on Education,[17] and open-ended interviews with several local leaders.

The relative importance of federal funds (item no. 11) in bringing about school desegregation in Greensboro is not discussed in any of the printed sources used for this study. From interviews with local school leaders, it appears that federal funds received prior to the beginning of Greensboro's desegregation had no antidiscriminatory regulations attached. If the funds came with antidiscriminatory "strings," the federal authorities chose not to emphasize or apply these regulations.

Federal court orders seem to have played little or no role in desegregating Greensboro's schools (item no. 13) because no legal action was instigated against the school system prior to its initial desegregation. At the same time this non-court-ordered, "voluntary" move by the school board does not diminish the importance of the threat of legal action (item no. 12) which is credited with being a major factor in bringing about local school desegregation.

The unimportance of federal agency pressure in bringing about Greensboro's school desegregation (item no. 14) is supported solely by information obtained in open-ended inter-

---

[17] U. S. Commission, *Civil Rights: Southern States*, p. 64; North Carolina Advisory Committee on Education, *Report to the Governor, the General Assembly, the State Board of Education, and the County and Local School Boards of North Carolina (April 1956)*, pp. 1–14.

views with Greensboro school leaders. Just as with the previously discussed funds, federal officials apparently did little or nothing about putting pressure on local school systems regarding school desegregation until after the 1964 Civil Rights Act became effective and the U. S. Department of Education's school desegregation guidelines were put into action.

The questionnaire findings held that the desegregation of other local facilities (item no. 18) prior to or at the same time as schools had little or no influence in bringing about school desegregation in Greensboro. Other sources either do not support this view or hold that the desegregation of other facilities was actually helpful in preparing the community for school desegregation. These sources include the 1959 *Conference on Education* report, a human relations report,[18] and background information from interviews.

The interviewee questionnaires give little or no importance to the view that a small black population ratio in the community was helpful in bringing about school desegregation (item no. 23). Most other sources do not mention the matter one way or another. One other source, the local press, offers a contrasting view, pointing to the low black population as a factor favoring peaceful change,[19] a view espoused by Ashmore in his 1954 study of the southern school situation.[20]

GREENVILLE—MOST IMPORTANT ITEMS

The factors which most leaders and groups in Greenville view as being of great importance in bringing about school desegregation locally are indicated on Table C. Eleven items are rated and ranked rather consistently as "most important" by

[18] Southern Regional Council, *Special Report on Charlotte, Greensboro and Winston-Salem, N. C.*, September 1957, pp. 8–9.

[19] *GDN*, editorials, May 20, 1954 and June 2, 1955.

[20] Harry Ashmore, *The Negro and the Schools*, p. 128. Ashmore refers to the "ratio of Negro to white population" as being "perhaps the most powerful single influence" in determining racial attitudes and influencing change.

most individual leaders, by the total group of leaders, and by most subgroups of leaders[21] (see last column on right on Table C). These items include:

4. clear and firm policy statement by law enforcement agencies and officials to support law and order.
7. firm support for desegregation from business and industrial leaders and groups.
10. firm support for desegregation from black leadership.
12. threat of court suit to seek desegregation.
13. court order to desegregate.
15. pressure from local civil rights or social action groups to desegregate.
16. efforts to prepare community for desegregation by human relations groups.
18. other facilities were desegregated prior to or at same time as schools.
21. communication and race relations between white and black leaders are good.
22. social climate and public opinion in community are moderate or liberal on racial matters.
23. black population is smaller than white population.

Not only do these eleven principles or factors appear from the interviewee questionnaire data to be of major importance in the local school desegregation process, but on most of the items there is agreement from several other sources.

According to the questionnaire, support for law and order by local law enforcement officials in connection with school desegregation (item no. 4) was an important factor in the peaceable desegregation of Greenville schools. Although no

---

[21] This category refers to principles or factors which meet three or more of the following criteria:

a) rated high by total interviewee group.
b) rated high by 60 percent or more of interviewee subgroups.
c) rated high by 60 percent or more of individual interviewees.
d) ranked high by total interviewee group.
e) ranked high by 60 percent or more of interviewee subgroups.
Actually, six of the items conform to all five of the criteria. The other five (items nos. 7, 12, 16, 21, and 22) conform to four of the criteria.

official statement to this effect was issued publicly, this support appears to have become a definite part of local law enforcement policy after state and local business and political leaders accepted desegregation as inevitable. Evidence for this can be found in the local press, speeches by at least one local law enforcement leader, and background interviews of several school and community leaders.

The view of Greenville interviewees that business and industrial support for desegregation (item no. 7) had a major role in the local social change is supported by several other sources. Just as in Greensboro, the business and industrial leadership in the South Carolina community is often looked upon also as being the major local power structure and decision-making force. This, plus the expressed determination of local and state leaders by 1963–64 not to jeopardize the growth of business and industry by permitting racial violence to occur, is borne out by articles in the local and area and national press,[22] scholarly studies of economic leadership patterns in the state and community by Key and Ladd, public statements by industrial leaders, and background interviews.

The opinion that support from black leaders in Greenville helped to bring about school desegregation (item no. 10) is validated to some extent by the Greenville School Board *Minutes,* news stories and editorials in the local and regional press, background interviews with local leaders, and Ladd's extensive study of local black leadership.[23] The support for change from Greenville's black leaders does not appear to have been as strong or as well organized as that in Greensboro.

Legal action both as a threat (item no. 12) and as a reality (item no. 13) are probably the strongest factors in the Greenville school desegregation situation, as shown by news stories and editorials in both the local and regional press, a public

[22] George McMillan, "Integration with Dignity," *Saturday Evening Post,* March 9, 1962.

[23] Ladd, *Negro Political Leadership,* pp. 2–4, 68–69, 94–95, 195–97, 303–306.

statement by the local school board, documents relating to the federal court order case against Greenville's schools,[24] local school board records, and interviews with local leaders.

Local civil rights pressure as a major factor in bringing about school desegregation (item no. 15) in Greenville can be supported somewhat from references in the local press, school board records, several confrontations between the school officials and civil rights groups from 1954 to 1964, news stories and editorials in the local press regarding the building up of civil rights pressure in the community in the early 1960s, interviews with local civil rights leaders and their public statements, and Ladd's intensive study of local leadership. Although the Greenville black and civil rights leadership was "weak and fragmented," its mere presence was enough to precipitate some action for change by white community leaders in the early 1960s.[25]

Efforts to prepare the community for desegregation by Greenville human relations groups (item no. 16) are credited by several sources with being important in the local school desegregation process. There are miscellaneous references to such activities in the local press, but the best accounts of such preparation and some evaluation of it come from Ladd's study, from records and reports of local human relations groups[26] and interviews with their officials, from a civil rights commission report,[27] and from interviews with various local leaders.

The prior existence of other desegregation in the community (item no. 18) as an important factor in the Greenville

[24] For a full synopsis of the litigation see "Elaine Whittenburg, etc. and Sara Thompson, etc., et al. v. The School District of Greenville County, South Carolina, etc., et al." *Race Relations Law Reporter,* 9:719–23, summer 1964.

[25] Ladd, *Negro Political Leadership,* pp. 77–83, 108–109, 263–70.

[26] See *Ibid.,* pp. 77–83, 251–52; the Greenville Council on Human Relations *Newsletter* (1956–65) ; and the Greenville Education Committee's *Minutes* (1964–65).

[27] U. S. Commission on Civil Rights, South Carolina Advisory Committee, "South Carolina Cities Meet the Challenge," (unpublished report), August 1, 1963, p. 2.

school desegregation process is supported by news stories in the local press, Ladd's study of Greenville, and background interviews. The fact that schools in the South Carolina community did not begin desegregation until 1964, seven years later than those in Greensboro, helps to account for the difference in importance given to this factor by the two places.

Good communications and race relations between black and white leaders in Greenville (item no. 21) are only mildly supported as factors having any importance in the local school desegregation situation by sources other than the questionnaire. When positive references are made to this factor in the local press, they are expressed in the paternalistic terms of the traditional white Southerner, namely, good relations exist as long as the status quo is not disturbed.[28] Ladd's study reiterates this point but interprets it negatively, pointing out that local race relations began to improve from poor to fairly good only as the status quo was disturbed and some desegregation began in the early 1960s. This view is supported by interviews with a number of local leaders.

Other sources, as well as the questionnaire, show that the social climate and public opinion concerning racial matters (item no. 22) in Greenville has been somewhat more moderate than in the rest of South Carolina. However, there is no clear indication from sources other than the questionnaire that this factor was important in bringing about school desegregation locally. Key and Ladd refer often to the amount of racism in the community.[29] While the local press, almost continuously from 1954 to 1963, reflected a strong racist editorial bias, this view changed in 1963 to one calling for law and order in the face of "federally forced integration."[30]

[28] See *GN*, editorials for May 18, 1954, and September 6, 1964; *GP*, September 30, 1965; *SSN*, May 1963.
[29] See Key, *Southern Politics*, pp. 130–31; Ladd, *Negro Political Leadership*, pp. 66–70, 279–80.
[30] For the best discussion of the local press and its race views, see two studies by Alfred S. Reid, "Literature in Greenville," *Furman Uni-*

The questionnaire findings regarding the major importance of a small black population to the school desegregation process (item no. 23) in Greenville is given varying degrees of importance by other sources. Numerous local leaders, in open-ended interviews, gave high priority to it as a factor. As mentioned earlier, Harry Ashmore called this factor a prime one in racial change, while Ladd's study negated its importance.[31]

GREENVILLE—LEAST IMPORTANT ITEMS

The principles or factors given little or no importance in the Greenville school desegregation situation by most local leaders and groups are shown in Table D. There are thirteen items rated and ranked rather consistently as "least important" by most individual leaders, by the total group of leaders, and by most subgroup leaders[32] (see last column on right in Table D). This list of items includes:

1. leadership from school board to desegregate.
2. leadership from school superintendent to desegregate.
3. clear and firm policy statement from school board to support desegregation.
5. firm support for desegregation from the press.

---

versity Bulletin, 7:124–25, November 1960; and "Recent Literary Developments in Greenville: 1959–1963," Furman University Bulletin, 12:24–30, November 1964.
    [31] Ashmore, The Negro and the Schools, p. 128; Ladd, Negro Political Leadership, pp. 76–77, 279.
    [32] The category refers to items which meet three or more of the following criteria:

a) rated low by total interviewee group.
b) rated low by 60 percent or more of interviewee subgroups.
c) rated low by 60 percent or more of individual interviewees.
d) ranked low by total interviewee group.
e) ranked low by 60 percent or more of interviewee subgroups.

Actually, five of the "least important" items meet all five of the criteria. One item (no. 9) conforms to four of the criteria, and seven items (nos. 2, 3, 5, 6, 17, 19, and 24) conform to three of the criteria.

6. firm support for desegregation from civic and religious groups and leaders.
9. firm support for desegregation from state political officials.
11. school system receives federal funds requiring nondiscrimination in their usage.
14. pressure from federal agencies to desegregate.
17. efforts to prepare community for desegregation by press.
19. educational level of white community is high.
20. educational level of black community is high.
24. political climate of community is moderate or liberal on racial issues.
25. legislation on state or local level permitted or encouraged desegregation.

Not only does the questionnaire data show these thirteen factors to be of little or no importance in the local desegregation situation, but other sources help to confirm this view about most of the items.

The majority opinion of Greenville interviewees regarding lack of leadership for desegregation from the local school board (item no. 1) is substantiated by sources other than the questionnaire. Even though some of the board's members evidently favored desegregation, the group as a whole openly expressed opposition to such a change from 1954 until even after being ordered to desegregate in 1964. This view is borne out by their statements as reported in the local press and in the Greenville School Board *Minutes*. Interviews with local school and community leaders help to corroborate this view.

The questionnaire information that the Greenville school superintendent usually reflected the attitude of the board and gave little or no leadership toward desegregation (item no. 2) is supported by accounts of his actions and statements as reported in the local press and the school board records. Background interviews with local leaders help to bear out this view, although some seem to have felt that the superintendent would have given more leadership if his board had approved such action.

The lack of a clear and firm policy from the school board

in support of desegregation (item no. 3) is confirmed not only by the questionnaire data but by other sources. Even after being ordered by a federal court to change its racial policies, the school leadership expressed strong disapproval of desegregation. At the same time the group apparently accepted the inevitability of such a change and began calling upon the public for law and order. This attitude of the board is confirmed by the *Minutes*, by local press reports, and by background interviews with local school leaders.

The majority opinion of Greenville interviewees, holding that local press support was not a factor in helping to bring about desegregation (item no. 5), is amply supported by other sources. These include editorials from the press itself, two scholarly studies of the local press, and background interviews with local leaders. In fact, the local press, especially the *Greenville News*, was an outspoken editorial foe of any form of desegregation from 1954 to 1963, and even then began only to plead for "law and order" in the face of "forced integration," which it labeled as "unconstitutional."[33] The *Greenville Piedmont* was milder in its attacks on desegregation, but there are no grounds for crediting it with any positive support for desegregation.

The questionnaire found that support from local religious and civic leaders (item no. 6) was not a significant factor in the local school desegregation process. The same conclusion was reached by news stories in the local and regional press, Ladd's study of Greenville, and background interviews. Local leaders point to the general silence of local religious and civic leaders on the racial issue from 1954 until 1963, when the state began to tone down what had previously been a strong segregation policy. The lack of existence of any local interracial ministerial or religious groups until 1963 is indicative of this situation. Even after the local schools had been ordered by

[33] See articles by Alfred Reid, "Literature in Greenville" and "Recent Literary Developments in Greenville: 1959–63," *Furman University Bulletin*, 7:124–25 and 12:24–30.

a federal court to desegregate in 1964, there is little to show that more than occasional and unorganized supportive activity was carried on by local religious and civic leaders and groups.

The lack of importance given by the questionnaire to the influence of state political officials in bringing about desegregation (item no. 9) is strongly supported by numerous news stories and editorials in the local and regional press, political studies by Ladd and Key,[34] Quint's historical study,[35] a human relations analysis of the state by a group of social scientists,[36] reports by the South Carolina School Committee, and background interviews with local leaders. The state's history of racism in politics, its political leaders' strong opposition to any form of desegregation from 1954 to 1962 and their gradual change afterwards towards becoming "law and order" advocates in the face of "federally forced integration" are amply documented.

The questionnaire indicates a lack of significant influence by federal funds or by federal agency pressure (items nos. 11 and 14) in bringing about desegregation in Greenville. This contention is not discussed in any of the printed sources. Federal funds have been received for many years locally, according to background interviews with school leaders. However, funds received prior to the beginning of school desegregation in 1964 apparently had no antidiscriminatory regulations attached. If so, compliance with the regulations was not required by the federal agencies involved.

The questionnaire item indicating the lack of community preparation for desegregation by the local press (item no. 17) is supported generally by the previously mentioned sources concerning the lack of press support for desegregation.

[34] Ladd, *Negro Political Leadership*, pp. 73–74, 94–95, 279, 303–306; Key, *Southern Politics*, pp. 130–55, 522.

[35] Howard H. Quint, *Profile in Black and White: A Frank Portrait of South Carolina.*

[36] Human Relations Programming in South Carolina (unpublished mimeographed report, circulated privately).

The questionnaire revealed that a high educational level among either whites or blacks in Greenville was of little if any importance in bringing about desegregation (items nos. 19 and 20). In fact, even though Greenville has been looked on as one of the leading educational centers in South Carolina, the educational level of its citizens, especially blacks, has been very low compared to national figures and considerably lower than the equivalent figures for Greensboro. The questionnaire findings are supported by data from the *U. S. Census of Population*, the local press, and studies by Ladd, Ashmore,[37] and the Southern Education Reporting Service.[38]

The negative view shown by the questionnaire in regard to whether a moderate or liberal political climate was important in bringing about desegregation in Greenville (item no. 24) is well supported by sources cited earlier in relation to state political leaders, especially the local and area press, studies by Key, Ladd, and Quint,[39] and interviews with local leaders. The overtones of racism in the state's political picture cast a shadow over the Greenville scene from 1954 to 1962.

The questionnaire's view that state and local legislation were not helpful factors in bringing about school desegregation in Greenville (item no. 25) is borne out by the local and regional press, studies by Ladd and Quint, the U. S. Civil Rights Commission's *Report on Education, 1961,* a special study on segregation legislation by the Southern Regional Council,[40] interim reports of the South Carolina School Committee, and interviews with local school and other community leaders. These sources point to the host of laws and resolutions

[37] Ladd, *Negro Political Leadership*, pp. 68–69, 195–96, 270; Ashmore *The Negro and the Schools*, pp. 6–23, 152–59.
[38] Patrick McCauley and Edward Bell (eds.), *Southern Schools: Progress and Problems*, pp. 32, 111, 140–50.
[39] See Key, *Southern Politics;* Ladd, *Negro Political Leadership*, pp. 66–70, 73–74, 90–93, 101–102, 278, 303–306; and Quint, *Profile in Black and White.*
[40] Southern Regional Council, *Special Report on Summary of Recent Segregation Laws Enacted in Southern States*, June 21, 1957.

approved or considered for approval by the state legislature from 1951 to 1963 aimed at maintaining segregation, at closing schools rather than desegregating them, at censuring or punishing those accused of advocating desegregation.

BOTH COMMUNITIES—MOST IMPORTANT ITEMS

The factors consistently rated highest by most leaders and groups in the two communities are compared on Table E. They include thirteen items in Greensboro and eleven in Greenville. There is agreement between most individual leaders and most groups in the two communities on seven of these "most important" principles or factors[41] (see last column on right on Table E):

4. clear and firm policy statement by law enforcement agencies and officials to support law and order.
10. firm support for desegregation from black leadership.
12. threat of court suit to seek desegregation.
15. pressure from local civil rights or social action groups to desegregate.
16. efforts to prepare community for desegregation by human relations groups.
21. communication and race relations between white and black leaders are good.

[41] This category refers to items which meet three or more of the following criteria:

a) rated high by total interviewee groups in both communities.
b) rated high by 60 percent or more of interviewee subgroups in both communities.
c) rated high by 60 percent or more of individual interviewees in both communities.
d) ranked high by total interviewee groups in both communities.
e) ranked high by 60 percent or more of interviewee subgroups in both communities.

Actually, three of the seven "most important" items conform to all of the five criteria (items nos. 4, 10, and 15). Two others (items nos. 12 and 22) conform to four of the criteria. The other two (items nos. 16 and 21) conform to three of the criteria.

22. social climate and public opinion in community is moderate or liberal on racial matters.

These seven factors not only appear in the interviewee questionnaire data as being of major importance in school desegregation situations in both communities, but on most of the items there is also support from several other sources.

The firm support for law and order given by local law enforcement officials during the school desegregation process (item no. 4) in each of the two communities was an important factor according to the questionnaire. Even though no official policy statements regarding this matter were issued by the law officials in either place, there is considerable evidence from other sources that officials in both places adopted and carried out such a policy firmly and effectively. As pointed out earlier in this chapter, supporting information is provided by the local press, public speeches by one or more law enforcement officials, at least one other research study, a federal civil rights report, and background information obtained from local interviewees.

The importance of local black leadership as a factor in bringing about desegregation (item no. 10) in both communities is supported by several sources other than the questionnaire, including local school board records, stories and editorials from the local and regional press, the 1959 federal report *Conference on Education,* Ladd's study of Negro leadership in the South,[42] and interviews with local leaders. It appears from these several sources that local black leadership was influential in the desegregation process in both communities, but that it was considerably stronger and better organized in Greensboro than in Greenville.

The threat of legal action as a factor in bringing about school desegregation in both communities (item no. 12) is rated as a fairly important factor by several sources. In Greenville such a threat was followed by litigation and a court order

[42] Ladd, *Negro Political Leadership,* pp. 2–4, 68–69, 94–95, 195–97, 303–306.

to desegregate, whereas in Greensboro there is evidence which indicates that a legal threat influenced the school officials to begin desegregation "voluntarily." News stories and editorials in the local and regional press, a federal report on civil rights in the South, statements by local school officials,[43] Greenville School Board *Minutes*, legal records,[44] and information obtained from interviews with local leaders in both communities helps to corroborate these views.

Local civil rights pressure was a major factor in bringing about school desegregation (item no. 15) in both communities, according to the questionnaire information and several other sources, including news stories and editorials in the local and regional press, school board records in both places, a federal report on civil rights, Ladd's study, and background information obtained from interviews with local leaders in both communities. Most of the sources mentioned earlier in the discussion of black leadership (item no. 10) apply here, for, on the most part, the only civil rights pressure in either of the communities in this study at the time school desegregation began was that from black leadership.

Community preparation by local human relations groups as a factor in helping to bring about desegregation (item no. 16) is given considerable credit by the local press, school board records, federal civil rights reports,[45] Ladd's study, records and reports of local human relations groups in both places,[46] and interviews with local leaders in both places.

---

[43] "Public Statement by the Greenville County School Board," *GN*, April 28, 1964.

[44] See synopsis of litigation, "Elaine Whittenberg, etc. and Sara Thompson, etc. et al. v. The School District of Greenville County, South Carolina, etc. et al.," *Race Relations Law Reporter*, 9:719–23, Summer 1964.

[45] U. S. Commission, "South Carolina Cities Meet the Challenge," p. 2.

[46] See Greensboro Interracial Commission, *Minutes*, January–September 1959; American Friends Service Committee, various unpublished staff reports in 1956–57 and 1963–64; Southern Regional Council, *Special Report on Charlotte, Greensboro and Winston-Salem, N. C. (September 1957)*, pp. 7–9; Greenville Council on Human Relations, *Newsletter*, 1955–56; and Greenville Education Committee, *Minutes*, 1964–65.

The presence of good relations and communication between the races as important factors in the school desegregation process (item no. 21) was minimal, according to all sources of data. From sources other than the questionnaire one can only come to the conclusion that interracial relations were stronger in Greensboro than in Greenville. Ladd's intensive study of the latter community concludes that interracial relations began to improve from being poor to being fairly good only as the status quo was disturbed and desegregation began.[47] The local and regional press, public statements by white and black leaders, the 1959 federal report *Conference on Education*, and background interviews with leaders in both places support the importance of these factors in varying degrees.

The presence of a moderate to liberal social climate and public opinion regarding racial matters and their importance in the school desegregation process (item no. 22) is well supported in both communities by the questionnaire information. Other sources point to the presence and considerable importance of these factors in Greensboro, but they give no clear indication that they existed to any appreciable degree in Greenville or that they exerted any particular influence on the desegregation situation there. These conclusions are borne out by numerous editorials in the local press, a federal report on civil rights, studies by Tumin, Key, Ladd, and Reid, and background interviews with local leaders in both communities.

BOTH COMMUNITIES—LEAST IMPORTANT ITEMS

On the other hand, the principles or factors which are rated lowest in both communities by most individual leaders and by most groups are shown on Table F. They include eight items in Greensboro and thirteen items in Greenville.

There is agreement between most individual leaders and

[47] Ladd, *Negro Political Leadership*, pp. 73–83.

groups in the two communities on only three of these "least important" items[48] (see last column on right on Table F) :

9. firm support for desegregation from state political leaders.
11. school system receives federal funds requiring nondiscrimination in their usage.
14. pressure from federal agencies to desegregate.

These three principles or factors not only appear in the interviewee questionnaire data as being of little or no importance in the local school desegregation situations in both communities, but there is agreement on most of these items by several other sources as to their relative importance.

The relative unimportance of the influence of state political leaders as a factor in the school desegregation process (item no. 9) is supported strongly by several sources in both communities, including the questionnaire. Political officials in both states, almost without exception, publicly opposed racial change until after the decision to desegregate had been announced by local school officials. After the decision had been made, most state officials in both states adopted a strong "law and order" pose. These conclusions are borne out by such sources of data as stories and editorials in the local and regional press, a federal report on civil rights, reports by the official segregation committees in both states, scholarly studies by Ladd, Key and Quint, a report on South Carolina by a group

---

[48] This category refers to items which meet three or more of these criteria:

a) rated low by total interviewee groups in both communities.
b) rated low by 60 percent or more of interviewee subgroups in both communities.
c) rated low by 60 percent or more of individual interviewees in both communities.
d) ranked low by total interviewee groups in both communities.
e) ranked low by 60 percent or more of interviewee subgroups in both communities.

Actually, two of the three items conform to all of the five criteria. The other one (item no. 9) conforms to four of the criteria.

of social scientists, and background interviews with local leaders in both places.

The lack of any significant influence by federal funds (item no. 11) or by federal agency pressure (item no. 14) in bringing about school desegregation in either of the communities in this study is strongly defended by information from questionnaire and background data from open-ended interviews with local leaders. However, there is no discussion of either of these factors in any of the printed sources.

From interviews with local school and community leaders, it appears that federal funds have been received for a number of years in both Greensboro and Greenville. Prior to the beginning of school desegregation in each community either there were no antidiscriminatory regulations attached to such funds or compliance was not required by the federal agencies involved. Interviews also give one the impression that little or no pressure to desegregate was exerted on either school system by any federal agencies until 1965. By this time school desegregation had already begun in both Greensboro and Greenville.

BOTH COMMUNITIES—RELATIVE IMPORTANCE OF ALL ITEMS

When all of the major sources for both communities are compared, it appears that there is general agreement by 60 percent or more of them on the relative importance of eighteen of the twenty-five principles or factors. These include the seven "most important" and the three "least important" ones, already described, plus eight others which fall within the range of "slightly important" to "fairly important."[49] According to the importance given to them by most sources, the eighteen fall into seven groupings:[50]

[49] See Tables E and F.
[50] No attempt has been made to determine the degree of importance of each item within a grouping.

Very Important Items
  10. firm support for desegregation from black leaders.
  15. pressure from local civil rights or social action groups to desegregate.

Very Important to Fairly Important Items
  4. clear and firm policy by law enforcement agencies and officials to support law and order.
  12. threat of court suit to seek desegregation.

Fairly Important Items
  16. efforts to prepare community for desegregation by human relations groups.
  21. communication and race relations between white and black leaders are good (more important in Greensboro than in Greenville).
  22. social climate and public opinion in community are moderate or liberal on racial matters (considerably more important in Greensboro than in Greenville).

Fairly Important to Slightly Important Items
  3. clear and firm policy statement from school board to support desegregation (fairly important in Greensboro but only slightly important in Greenville).
  5. firm support for desegregation from the press (considerably more important in Greensboro than in Greenville).
  6. firm support for desegregation from religious and civic groups and leaders (more important in Greensboro than in Greenville).
  7. firm support for desegregation from business and industrial leaders and groups.
  8. firm support for desegregation from power structure leaders and groups.
  17. efforts to prepare community for desegregation by press.

Slightly Important Items
  24. political climate of community is moderate or liberal on racial issues. (This item opposed desegregation in both communities, according to most sources, and it gave "law and order" support in both places only after the decision to desegregate had been made in the individual communities.)

Slightly Important to Not Important Items
  25. legislation on state or local level permitted or encouraged desegregation. (This was of slight importance in encouraging

desegregation in Greensboro, but in Greenville it acted as a negative factor according to most sources.)

Unimportant Items

9. firm support for desegregation from state political leaders. (Most sources agree that this factor opposed desegregation in both places.)
11. school system receives federal funds requiring nondiscrimination in their usage (not applicable in either community).
14. pressure from federal agencies to desegregate (not applicable in either community).

As for the remaining seven items, out of the total list of twenty-five principles or factors, there is strong agreement within each community by 60 percent or more of the total sources as to the importance of each item. There is no agreement between communities on these seven items however. Each is considered of great importance in one community, but of little or no importance in the other. They can be grouped as follows:

Very Important in One Community—Not Important in the Other

13. court order to desegregate (the most important factor in Greenville, but of no relevance in Greensboro).
20. high education level of black community (very important in Greensboro, but not relevant in Greenville).

Very Important in One Community—Slightly Important in the Other

2. leadership from school superintendent to desegregate (very important in Greensboro, but of little or no importance in Greenville).
18. other facilities were desegregated prior to or at same time as schools (supported by Greenville sources as very important, but judged only slightly importance by Greensboro sources).
19. educational level of white community is high (very important in Greensboro, but only slightly important in Greenville).
23. black population is smaller than white population (very important to the desegregation process in Greenville, but looked on as only slightly important in Greensboro).

Fairly Important in One Community—Not Important in the Other

1. leadership from school board to desegregate (fairly important in Greensboro, but unimportant in Greenville).

Chapter V

SUMMARY AND CONCLUSIONS

On the basis of the findings in the last chapter, it seems logical to draw certain conclusions regarding the twenty-five human relations principles or factors which we have been seeking to validate in this study.

These conclusions must be drawn with care, however, and only after the findings have been subjected to a well-formulated set of criteria. These criteria, while objective, must be universal enough that any resulting conclusions will be valid in the local situation and may reliably apply to other similar desegregation situations.

Three groups of criteria which seem to meet these standards have been applied to each of the selected principles or factors in this study. The applicability of each criteria to a specific principle or factor is determined by whether a majority of the sources of data in one or both communities in the study support the finding.[1]

The three groups of criteria used in testing each principle or factor in both Greensboro, North Carolina, and Greenville, South Carolina, are as follows:

---

[1] A majority of the sources in each community totals four (60 percent) or more of the seven sources from which data was obtained. Data for each community was obtained from twenty interviewee questionnaires, other background material from the twenty interviewees, mass media, official records, public statements by local leaders, other research studies, and the participant-observer experience of this investigator.

	In both places	In one place only	In neither place
I. Presence of each principle or factor			
1. It appears to be present.			
2. It appears to be present for certain time only.			
3. It appears to be operational.			
4. It appears to be operational for certain time only.			
II. Importance of each principle or factor			
1. It appears to have no importance.			
2. It appears to be slightly important.			
3. It appears to be fairly important.			
4. It appears to be very important.			
5. It appears to be so important that the successful outcome of desegregation depends on its presence.			
6. It appears to be so unimportant that it apparently could be removed or omitted without affecting the desegregation process.			
7. It appears to be important only in opposition to desegregation.			
III. Relationship of each principle or factor to other principles or factors			
1. Its influence appears to have no dependence on other principles or factors.			

2. Its influence appears to depend partially on the presence and importance of one or more other principles or factors. (Explain)

---

3. Its influence appears to depend completely on the presence and importance of one or more other principles or factors. (Explain)

---

4. Its influence appears to oppose that of one or more other principles or factors. (Explain)

CONCLUSIONS APPLICABLE TO BOTH COMMUNITIES

After applying the foregoing criteria to each of the selected principles or factors, twelve conclusions applicable to both communities in this study seem to be justified:

1. Firm support and pressure from local black leadership and civil rights or social action groups are very important in bringing about school desegregation. This is supported strongly by most information relating to the desegregation process in both communities.

2. A clear and firm policy by law enforcement agencies and officials to support law and order is very important to the success of school desegregation. This is supported strongly by most information relating to the experiences of the two communities.

3. Legal action, or the threat of legal action, is very important in bringing about school desegregation. In Greenville almost all sources list legal action as the most important factor in bringing about desegregation. In Greensboro the threat of legal action is given high importance by most sources.

4. The efforts of local human relations groups which prepare a community for desegregation are fairly important to the success of school desegregation, as shown by the experiences of both communities in this study.

5. A local social climate involving moderate to liberal public opinion on racial matters, good communication between racial leaders, and good overall race relations appears to be fairly important to the success of the school desegregation process. This is supported

by most sources relating to the experiences of the two communities.

6. A firm policy by the school board in support of desegregation is helpful to the school desegregation process. This is shown by the experiences of both communities in this study, although only the board in Greensboro can be credited with firmly supporting desegregation. The Greenville board adopted a firm "law and order" policy after being ordered by a federal court to desegregate.

7. The local press can have a fairly important influence on the success of the desegregation process by giving it firm support and by helping to prepare the community for it. This is shown in the experiences of both communities in this study, although in only one of them can the press be credited highly for its role in being helpful to desegregation. In the other community, Greenville, the press, a longtime opponent of racial changes, adopted a strong "law and order" policy shortly before the beginning of the local school desegregation.

8. Firm support from religious and civic leaders and groups is helpful but not vital to the success of school desegregation.

9. Firm support from business and industrial leaders and groups is helpful to the success of school desegregation, even though such support may not be highly visible to the public. This factor, borne out by the experiences of the two communities in this study, is linked closely with the next factor by some sources.

10. Firm support from power structure leaders and groups, which also may not be publicly visible, is very helpful to the success of school desegregation.

11. The lack of a moderate or liberal political climate and the lack of support from political leaders are detrimental, but not necessarily fatal, to the success of school desegregation, as shown by the experiences of both communities in this study. The influence of strong political opposition in delaying the beginning of school desegregation in both places is borne out by most sources.

12. The application of pressure on local school boards by federal agencies and the nondiscriminatory use of federal funds are not necessarily relevant as factors in bringing about school desegregation, as shown by the experience of the two communities in this study.[2]

---

[2] This conclusion is made on the basis of the experiences of two communities which began school desegregation prior to 1965 and prior to the enforcement of the 1964 Federal Civil Rights Act. For communities which have begun desegregation since 1965, such a conclusion may not be apropos, in that federal agency pressure and the threat of the cut-off

CONCLUSIONS APPLICABLE TO ONLY ONE COMMUNITY

Four other conclusions regarding specific principles or factors are applicable to one community but not to both of the ones in this study:

1. A high educational level in the white and/or black communities may be very important to the school desegregation process. This is supported strongly by the experience of Greensboro.

2. Leadership from the school superintendent or from the school board may be very important in bringing about school desegregation, as indicated by the experience of Greensboro.

3. The desegregation of other community facilities prior to, or at the same time as, schools may be highly important to the success of school desegregation. This is supported strongly by the experiences of Greenville. In Greensboro this factor appears to be only slightly important.

4. A local black population considerably smaller than the white population may aid school desegregation. This conclusion is supported by most sources concerning Greenville, which has a 20 percent black population. In the other community, where a similar population ratio exists, this factor appears to be only slightly important.

OTHER CONCLUSIONS

Five additional conclusions drawn from the overall research findings and based on individual criteria[3] follow:

1. Various leadership groups (vocational and racial) within a community tend to view the forces operating in the school desegre-

---

of federal funds to local school systems are major aspects of the U. S. Department of Education's desegregation guidelines, to which most southern school systems have been required to comply since 1965.

[3] The criteria for the first four of these conclusions is statistical and is based on questionnaire data, as indicated in the explanation of each conclusion. The last conclusion, a general one referring to the overall process of desegregation in each of the communities in this study, is based on background data and the historical experience of desegregation in the two places.

gation process much more similarly than do comparable leaders or groups in different communities. This is evident in the interview data. Within each community a highly significant statistical correlation exists between the various leadership groups (white leaders, black leaders, school leaders, religious and civic leaders, business leaders).[4] The views of comparable groups in the two communities show little or no correlation however.[5]

2. Certain leadership groups within each community tend to view the school desegregation forces much more similarly than do other groups. In each of the communities in this study, business leaders and religious and civic leaders are considerably closer to each other in how they view these forces than are any other groups. Business leaders in each community are nearer also to all other leaders within the community in their views on these matters than are any other leadership subgroups.[6]

3. Black leaders in different communities tend to view the forces of school desegregation somewhat more similarly than do any other leadership groups. In the two communities in this study, these two groups are the only ones whose views regarding the intergroup principles or factors come near to having any significant correlation.[7]

4. Some special interest groups (vocational and racial) tend to give particular importance to those principles or factors in the school desegregation process which affect or reflect their group image. This is especially true of school leaders and religious leaders and somewhat true of black leaders. Each of these leadership groups in both communities tends to rank the items relating to their roles several points higher than do other groups.[8]

---

[4] For details concerning correlation of viewpoints by various subgroups in each community, see discussion and Tables A-4 (Greensboro) and C-4 (Greenville) in Appendix E.

[5] For comparison of viewpoints of interviewees in both communities see discussion and Table E-4 in Appendix E.

[6] See Tables A-4 and C-4 in Appendix E.

[7] See Table E-4 in Appendix E.

[8] School leaders in both communities tend to rank three items (no. 1—school board leadership, no. 2—school superintendent leadership, and no. 3—board policy clear) higher than do other groups. Black leaders tend to rank two items (no. 10—black leaders support, and no. 15—civil rights pressure) higher than do other groups. Religious leaders tend to give a higher rank to one item (no. 6—religious support) than do other groups. See Tables A-7 and C-7 for comparison of rankings on all items by all leadership subgroups within each community. (See Appendix E for these tables.)

5. Even though two communities may have many similar characteristics, each is a unique combination of these and other characteristics, and there may be little or no similarity in how the two react to a specific social change. This is borne out by the experiences of the communities in this study. The two have many similarities—demographic, geographic, economic, religious, racial, and historical—but their reactions to the school desegregation issue were quite different. Greensboro began desegregation in 1957 "voluntarily," whereas Greenville waited until seven years later and then desegregated only under a court order.

These conclusions appear to substantiate the view that the purpose of this study has been achieved to a considerable degree. No major evidence has been discovered in the course of the study to indicate that any significant principles or factors other than those being tested were of particular importance in the two desegregation situations under investigation.

At the same time, the relative importance given to some of the principles or factors in this study, especially in the questionnaire, is not in full accord with the supporting data from other sources. This is particularly evident with the two factors relating to the influence of business and industrial and power structure groups and leaders. Both factors are given much less importance in the questionnaire results than in other sources, but then these factors are not easily amenable to quantification.

Other principles or factors on which there is some variation in the amount of support given by questionnaire results and by other sources in one or both communities include other desegregation, good race communication, moderate social climate, and low black population. The above comment about quantification probably applies to these items, too.

HYPOTHESES

As a result of these conclusions, there seems to be sufficient evidence to warrant the formulation of the following hypotheses:

1. The speed and extent of the school desegregation process in a particular community are directly dependent on the presence or absence of pressure on the local school officials by one or more power forces to which they accede. These forces may be in the form of federal pressure (court action or other), civil rights pressure (litigation or other), or economic pressure (pressure on schoolmen by local economic leaders who themselves fear a loss of community business and industry if "racial unrest" should develop).

2. The success or failure of the school desegregation process in a community is directly related to the quality and amount of support given to it by law enforcement officials and agencies. A clear and firm policy in support of law and order in connection with the social change is very important to a peaceful, orderly transition.

3. The success or failure of the school desegregation process in a community is directly affected by the quality and amount of support given to it by local black leadership. Firm support for desegregation from this group is very important in gaining support for the change from the black community and in determining the quality and the extent of change.

4. The quality of the overall success or failure of the school desegregation process in a community is largely dependent on a variety of often interrelated factors. Most of these factors should support desegregation if the change is to occur in a peaceful and constructive manner. These factors include a moderate to liberal social climate and public opinion regarding racial matters, good communication between racial leaders, good overall race relations, community preparation for desegregation by human relations groups and the press, and firm support for desegregation from local leaders and groups representative of the school board, business, industry, law enforcement, the black community, religion, civic groups, mass media, and the power structure.

5. Each community represents a unique combination of characteristics, even though it may have some or many characteristics similar to those possessed by one or more other communities. Because of this uniqueness, each may be directly affected in a social change by one or more factors which have little or no influence on another community. Examples of such factors would be a court order to desegregate, leadership from a school superintendent, the presence of certain other desegregated facilities in the community. a high degree of education among local blacks and/or whites, and the local population racial ratio.

TOPICS FOR FURTHER STUDY

On the basis of questions growing out of this study which have not been answered because of the limitations of purpose and scope of this research, several topics stand out as worthy of further scholarly exploration. Additional studies of this kind in a variety of types and sizes of communities, making use of methodology, procedures, and instruments similar to those used in this study, are needed to further validate the presence, importance, and relationship of such intergroup relations principles or factors as the ones in this study. Such studies are essential to the development of a body of knowledge that will be helpful to social scientists in predicting the possibilities for success in specific situations of social change.

Research to determine the particular influence of economic factors and to determine the role of power structure forces in similar social changes is gravely needed.

APPENDIX A

LIST OF FIFTY-NINE INTERGROUP RELATIONS PRINCIPLES AND FACTORS SUBMITTED TO A NATIONAL PANEL OF JUDGES

I. LEADERSHIP PRINCIPLES AND FACTORS WHICH OPERATE TO BRING ABOUT SCHOOL DESEGREGATION

FACTORS	Not Important	Slightly Important	Fairly Important	Very Important
1. Leadership from one or more members of school board to desegregate	——	——	——	——
2. Leadership from school board to desegregate	——	——	——	——
3. Leadership from school superintendent to desegregate	——	——	——	——
4. Clear and firm policy statement from board to support desegregation	——	——	——	——
5. Clear and firm policy statement by law enforcement agencies and officials to support law and order	——	——	——	——
6. Firm support for desegregation from the press	——	——	——	——
7. Firm support for desegregation from religious leaders and groups	——	——	——	——
8. Firm support for desegregation from civic leaders and groups	——	——	——	——
9. Firm support for desegregation from local political leaders and groups	——	——	——	——
10. Firm support for desegregation from business and industrial leaders and groups	——	——	——	——
11. Firm support for desegregation from power structure leaders and groups	——	——	——	——

FACTORS	Not Important	Slightly Important	Fairly Important	Very Important
12. Firm support for desegregation from state political officials	___	___	___	___
13. Firm support for desegregation from state educational leaders	___	___	___	___
14. Firm support for desegregation from state agencies	___	___	___	___
15. Firm support for desegregation from black leadership	___	___	___	___

II. PHYSICAL PRINCIPLES AND FACTORS WHICH OPERATE TO BRING ABOUT SCHOOL DESEGREGATION

FACTORS	Not Important	Slightly Important	Fairly Important	Very Important
16. Physical condition of black schools is inferior to that of white schools	___	___	___	___
17. Many black children live nearer to white schools than to Negro schools	___	___	___	___
18. Some black children live nearer to white schools than to Negro schools	___	___	___	___
19. Number of black or white children in community is too small to operate schools for both	___	___	___	___

III. FINANCIAL AND ADMINISTRATIVE PRINCIPLES AND FACTORS WHICH
OPERATE TO BRING ABOUT SCHOOL DESEGREGATION

FACTORS	Not Important	Slightly Important	Fairly Important	Very Important
20. School system receives federal funds requiring no discrimination in their usage (for education of military personnel's children, etc.)	——	——	——	——
21. School bond issues whose approval depend on black vote are at stake	——	——	——	——
22. Cost to operate dual school facilities (black and white) is excessive	——	——	——	——
23. School board members are appointed; this gives them freedom to desegregate schools	——	——	——	——
24. School board members are named by popular election; this gives them freedom to desegregate schools	——	——	——	——

IV. COERCIVE PRINCIPLES AND FACTORS WHICH OPERATE TO BRING ABOUT
SCHOOL DESEGREGATION

FACTORS	Not Important	Slightly Important	Fairly Important	Very Important
25. Threat of court suit to seek desegregation	——	——	——	——
26. Court suit is pending	——	——	——	——
27. Court order to desegregate	——	——	——	——
28. Pressure from federal agencies (such as the Department of Defense or Education) to desegregate	——	——	——	——

FACTORS	Not Important	Slightly Important	Fairly Important	Very Important
29. Pressure from state agencies (such as the Department of Education) to desegregate	——	——	——	——
30. Pressure from local official agencies (such as biracial committee or city council) to desegregate	——	——	——	——
31. Press (newspaper, TV, radio) campaign for desegregation	——	——	——	——
32. Public opinion campaign for desegregation	——	——	——	——
33. Pressure from local civil rights or social action groups to desegregate	——	——	——	——

V. PREPARATION PRINCIPLES AND FACTORS WHICH OPERATE TO BRING ABOUT SCHOOL DESEGREGATION

FACTORS	Not Important	Slightly Important	Fairly Important	Very Important
34. Effort to prepare community for desegregation by school officials	——	——	——	——
35. Efforts to prepare community for desegregation by other agencies (city council, biracial committee, etc.)	——	——	——	——
36. Efforts to prepare community for desegregation by human relations groups	——	——	——	——
37. Efforts to prepare community for desegregation by press	——	——	——	——
38. Efforts to prepare teachers and/or students for desegregation by school officials	——	——	——	——

FACTORS	Not Important	Slightly Important	Fairly Important	Very Important
39. Efforts to prepare other groups in the community for school desegregation (low-income groups, civic clubs, etc.) by school or community leaders	——	——	——	——
40. Amount of such preparation is pertinent	——	——	——	——
41. Kind of such preparation is pertinent	——	——	——	——
42. Quality of such preparation is pertinent	——	——	——	——

VI. OTHER PRINCIPLES AND FACTORS WHICH OPERATE TO BRING ABOUT SCHOOL DESEGREGATION

FACTORS	Not Important	Slightly Important	Fairly Important	Very Important
43. Other facilities (libraries, hospitals, restaurants, etc.) are desegregated prior to or at same time as schools	——	——	——	——
44. Other minority groups (Jews, Catholics, foreign-born, etc.) in community are already accepted by majority group	——	——	——	——
45. Educational level of white community is high (such as college community)	——	——	——	——
46. Educational level of black community is high	——	——	——	——
47. Educational level of both white and black community is high	——	——	——	——
48. Economic level of white and black community is high	——	——	——	——

FACTORS	Not Important	Slightly Important	Fairly Important	Very Important
49. Economic level of black community is high	___	___	___	___
50. Communication between white and black leaders is good	___	___	___	___
51. Communication between school officials and black parents is good	___	___	___	___
52. Public opinion in community is moderate or liberal on racial matters	___	___	___	___
53. There is co-operation between various local agencies and levels of local government	___	___	___	___
54. Amount of urbanization in community makes it easier to desegregate schools	___	___	___	___
55. History and background of race relations in the community is good	___	___	___	___
56. Black population is smaller than white population	___	___	___	___
57. Social climate of community and area is moderate or liberal on racial issues	___	___	___	___
58. Political climate of community and area is moderate or liberal on racial issues	___	___	___	___
59. Legislation on state or local level permits or encourages desegregation	___	___	___	___

APPENDIX B

SELECTED LIST OF TWENTY-FIVE PRINCIPLES AND FACTORS TESTED IN LOCAL COMMUNITIES

_____ DATE

_____ COMMUNITY

Source: 1. Interview   _____
2. Public statements _____
3. Official records   _____
4. Newspapers   _____

PRINCIPLES AND FACTORS WHICH OPERATED TO BRING ABOUT
SCHOOL DESEGREGATION IN YOUR COMMUNITY

(DIRECTIONS: Please check one of the blocks to the right of each item to show how that item has related to school desegregation in your community. If the particular principle or factor *did not exist* or *did not seem to have any effect* in your community, *mark the first block.* If it had a *major effect* in your community, *mark the last block.* If it was *slightly important* or *fairly important*, mark the appropriate block. Mark each item as accurately as possible. Omit any item on which you have no opinion or knowledge.)

FACTORS	Not Important	Slightly Important	Fairly Important	Very Important
1. Leadership from school board to desegregate	_____	_____	_____	_____
2. Leadership from school superintendent to desegregate	_____	_____	_____	_____
3. Clear and firm policy statement from school board to support desegregation	_____	_____	_____	_____
4. Clear and firm policy statement by law enforcement agencies and officials to support law and order	_____	_____	_____	_____
5. Firm support for desegregation from the press	_____	_____	_____	_____
6. Firm support for desegregation from civic and religious groups and leaders	_____	_____	_____	_____

FACTORS	Not Important	Slightly Important	Fairly Important	Very Important
7. Firm support for desegregation from business and industrial leaders and groups	___	___	___	___
8. Firm support for desegregation from power structure leaders and groups	___	___	___	___
9. Firm support for desegregation from state political officials	___	___	___	___
10. Firm support for desegregation from black leadership	___	___	___	___
11. School system receives federal funds requiring no discrimination in their usage (for education of military personnel's children, etc.)	___	___	___	___
12. Threat of court suit to seek desegregation	___	___	___	___
13. Court order to desegregate	___	___	___	___
14. Pressure from federal agencies (Department of Defense or Education) to desegregate	___	___	___	___
15. Pressure from local civil rights or social action groups to desegregate	___	___	___	___
16. Efforts to prepare community for desegregation by human relations groups	___	___	___	___
17. Efforts to prepare community for desegregation by press	___	___	___	___
18. Other facilities (libraries, restaurants, etc.) were desegregated prior to or at same time as schools	___	___	___	___

FACTORS	Not Important	Slightly Important	Fairly Important	Very Important
19. Educational level of white community is high (such as college community)	——	——	——	——
20. Educational level of black community is high	——	——	——	——
21. Communication and race relations between white and black leaders is good	——	——	——	——
22. Social climate and public opinion in community is moderate or liberal on racial matters	——	——	——	——
23. Black population is smaller than white population	——	——	——	——
24. Political climate of community is moderate or liberal on racial issues	——	——	——	——
25. Legislation on state or local level permitted or encouraged desegregation	——	——	——	——

APPENDIX C

BACKGROUND DATA ON TWENTY-SIX COMMUNITIES CONSIDERED FOR THIS STUDY

North Carolina Communities

Community	Population 1960 Total	Negro (%)	School Deseg-regation Begins	Background Studies Available	Economics and Geography	Commu-nity Accessible Easily	Special Research Difficulty
Asheville	60,192	19%	1961	yes	mountain, commerce, tourists	no	no
Burlington	33,199	10%	1963	no	Piedmont, industry	yes	no
Charlotte	201,564	27%	1957	yes	Piedmont, commerce	yes	no
Durham	78,302	36%	1959	yes	Piedmont, commerce	yes	yes
Fayetteville	47,106	36%	1962	no	military, commerce	no	no
Gastonia	37,276	18%	1963	no	Piedmont, industry	no	no
Goldsboro	28,873	41%	1962	no	commerce, farm area	no	no
Greensboro	119,574	26%	1957	yes	Piedmont, commerce, industry	yes	no
Greenville	22,860	33%	1964	no	commerce, farm area	no	no
High Point	62,063	17%	1959	yes	Piedmont, industry	yes	yes
Kannapolis	34,647	12%	1965	no	Piedmont, industry	yes	no
Kinston	24,819	40%	1964	no	commerce, farm area	no	no
Raleigh	93,931	24%	1960	yes	capitol, commerce	yes	no
Rocky Mount	32,147	35%	1963	no	commerce, farm area	no	no
Salisbury	21,297	28%	1962	no	Piedmont, commerce	yes	no
Wilmington	44,013	36%	1962	no	seaport, commerce	no	no
Wilson	28,753	40%	1965	no	commerce, farm area	no	no
Winston-Salem	111,135	37%	1957	yes	Piedmont, industry	yes	no

South Carolina Communities

Community	Population 1960		School Deseg-regation Begins	Background Studies Available	Economics and Geography	Community Accessible Easily	Special Research Difficulty
	Total	Negro (%)					
Anderson	41,316	20%	1964	no	Piedmont, industry, commerce	yes	no
Charleston	65,925	50%	1963	yes	seaport, trade	no	no
Columbia	97,433	30%	1964	no	capitol, commerce	no	no
Florence	24,722	37%	1964	no	commerce, farm area	no	no
Greenville	66,188	30%	1964	yes	Piedmont, commerce, industry	yes	no
Rock Hill	29,404	25%	1964	no	Piedmont, commerce, industry	yes	yes
Spartanburg	44,352	32%	1964	no	Piedmont, commerce, industry	yes	no
Sumter	23,062	35%	1964	no	military, commerce, farm area	no	no

APPENDIX D

BACKGROUND DATA QUESTIONNAIRE

Used as guide in semi-
structured interviews by
researcher with leaders
in local communities.

Date _____   Source: 1. Interview _____
                                          2. Public statement _____
Community _____   3. Official record _____
                                          4. News media _____

INTERVIEW QUESTIONNAIRE

PRINCIPLES AND FACTORS WHICH OPERATED TO
BRING ABOUT SCHOOL DESEGREGATION

Background Data

1. When did school desegregation begin in your community? _____

2. How was it done?
   In stages _____
   All at once _____
   Explain _____

3. How many students were involved?
   At first ____   Elementary ____   High ____
   Later ____   Elementary ____   High ____

4. How many schools were involved?
   At first ____   Elementary ____   High ____
   Later ____   Elementary ____   High ____

5. What was general reaction to 1954 Supreme Court Ruling?

	Favor-able	Unfa-vorable	State-ment Issued	Date and Place
by school superintendent?	____	____	____	____
by school board?	____	____	____	____
by other community leaders (specify)?	____	____	____	____
by civil rights groups or leaders?	____	____	____	____
by segregationist groups or leaders?	____	____	____	____
by religious leaders?	____	____	____	____
by newspaper or radio or TV leaders?	____	____	____	____

6. What was reaction to school
board's decision to desegregate?

	Favorable	Unfavorable	Statement Issued	Date and Place
by civil rights groups or leaders?	___	___	___	___
by religious leaders or groups?	___	___	___	___
by news media?	___	___	___	___
by law enforcement officials?	___	___	___	___
by political leaders?	___	___	___	___
by city officials?	___	___	___	___
by opposition groups or leaders?	___	___	___	___

7. What was reaction to issue of
desegregation being raised locally?

by school board?	___	___	___	___
by school superintendent?	___	___	___	___
by religious leaders or groups?	___	___	___	___
by news media?	___	___	___	___
by law officials?	___	___	___	___
by political leaders?	___	___	___	___
by city officials?	___	___	___	___
by civil rights leaders or groups?	___	___	___	___
by opposition leaders or groups?	___	___	___	___

8. Who initiated first action toward school desegregation in local community?
    (a) school board?
    (b) school superintendent or other school officials?
    (c) individual white leaders?
    (d) individual Negro leaders?
    (e) parents who wanted their children transferred?
    (f) students?
    (g) social action group or groups (specify)?

I. LEADERSHIP FACTORS AND PRINCIPLES

Leadership pattern in community
    1. In the white community, are there one or more individuals or groups who are considered to be top decision makers on major issues, such as racial changes, etc.?

    2. Who are these persons or groups? _____

3. Why are these person(s) and/or group(s) in such a position?
   because of economic power? ____
   because of political power? ____
   because of other power? (specify)_____

4. Were these person(s) and/or group(s) influential in school desegregation situation? Explain.

5. In the black community, are there one or more individuals or groups who are considered to be top decision makers on major issues, such as racial changes, etc.?

6. Who are these persons or groups? _____

7. Why are these person(s) and/or group(s) in such a position?
   because of economic power? ____
   because of political power? ____
   because of other power (specify)? _____

8. Were these person(s) and/or group(s) influential in school desegregation situation? Explain.

9. Did school board or any official in school system:
(a) give support to 1954 Court ruling in 1954? ____
(b) give encouragement to parents or community groups to initiate desegregation action? ____
(c) initiate efforts to desegregate the schools? ____
(d) give support to desegregation issue after it was raised locally? ____
(e) give leadership to bringing about constructive, peaceful desegregation once the decision to desegregate was made by the board? ____
(f) give clear and firm support to desegregation at any time (specify when, etc.)?

10. Was firm and positive support for desegregation given:

	Before 1954	Before issue was raised locally	After issue was raised locally
(a) by law enforcement agencies and officials?	____	____	____
(b) by press (radio, TV, news-paper)?	____	____	____
(c) by religious leaders and groups?	____	____	____
(d) by civic leaders and groups?	____	____	____

	Before 1954	Before issue was raised locally	After issue was raised locally
(e) by local political leaders and groups?			
(f) by business and industrial leaders and groups?			
(g) by power structure leaders and groups?			
(h) by state political leaders and groups?			
(i) by state educational leaders and groups?			
(j) by state agencies (Department of Education)?			
(k) by black leaders and groups?			
(l) by civil rights groups and leaders?			

II. PHYSICAL FACTORS AND PRINCIPLES

1. Was there much difference in physical condition of local Negro and white schools
   (a) before 1954? _____
   (b) before desegregation issue was raised? _____
   Was this a factor in bringing about desegregation? Explain.

2. What part of black students live nearer to white schools?
   Few? _____   Most? _____
   Were any real hardship cases involved? _____
   Were these factors involved in bringing about desegregation? ___

3. What has been local population, by race?
   (a) before 1954? (number or percent) _____
   (b) since 1954? (number or percent) _____

4. What geographical area does school system serve
   (a) only local community? _____
   (b) a county or other wider area? _____

III. FINANCIAL AND ADMINISTRATIVE FACTORS AND PRINCIPLES

1. How are schools financed?
   (a) Is federal money involved? _____
   Was this a factor in desegregating the schools? ___

(b) Have school bonds been voted on since 1954? _____
Did this influence desegregation? _____

(c) Has high cost of dual school facilities influenced desegregation? _____

2. How is school board chosen? by appointment? _____ by election? _____
Was this a factor in desegregation? _____
Does the board have representatives from black or other minority groups? _____
Does the board seem to be controlled by special interest groups or persons? _____

IV. COERCIVE FACTORS AND PRINCIPLES

1. Was court action involved in desegregating your schools?
(a) threat of court action? _____
(b) actual filing of court suit? _____
(c) court order to desegregate? _____

2. Was this to begin or to increase desegregation? _____

3. Who initiated such action?
(a) parents _____
(b) school officials _____
(c) group or groups (specify) _____

4. What was result of such action?

5. Was pressure from other sources involved in desegregating local schools?
(a) federal agencies (Departments of Defense or Education, etc.) _____
(b) state agencies (governor, Department of Education, etc.) _____
(c) local officials (mayor, city council, biracial commission) _____
(d) civil rights groups (NAACP, C.O.R.E., etc.) _____
(e) human relations groups _____
(f) religious groups (ministerial groups, etc.) _____
(g) other civic groups _____
(h) press _____
(i) public opinion campaign _____

V. COMMUNITY PREPARATION FACTORS AND PRINCIPLES

1. Were efforts made to prepare community for school desegregation

	When	How
(a) by school officials?		
(b) by other official groups?		
(c) by human relations groups?		
(d) by press?		
(e) by religious forces?		

2. Did such efforts have much effect
(a) in bringing about school desegregation? _____
(b) in making it operate more smoothly? _____

VI. OTHER PRINCIPLES AND FACTORS WHICH OPERATED TO BRING ABOUT
SCHOOL DESEGREGATION

1. What was the situation in race relations in your community

	Very Good	Fair	Poor	Critical
before 1954?				
after 1954 ruling?				
after desegregation issue raised locally?				
after school board decided to desegregate?				
after desegregation began?				

2. What was communication situation between white and black leaders

	Very Good	Fair	Poor	Critical
before 1954?				
after 1954 ruling?				
after desegregation issue was raised locally?				
after school board decided to desegregate?				
after desegregation began?				

3. What was political climate in local community (as to race, etc.)

	Very Good	Fair	Poor	Critical
before 1954?				
after 1954 ruling?				
after desegregation issue was raised locally?				
after school board decided to desegregate?				
after desegregation began?				

	Very Good	Fair	Poor	Criti-cal

4. What was communication situation between school officials and black parents
before 1954? ⎯⎯ ⎯⎯ ⎯⎯ ⎯⎯
after 1954 ruling? ⎯⎯ ⎯⎯ ⎯⎯ ⎯⎯
after desegregation issue was raised locally? ⎯⎯ ⎯⎯ ⎯⎯ ⎯⎯
after school board decided to desegregate? ⎯⎯ ⎯⎯ ⎯⎯ ⎯⎯
after desegregation began? ⎯⎯ ⎯⎯ ⎯⎯ ⎯⎯

5. What has been economic level in local community

	High	Aver-age	Low
of most whites?	⎯⎯	⎯⎯	⎯⎯
of most blacks?	⎯⎯	⎯⎯	⎯⎯

6. What has been educational level in local community
of most whites? ⎯⎯ ⎯⎯ ⎯⎯
of most blacks? ⎯⎯ ⎯⎯ ⎯⎯

7. Was there other desegregation besides school desegregation in local community

	None	Some	Much
before 1954?	⎯⎯	⎯⎯	⎯⎯
before school issue was raised locally?	⎯⎯	⎯⎯	⎯⎯
before school desegregation began?	⎯⎯	⎯⎯	⎯⎯

8. Were there other racial or cultural minority groups in community before school desegregation began? ⎯⎯⎯⎯
Who (Jews, Catholics, etc.)? ⎯⎯⎯⎯⎯⎯⎯⎯⎯⎯⎯⎯⎯⎯⎯⎯⎯⎯
Did their presence affect desegregation? ⎯⎯⎯⎯

9. Has there been local or state legislation relating to school desegregation in local community?
What was it?
When was it passed?
By whom was it passed?
Was it passed to stop desegregation, to slow it down, or to aid it?

10. Is your community an urban one? ⎯⎯⎯⎯⎯
Does this have an influence on desegregation?

11. Do official agencies in local community (school board, city council, police department, county commissioners, etc.) co-operate, or is there considerable conflict between them? What effect has this had on desegregation?

12. Did school desegregation begin locally with tokenism or with a large number of students? How did this affect the beginning of desegregation?

APPENDIX E

ANALYSIS OF QUESTIONNAIRE DATA

A considerable body of data showing a detailed analysis of the desegregation process in each of the communities in this study was omitted from Chapter IV in an effort to keep the main text from becoming too tedious for the general reader. However, since there are scholars and researchers who would find this material helpful, it is included in the following pages.

TECHNIQUES USED TO ANALYZE QUESTIONNAIRE DATA

Techniques used to analyze the questionnaire data include a series of simple frequency distributions and rank order lists and the computation of rank order correlation coefficients between various groups and subgroups of interviewees.[1] The use of these techniques is based primarily on the series of weightings assigned to each of the questionnaire's twenty-five items by each of the forty interviewees involved in the study.[2] To make the analysis more meaningful, this data may be observed and studied from various viewpoints by applying these techniques to several interviewee groupings, namely (1) each of the twenty interviewees in each community as individuals, (2) the twenty interviewees as a total group in each community, and (3) five smaller subgroups of interviewees in each community. The subgroups include white leaders, black leaders, school leaders, religious leaders, and business leaders.

Frequency distribution charts are especially helpful for showing which of the twenty-five factors are operative in each or both communities, how often each is mentioned or emphasized, what relative value each is given by interviewees, and whether any one or more of the items might be removed or omitted without affecting the desegregation situation in one or both communities. Such frequency distributions may be developed from the individual weightings assigned to each factor in the questionnaire by each of

[1] Computed by formula: $\text{Rho} = 1 - \dfrac{6 \Sigma \, D^2}{n(n^3 - 1)}$. See Allen L. Edwards, *Statistical Methods for the Behavioral Sciences*, New York: Rinehart, 1956, pp. 193–97.

[2] Each interviewee was asked to assign a numerical weight of 1, 2, 3, or 4 to each principle or factor on the questionnaire to indicate its importance, if any, in the local school desegregation situation, namely: 1—not important; 2—slightly important; 3—fairly important; 4—very important.

the interviewees, as well as from the totaled weightings assigned to each item by a group or subgroup of interviewees. For purposes of this study items weighted as "1—not important" or "2—slightly important" by interviewees are considered as being rated "low" or "least important." Items weighted as "3—fairly important" or "4—very important" are considered as being rated "high" or "most important."

From these same totaled weightings, rank order lists can be established. Such lists are helpful in determining the relative importance of each factor in a particular community, and how each relates to others in order of importance. By selecting reasonable upper and lower cutoff points on the ranked lists, the most important and least important items may be designated as viewed by various groups and subgroups. For purposes of this study, factors ranked from 1.0 to 11.0 are considered to be "most important," and those ranked from 20.0 to 25.0 are considered to be "least important."

By computing the rank order correlation coefficient between the overall groups and between various pairs of subgroups, one can determine whether there is any significant relationship between the importance attached to various factors by comparable or related interviewee groups, such as white and black leaders in a particular community, school leaders in both communities, and so on. In analyzing the questionnaire data, it seems useful to apply these techniques to each community separately at first so as to determine which principles or factors appear to be operative, what importance, if any, they are judged to have in each place, and whether there is any correlation in how various groups of interviewees in each community view the various items.

After studying each community separately, the questionnaire information from both may be compared and analyzed jointly to determine the presence and importance, if any, of the factors in the two places and whether there is any correlation in how comparable interviewee groups in the two communities view the items.

Other data obtained during the interviews, as well as material from other sources and from earlier sections of this study, are useful in providing a check against the questionnaire findings. This includes verbal data obtained from each interviewee about his community's background and how school desegregation came about there and information from the mass media, official records, other research studies, public statements by officials, and the participant-observer experience of this researcher.

GREENSBORO, NORTH CAROLINA—QUESTIONNAIRE DATA ANALYZED

From the frequency distribution tables showing the weightings assigned to the twenty-five principles or factors by twenty Greensboro leaders as individuals (Table A-1), by the same interviewees as a total group (Table A-2), and by five subgroups among them (Table A-2), some determination can be made as to how frequently each item is mentioned or emphasized, what relative value each is given by the interviewees, and whether any items could be omitted without affecting the local desegregation process.

For instance, thirteen factors, as shown in Table A-3, are considered by 60 percent or more of the individual interviewees to be "very important" or "fairly important." Three of these items— school superintendent leadership, black leaders' support, and civil rights pressure—are rated as "very important" by most interviewees, while three other items—religious support and a high level of education among blacks and whites—are rated as "fairly important" by most interviewees. These six items, plus the threat of legal action are looked on as "fairly important" to "very important" by 70 percent or more of the Greensboro leaders. Two are rated as such by 85 to 90 percent of the interviewees.

The Greensboro leaders as a total group, as shown on Table A-4, give an average rating of "very important" or "fairly important," to seventeen factors. These include the thirteen items rated similarly by the interviewees as individuals. The total interviewee group gives a "very important" rating to five items: leadership of the school superintendent, black leaders' support, civil rights pressure, and a high level of education among both blacks and whites. Three of these rate similarly among most interviewees as individuals.

Of the five interviewee subgroups, shown also on Table A-4, 60 percent or more rate eighteen of the principles or factors as "very important" or "fairly important." Included among these eighteen items are all of those rated similarly by most individual interviewees and by all interviewees as a total group. Black leaders' support, the threat of legal action, and civil rights pressure are given a "very important" rating by most subgroups.

There is agreement among the three major interviewee groupings[3] in assigning a "very important" rating to black leaders' support

---

[3] This includes 60 percent or more of the individual interviewees, all interviewees as a group, and 60 percent or more of the interviewee subgroups.

Table A
MOST IMPORTANT PRINCIPLES OR FACTORS
(as rated and/or ranked by Greensboro leaders)

Explanatory code:
A. Total interviewee group
B. 60 percent or more of subgroups (three or more out of five)
C. 60 percent or more of individual interviewees (twelve or more from total of twenty)
D. Most groups and individuals

As *rated* and/or *ranked** by total group of Greensboro interviewees, by most individual interviewees, and by majority of interviewee subgroups

Item no. DESCRIPTION	Rated high by			Ranked high by		Rated and/or ranked high by: D
	A	B	C	A	B	
1. School board leadership	X	X				
2. School superintendent leadership	X	X	X	X	X	X
3. Board policy clear	X	X	X		X	X
4. Police policy clear	X	X	X	X	X	X
5. Press support	X	X	X	X	X	X
6. Religious support	X	X	X	X	X	X
7. Business support						
8. Power structure support						
9. Political support						
10. Negro leaders' support	X	X	X	X	X	X
11. Federal funds influence						
12. Legal action threat	X	X	X	X	X	X
13. Federal court order						
14. Federal agency pressure						
15. Civil rights pressure	X	X	X	X	X	X
16. Human relations groups prepare community	X	X	X	X		X
17. Press prepares community	X	X				
18. Other desegregation		X				
19. White education high	X	X	X	X	X	X
20. Negro education high	X	X	X	X	X	X
21. Race communication good	X	X	X		X	X
22. Social climate moderate	X	X	X	X	X	X
23. Negro population low						
24. Political climate good	X	X				
25. Legislation favorable	X	X				

* *Rated* refers to a rating of "very important" or "fairly important" given to items by interviewees. *Ranking* refers to rank of 1 to 11 assigned to items by interviewees.

256

Table A-1
IMPORTANCE GIVEN TO TWENTY-FIVE PRINCIPLES OR FACTORS
(by Greensboro leaders)

Explanatory code: N—Number of interviewees (out of total of twenty) (P)—Percent of interviewees (based on total of twenty interviewees)	Based on individual weightings* given to each item by all interviewees in Greensboro					
	Rating given to items by individual interviewees					
	(A) Very important	(B) Fairly important	(A) + (B) = High rating	(C) Slightly important	(D) Not important	(C) + (D) = Low rating
Item no. DESCRIPTION	by: N(P)	by: N(P)	by: N(P)	by: N(P)	by: N(P)	by: N(P)
1. School board leadership	6(30%)	4(20%)	10(50%)	1(5%)	9(45%)	10(50%)
2. School superintendent leadership	11(55%)	3(15%)	14(70%)	3(15%)	3(15%)	6(30%)
3. Board policy clear	8(40%)	4(20%)	12(60%)	1(5%)	7(35%)	8(40%)
4. Police policy clear	8(40%)	4(20%)	12(60%)	3(15%)	5(25%)	8(40%)
5. Press support	7(35%)	6(30%)	13(65%)	5(25%)	2(10%)	7(35%)
6. Religious support	3(15%)	11(55%)	14(70%)	3(15%)	3(15%)	6(30%)
7. Business support	1(5%)	6(30%)	7(35%)	5(25%)	8(40%)	13(65%)
8. Power structure support	3(15%)	2(10%)	5(25%)	3(15%)	12(60%)	15(75%)
9. Political support	1(5%)	2(10%)	3(15%)	2(10%)	15(75%)	17(85%)
10. Negro leaders' support	11(55%)	3(15%)	14(70%)	5(25%)	1(5%)	6(30%)
11. Federal funds influence	1(5%)	—	1(5%)	2(10%)	17(85%)	19(95%)
12. Legal action threat	9(45%)	5(25%)	14(70%)	1(5%)	5(25%)	6(30%)
13. Federal court order	—	2(10%)	2(10%)	—	18(90%)	18(90%)
14. Federal agency pressure	1(5%)	1(5%)	2(10%)	—	18(90%)	18(90%)
15. Civil rights pressure	13(65%)	2(10%)	15(75%)	3(15%)	2(10%)	5(25%)
16. Human relations groups prepare community	6(30%)	7(35%)	13(65%)	4(20%)	3(15%)	7(35%)
17. Press prepares community	2(10%)	9(45%)	11(55%)	6(30%)	3(15%)	9(45%)
18. Other desegregation	2(10%)	4(20%)	6(30%)	4(20%)	10(50%)	14(70%)
19. White education high	4(20%)	14(70%)	18(90%)	2(10%)	—	2(10%)
20. Negro education high	6(30%)	11(55%)	17(85%)	3(15%)	—	3(15%)
21. Race communication good	3(15%)	9(45%)	12(60%)	6(30%)	2(10%)	8(40%)
22. Social climate moderate	4(20%)	9(45%)	13(65%)	5(25%)	2(10%)	7(35%)
23. Negro population low	—	4(20%)	4(20%)	12(60%)	4(20%)	16(80%)
24. Political climate good	3(15%)	4(20%)	7(35%)	9(45%)	4(20%)	13(65%)
25. Legislation favorable	6(30%)	2(10%)	8(40%)	10(50%)	2(10%)	12(60%)

* Each interviewee was asked to assign a weight to each item to indicate its importance, namely, not important, slightly important, fairly important, or very important.

Table A-2
IMPORTANCE GIVEN TO TWENTY-FIVE PRINCIPLES OR FACTORS
(by groups in Greensboro)

Interviewee groups:
A—All leaders
B—White leaders
C—Negro leaders
D—Religious leaders
E—School leaders
F—Business leaders

Based on group and subgroup averages of weightings given to each item by all of the interviewees in Greensboro*

Item no. DESCRIPTION	Very important						Fairly important						Slightly important						Not important					
	A	B	C	D	E	F	A	B	C	D	E	F	A	B	C	D	E	F	A	B	C	D	E	F
1. School board leadership							X	X		X	X	X			X									
2. School superintendent leadership	X	X	X							X	X	X												
3. Board policy clear							X	X	X	X	X	X												
4. Police policy clear							X	X	X	X	X	X												
5. Press support		X					X		X	X	X													
6. Religious support							X	X	X	X	X	X												
7. Business support							X						X		X	X	X	X						
8. Power structure support												X	X	X	X	X	X							
9. Political support													X	X	X	X	X							X
10. Negro leaders' support	X		X	X	X		X																	
11. Federal funds influence													X	X	X	X	X	X						
12. Legal action threat		X	X	X	X		X	X																
13. Federal court order													X	X	X			X				X	X	
14. Federal agency pressure																X		X	X	X	X		X	
15. Civil rights pressure	X		X	X			X					X												
16. Human relations groups prepare community			X	X			X	X			X	X												
17. Press prepares community							X	X	X	X	X	X												
18. Other desegregation									X	X	X		X	X				X						
19. White education high	X	X			X		X		X	X														
20. Negro education high	X	X			X		X		X	X														
21. Race communication good							X	X	X	X	X	X												
22. Social climate moderate							X	X	X	X	X	X												
23. Negro population low							X						X		X	X	X	X						
24. Political climate good							X	X	X	X	X							X						
25. Legislation favorable							X	X	X	X	X	X												

* Each interviewee was asked to assign a weight of 1, 2, 3, or 4 to each item to indicate its importance, namely, 1—not important, 2—slightly important, 3—fairly important, and 4—very important.

Table A-3
PRINCIPLES OR FACTORS RATED HIGH
(by individuals in Greensboro)

Explanatory code: N—Number of interviewees (out of total of twenty) (P)—Percent of interviewees (based on total of twenty interviewees) Item no.—DESCRIPTION	Based on individual weightings given to each item by all interviewees in Greensboro*			
	Rating given to items		Items rated high	
	Very important by: N(P)	Fairly important by: N(P)	by (P)	by 60 percent or more of interviewees
1. School board leadership	6(30%)	4(20%)	50%	
2. School superintendent leadership	11(55%)	3(15%)	70%	X
3. Board policy clear	8(40%)	4(20%)	60%	X
4. Police policy clear	8(40%)	4(20%)	60%	X
5. Press support	7(35%)	6(30%)	65%	X
6. Religious support	3(15%)	11(55%)	70%	X
7. Business support	1(5%)	6(30%)	35%	
8. Power structure support	3(15%)	2(10%)	25%	
9. Political support	1(5%)	2(10%)	15%	
10. Negro leaders' support	11(55%)	3(15%)	70%	X
11. Federal funds influence	1(5%)	—	5%	
12. Legal action threat	9(45%)	5(25%)	70%	X
13. Federal court order	—	2(10%)	10%	
14. Federal agency pressure	1(5%)	1(5%)	10%	
15. Civil rights pressure	13(65%)	2(10%)	75%	X
16. Human relations groups prepare community	6(30%)	7(35%)	65%	X
17. Press prepares community	2(10%)	9(45%)	55%	
18. Other desegregation	2(10%)	4(20%)	30%	
19. White education high	4(20%)	14(70%)	90%	X
20. Negro education high	6(30%)	11(55%)	85%	X
21. Race communication good	3(15%)	9(45%)	60%	X
22. Social climate moderate	4(20%)	9(45%)	65%	X
23. Negro population low	—	4(20%)	20%	
24. Political climate good	3(15%)	4(20%)	35%	
25. Legislation favorable	6(30%)	2(10%)	40%	

* Each interviewee was asked to assign a weight of 1, 2, 3, or 4 to each item to indicate its importance, namely, 1—not important, 2—slightly important, 3—fairly important, 4—very important.

259

Table A-4
PRINCIPLES OR FACTORS RATED HIGH
(by groups in Greensboro)

Interviewee groups:
A—All leaders
B—White leaders
C—Negro leaders
D—Religious leaders
E—School leaders
F—Business leaders
B–F—60 percent or more of subgroups (three or more)

Based on averages of weightings* given to each item by total interviewee group and by the five interviewee subgroups in Greensboro

Item no. DESCRIPTION	Very important A	B	C	D	E	F	Fairly important A	B	C	D	E	F	Items rated high by A	B–F
1. School board leadership							X	X		X	X	X	X	X
2. School superintendent leadership	X	X	X							X	X	X	X	X
3. Board policy clear							X	X	X	X	X	X	X	X
4. Police policy clear							X	X	X	X	X	X	X	X
5. Press support		X					X		X	X	X	X	X	X
6. Religious support							X	X	X	X	X	X	X	X
7. Business support								X						
8. Power structure support											X			
9. Political support														
10. Negro leaders' support	X		X	X	X	X		X					X	X
11. Federal funds influence														
12. Legal action threat			X	X	X	X	X	X					X	X
13. Federal court order														
14. Federal agency pressure														
15. Civil rights pressure	X		X	X							X		X	X
16. Human relations groups prepare community			X	X			X	X			X	X	X	X
17. Press prepares community							X	X	X	X	X	X	X	X
18. Other desegregation								X	X	X				X
19. White education high	X	X		X					X		X		X	X
20. Negro education high	X	X		X					X		X		X	X
21. Race communication good							X	X	X	X	X	X	X	X
22. Social climate moderate							X	X	X	X	X	X	X	X
23. Negro population low								X						
24. Political climate good							X	X	X	X	X		X	X
25. Legislation favorable							X	X	X	X	X	X	X	X

* Each interviewee was asked to assign a weight of 1, 2, 3, or 4 to each item to indicate its importance, namely, 1—not important, 2—slightly important, 3—fairly important, 4—very important.

and civil rights pressure. School superintendent leadership receives a top rating by two of the interviewee groupings.[4] The three major groupings are also in agreement in rating thirteen items as "very important" or "fairly important." The total interviewee group and most subgroups give a similar rating to four other items.

In contrast to the principles or factors given high ratings in Greensboro, ten items are considered as "not important" or only "slightly important" by 60 percent or more of the individual leaders, as shown on Table A-5. Five of these items are looked upon by most of the leaders as having no importance in the local situation: power structure support, political support, federal funds influence, federal court order, and federal agency pressure. A low black population is considered by most individuals as being "slightly important." The six items just mentioned, plus other desegregation, are looked upon as having little or no importance by 70 percent or more of the Greensboro leaders. Four of the items are so rated by 85 to 95 percent of the interviewees.

The total group of Greensboro interviewees, as shown on Table A-6, give little or no importance to eight of the same items rated similarly by most individual leaders. The group, however, seems to consider only federal agency pressure as having no importance locally. The seven others are rated as "slightly important." Most of the interviewee subgroups, as shown on Table A-6, give a rating of "not important" or "slightly important" to seven items. Again federal agency pressure is looked upon by most subgroups as having no importance. There is agreement among the three major interviewee groupings in assigning a rating of "not important" to federal agency pressure. Seven other items, however, are also looked upon by all the major interviewee groupings as having little if any importance in the local school desegregation situation.

The relative importance of each of the twenty-five factors and how each relates to the others in order of importance in the Greensboro school desegregation process can be seen by examining the rank order listings in Table A-7.[5]

Table A-8 shows the factors ranked as "most important" by the

---

[4] These include 60 percent or more of the individual interviewees and all interviewees as a group (Tables A-3 and A-4).

[5] Upper and lower cutoff points on the rank order lists have been established for this study in order to set up categories of "most important" (ranks 1.0 to 11.0) and "least important" (ranks 20.0 to 25.0) factors. The upper group includes about 45 percent of the ranks and the lower one about 25 percent. The cutoff points were first set to include the top ten and the bottom five ranks, but each had to be adjusted to include an extra rank.

Table A-5
PRINCIPLES OR FACTORS RATED LOW
(by individuals in Greensboro)

| *Explanatory code:* N—Number of interviewees (out of total of twenty) (P)—Percent of interviewees (based on total of twenty interviewees) | Based on individual weightings* given to each item by all interviewees in Greensboro | | | |
| Item no. DESCRIPTION | Rating given to item | | Items rated low | |
	Slightly important by: N(P)	Not important by: N(P)	by (P)	by 60 percent or more of interviewees
1. School board leadership	1(5%)	9(45%)	50%	
2. School superintendent leadership	3(15%)	3(15%)	30%	
3. Board policy clear	1(5%)	7(35%)	40%	
4. Police policy clear	3(15%)	5(25%)	40%	
5. Press support	5(25%)	2(10%)	35%	
6. Religious support	3(15%)	3(15%)	30%	
7. Business support	5(25%)	8(40%)	65%	X
8. Power structure support	3(15%)	12(60%)	75%	X
9. Political support	2(10%)	15(75%)	85%	X
10. Negro leaders' support	5(25%)	1(5%)	30%	
11. Federal funds influence	2(10%)	17(85%)	95%	X
12. Legal action threat	1(5%)	5(25%)	30%	
13. Federal court order	—	18(90%)	90%	X
14. Federal agency pressure	—	18(90%)	90%	X
15. Civil rights pressure	3(15%)	2(10%)	35%	
16. Human relations groups prepare community	4(20%)	3(15%)	35%	
17. Press prepares community	6(30%)	3(15%)	45%	
18. Other desegregation	4(20%)	10(50%)	70%	X
19. White education high	2(10%)	—	10%	
20. Negro education high	3(15%)	—	15%	
21. Race communication good	6(30%)	2(10%)	40%	
22. Social climate moderate	5(25%)	2(10%)	35%	
23. Negro population low	12(60%)	4(20%)	80%	X
24. Political climate good	9(45%)	4(20%)	65%	X
25. Legislation favorable	10(50%)	2(10%)	60%	X

* Each interviewee was asked to assign a weight of 1, 2, 3, or 4 to each item to indicate its importance, namely, 1—not important, 2—slightly important, 3—fairly important, 4—very important.

Table A-6
PRINCIPLES OR FACTORS RATED LOW
(by groups in Greensboro)

Interviewee groups:
A—All leaders
B—White leaders
C—Negro leaders
D—Religious leaders
E—School leaders
F—Business leaders
B-F—60 percent or more of subgroups (three or more)

Based on averages of weightings* given to each item by total interviewee group and by the five interviewee subgroups in Greensboro

Item no. DESCRIPTION	Slightly important						Not important						Items rated low by	
	A	B	C	D	E	F	A	B	C	D	E	F	A	B-F
1. School board leadership			X											
2. School superintendent leadership														
3. Board policy clear														
4. Police policy clear														
5. Press support														
6. Religious support														
7. Business support	X		X	X	X	X							X	X
8. Power structure support	X	X	X	X	X								X	X
9. Political support	X	X	X	X	X					X			X	X
10. Negro leaders' support														
11. Federal funds influence	X	X	X	X	X	X							X	X
12. Legal action threat														
13. Federal court order	X	X	X			X				X	X		X	X
14. Federal agency pressure		X				X	X	X	X		X		X	X
15. Civil rights pressure														
16. Human relations groups prepare community														
17. Press prepares community														
18. Other desegregation	X	X			X								X	
19. White education high														
20. Negro education high														
21. Race communication good														
22. Social climate moderate														
23. Negro population low	X		X	X	X	X							X	X
24. Political climate good						X								
25. Legislation favorable														

* Each interviewee was asked to assign a weight of 1, 2, 3, or 4 to each item to indicate its importance, namely, 1—not important, 2—slightly important, 3—fairly important, 4—very important.

263

Table A-7
PRINCIPLES OR FACTORS
(as ranked by Greensboro groups)

Interviewee groups: A—All leaders B—White leaders C—Negro leaders D—Religious leaders E—School leaders F—Business leaders	Rankings given by total group of twenty interviewees, and by five subgroups of interviewees					
Item no. DESCRIPTION	Rank assigned to twenty-five items by groups					
	A	B	C	D	E	F
1. School board leadership	16.	13.	18.	16.5	8.5	13.
2. School superintendent leadership	4.5	2.	7.	3.5	2.5	6.
3. Board policy clear	12.5	4.5	15.	8.	5.	10.5
4. Police policy clear	9.5	11.	9.	14.5	8.5	14.5
5. Press support	6.5	1.	12.	3.5	1.	6.
6. Religious support	11.	8.	12.	5.	8.5	10.5
7. Business support	18.5	18.	19.	12.	18.	18.5
8. Power structure support	21.	20.	23.5	20.	21.	16.5
9. Political support	22.	22.	20.5	20.	21.	25.
10. Negro leaders' support	2.	8.	2.	1.5	13.	3.
11. Federal funds influence	23.	24.	22.	23.5	24.5	24.
12. Legal action threat	6.5	14.5	3.	8.	14.5	3.
13. Federal court order	24.	23.	25.	23.5	24.5	22.5
14. Federal agency pressure	25.	25.	23.5	25.	23.	22.5
15. Civil rights pressure	1.	8.	1.	1.5	14.5	6.
16. Human relations groups prepare community	8.	16.	4.5	12.	16.5	8.
17. Press prepares community	15.	14.5	12.	14.5	11.5	14.5
18. Other desegregation	20.	21.	16.5	22.	21.	21.
19. White education high	4.5	4.5	4.5	8.	5.	3.
20. Negro education high	3.	3.	6.	8.	2.5	1.
21. Race communication good	12.5	8.	10.	8.	5.	10.5
22. Social climate moderate	9.5	12.	8.	16.5	11.5	10.5
23. Negro population low	18.5	18.	20.5	18.	19.	20.
24. Political climate good	17.	18.	14.	20.	16.5	18.5
25. Legislation favorable	14.	8.	16.5	12.	8.5	16.5

Table A-8
PRINCIPLES OR FACTORS RANKED HIGH
(by groups in Greensboro)

Interviewee groups: A—All leaders B—White leaders C—Negro leaders D—Religious leaders E—School leaders F—Business leaders B–F—60 percent or more of subgroups (three or more)	Principles or factors ranked from 1 to 11 by all interviewees and/ or by one or more subgroups of interviewees in Greensboro							
	Rank assigned by						Items ranked 1 to 11 by	
Item no. DESCRIPTION	A	B	C	D	E	F	A	B–F
1. School board leadership	—	—	—	—	8.5	—		
2. School superintendent leadership	4.5	2.	7.	3.5	2.5	6.	X	X
3. Board policy clear	—	4.5	—	8.	5.	10.5		X
4. Police policy clear	9.5	11.	9.	—	8.5	—	X	X
5. Press support	6.5	1.	—	3.5	1.	6.	X	X
6. Religious support	11.	8.	—	5.	8.5	10.5	X	X
7. Business support								
8. Power structure support								
9. Political support								
10. Negro leaders' support	2.	8.	2.	1.5	—	3.	X	X
11. Federal funds influence								
12. Legal action threat	6.5	—	3.	8.	—	3.	X	X
13. Federal court order								
14. Federal agency pressure								
15. Civil rights pressure	1.	8.	1.	1.5	—	6.	X	X
16. Human relations groups prepare community	8.	—	4.5	—	—	8.	X	
17. Press prepares community	—	—	—	—	11.5	—		
18. Other desegregation								
19. White education high	4.5	4.5	4.5	8.	5.	3.	X	X
20. Negro education high	3.	3.	6.	8.	2.5	1.	X	X
21. Race communication good	—	8.	10.	8.	5.	10.5		X
22. Social climate moderate	9.5	—	8.	—	11.5	10.5	X	X
23. Negro population low								
24. Political climate good								
25. Legislation favorable	—	8.	—	—	8.5	—		

several groupings of Greensboro leaders. The item which ranks highest among the interviewees as a total group is pressure from civil rights groups. The next four items, in order of importance, are black leaders' support, a high level of education among blacks, the school superintendent's leadership, and a high level of education among whites. Most of the subgroups rank each of these five factors also within the same range of 1.0 to 5.0.

Of all the factors ranked by all groups within the "most important" range (ranks 1.0 to 11.0), there is agreement by the total interviewee group and at least 60 percent of the subgroups on ten items.[6] On seven of these items, there is agreement by the total interviewee group and 80 percent or more of the subgroups as to ranking within the "most important" range, and on three items there is agreement by the total group and all subgroups.

Among the principles or factors ranked as "least important" (ranks 20.0 to 25.0) in Greensboro as shown on Table A-9, the item which ranks at the bottom of the list, insofar as the total group is concerned, is federal agency pressure. Other items ranked within the "least important" range by the total interviewee group include power structure support, political support, federal funds influence, federal court order, and other desegregation. Four out of the five interviewee subgroups are in agreement with the total interviewee group in ranking each of these six items within the same "least important" range.

In order to determine whether there are any important relationships or differences in how various groups of the Greensboro leaders view the principles or factors involved in the local desegregation situation, the computation of rank order correlation coefficients is used. The results of such computations, as presented on Table A-10, show that the relationships between various pairs of the five Greensboro interviewee subgroups and between each subgroup and all other interviewees in the community are all very close.[7] Statistically, all of the correlations are highly significant (beyond the 1 percent level).[8]

[6] Item no. 16 is ranked also within this range by the total interviewee group, but only by 40 percent of the subgroups. Items nos. 3 and 21 are ranked within this range by most subgroups but not by the total interviewee group.

[7] Correlations have been computed between twelve white leaders and eight black leaders, between six religious and seven school leaders, between six religious and six business leaders, between seven school and six business leaders, and between each of these subgroups and all other interviewees in the community.

[8] Significance here means that the observed value of Rho is significantly greater than zero so that it can be concluded that there is suffi-

Table A-9
PRINCIPLES OR FACTORS RANKED LOW
(by groups in Greensboro)

Interviewee groups: A—All leaders B—White leaders C—Negro leaders D—Religious leaders E—School leaders F—Business leaders B-F—60 percent or more of subgroups (three or more)		Principles or factors ranked from 20 to 25 by all interviewees and/ or by one or more subgroups of interviewees in Greensboro						
		Rank assigned by						Items ranked 20 to 25 by
Item no. DESCRIPTION	A	B	C	D	E	F	A	B-F
1. School board leadership								
2. School superintendent leadership								
3. Board policy clear								
4. Police policy clear								
5. Press support								
6. Religious support								
7. Business support								
8. Power structure support	21.	20.	23.5	20.	21.	—	X	X
9. Political support	22.	22.	20.5	20.	21.	25.	X	X
10. Negro leaders' support								
11. Federal funds influence	23.	24.	22.	23.5	24.5	24.	X	X
12. Legal action threat								
13. Federal court order	24.	23.	25.	23.5	24.5	22.5	X	X
14. Federal agency pressure	25.	25.	23.5	25.	23.	22.5	X	X
15. Civil rights pressure								
16. Human relations groups prepare community								
17. Press prepares community								
18. Other desegregation	20.	21.	—	22.	21.	21.	X	X
19. White education high								
20. Negro education high								
21. Race communication good								
22. Social climate moderate								
23. Negro population low	—	—	20.5	—	—	20.		
24. Political climate good	—	—	—	20.	—	—		
25. Legislation favorable								

Table A-10
RANK ORDER CORRELATIONS*
(for groups in Greensboro)

Read across and up		Based on rankings assigned to twenty-five principles or factors by total interviewee group and by five interviewee subgroups					
		GREENSBORO INTERVIEWEES					
		White leaders	Negro leaders	Religious leaders	School leaders	Business leaders	All other leaders
GREENSBORO INTERVIEWEES	White leaders	——	.682				.682
	Negro leaders	.682	——				.682
	Religious leaders			——	.752	.863	.845
	School leaders			.752	——	.746	.648
	Business leaders			.863	.746	——	.872
	All other leaders	.682	.682	.845	.648	.872	——

* Computed by formula for rank order correlation coefficient:

$$\text{Rho} = 1 - \frac{6\Sigma D^2}{n(n^2 - 1)}$$

Correlation significance:
.396 = 5 percent significance
.505 = 1 percent significance

∴ All of the correlations on the above chart are statistically significant beyond the 1 percent level.

This would seem to indicate that all Greensboro leaders, regardless of their racial or vocational category, tend to view the forces operating in the local school desegregation process quite similarly. At the same time, there are several differences and relationships worth noting specifically between various interviewee groups.

The white and black leaders seem to be further apart in their thinking (Rho = .682) than any other two subgroups. Their group rankings are either identical or vary only slightly (4.0 points or

cient evidence to indicate that the two rankings in each case show more than chance agreement (Edwards, *Statistical Methods*, pp. 400–402). For purposes of this study, statistical significance is .396 at the 5 percent level and .505 at the 1 percent level.

Table B
LEAST IMPORTANT PRINCIPLES OR FACTORS
(as rated and/or ranked by Greensboro leaders)

Explanatory code:
A. Total interviewee group
B. 60 percent or more of subgroups (three or more out of five)
C. 60 percent or more of individual interviewees (twelve or more from total of twenty)
D. Most groups and individuals (60 percent or more)

As *rated* and/or *ranked* by total group of Greensboro interviewees, by most individual interviewees, and by majority of interviewee subgroups

Item no. DESCRIPTION	Rated low by			Ranked low by		Rated and/ or ranked low by: D
	A	B	C	A	B	
1. School board leadership						
2. School superintendent leadership						
3. Board policy clear						
4. Police policy clear						
5. Press support						
6. Religious support						
7. Business support	X	X	X			X
8. Power structure support	X	X	X	X	X	X
9. Political support	X	X	X	X	X	X
10. Negro leaders' support						
11. Federal funds influence	X	X	X	X	X	X
12. Legal action threat						
13. Federal court order	X	X	X	X	X	X
14. Federal agency pressure	X	X	X	X	X	X
15. Civil rights pressure						
16. Human relations groups prepare community						
17. Press prepares community						
18. Other desegregation	X		X	X	X	X
19. White education high						
20. Negro education high						
21. Race communication good						
22. Social climate moderate						
23. Negro population low	X	X	X			X
24. Political climate good			X			
25. Legislation favorable			X			

269

less) on fifteen factors. Sharp contrasts (10.0 points or more) exist, however, between the rankings given by the two groups to four items. Two of these—threat of legal action and human relations support—are ranked much higher by black leaders than by whites. The other two, a clear school board policy and press support, are ranked much higher by whites than by blacks.

In contrast, religious leaders and business leaders (Rho = .863) seem to be nearer to each other in their views on these matters than any other two subgroups. Their rankings are identical or vary only slightly (4.0 points or less) on sixteen of the items. On five of these, the variation in ranking is 1.0 or less. There are no variations in rank between the two groups of more than 7.0 points.

School leaders seem to be slightly closer to religious leaders (Rho = .752) than to business leaders (Rho = .746) in their rankings on the twenty-five factors, although the correlations are almost the same. On sixteen items the rankings vary only slightly (4.0 points or less) between the school leaders and religious leaders. A similar relationship exists between the schoolmen and business leaders on fourteen items. The school leaders tend to differ quite sharply (8.5 to 13.0 points) with each of the other groups in ranking black leaders' support, threat of legal action, and civil rights pressure. The schoolmen rank each of these items fairly low, while the other groups rank them very high. At the same time, the Greensboro school leaders tend to differ more from all other leaders in the community (Rho = .648) in their rankings than do any of the other subgroups. There are no factors on which the rankings of these two groups are identical, although there are sixteen items on which their deviation is rather small (4.0 points or less). Sharp differences (10.0 to 13.5 points) in rank show up on five items. School board leadership is ranked considerably higher by the schoolmen than by all other leaders combined.[9] Support from black leaders, threat of legal action, civil rights pressure, and human relations preparation are ranked rather low by the school leaders but very high by all other leaders.

Business leaders seem to differ less in their views on these matters from all other leaders combined (Rho = .872) than do any of the other subgroups. On nineteen of the items, the deviation in ranking is 4.0 points or less, and on eight the deviation is 1.0 or less. Only one item—a clear police policy—does the ranking vary as much as 8.0 points, with the businessmen ranking this factor considerably lower than the other leaders. Greensboro's business leaders seem to

[9] Item no. 1 is ranked 8.5 by schoolmen but 18.5 by all others combined.

be nearer to religious leaders (Rho = .863) than to school leaders (Rho = .746) in their views on these issues.

Religious leaders, when compared with all other leaders combined (Rho = .845) tend to give similar rankings to most items. On seventeen items the deviation in ranking is 4.0 or less, and on ten the difference is 1.0 or less. There are no sharp differences in rankings between religious and other leaders, the greatest variation being 9.0 points difference on one item—a moderate social climate. The religious leaders tend to view this item as less important than do the other leaders.

GREENVILLE, SOUTH CAROLINA—QUESTIONNAIRE DATA ANALYZED

In Greenville some indication as to how often each factor is mentioned or emphasized, what relative value, if any, is attached to each, and whether any items could be omitted without affecting the local desegregation situation can be obtained by examining the frequency tables showing the weightings assigned to each of the twenty-five items by the twenty individual interviewees (Table C-1) and the various groupings of interviewees (Table C-2).

Most of the individual leaders, as shown on Table C-3, give considerable importance to six factors. One of these items—federal court order—is rated "very important" by all of the interviewees. A clear police policy, black leaders' support, civil rights pressure, other desegregation, and a low black population are rated as "very important" to "fairly important" by 65 percent or more of the leaders.

The Greenville leaders as a total group, as shown by Table C-4, give an averaged weighting of "very important" or "fairly important" to eleven factors. These include the six above-mentioned items plus five additional items.

The total interviewee group rates only black leaders' support and federal court order as "very important." The same two items are rated similarly by 80 percent or more of the individual leaders and by all of the five interviewee subgroups. Sixty percent or more of the subgroups are in agreement also with the total interviewee group in rating nine items as "fairly important."

There is agreement in Greenville among most individual leaders, all leaders as a group, and most subgroups of leaders in assigning the "very important" rating to only one item, a federal court order. Black leaders' support is given a top rating by the leaders as a total group and by all subgroups.

Table C
MOST IMPORTANT PRINCIPLES OR FACTORS
(as rated and/or ranked by Greenville leaders)

Explanatory code:
A. Total interviewee group
B. 60 percent or more of subgroups (three or more out of five)
C. 60 percent or more of individual interviewees (twelve or more from total of twenty)
D. Most groups and individuals (60 percent or more)

As *rated* and/or *ranked** by total group of Greenville interviewees, by most individual interviewees, and by majority of interviewee subgroups

Item no. DESCRIPTION	Rated high by A	B	C	Ranked high by A	B	Rated and/or ranked high by: D
1. School board leadership						
2. School superintendent leadership						
3. Board policy clear						
4. Police policy clear	X	X	X	X	X	X
5. Press support						
6. Religious support						
7. Business support	X	X		X	X	X
8. Power structure support		X				
9. Political support						
10. Negro leaders' support	X	X	X	X	X	X
11. Federal funds influence						
12. Legal action threat	X	X		X	X	X
13. Federal court order	X	X	X	X	X	X
14. Federal agency pressure						
15. Civil rights pressure	X	X	X	X	X	X
16. Human relations groups prepare community	X	X		X	X	X
17. Press prepares community						
18. Other desegregation	X	X	X	X	X	X
19. White education high						
20. Negro education high						
21. Race communication good	X	X		X	X	X
22. Social climate moderate	X	X		X	X	X
23. Negro population low	X	X	X	X	X	X
24. Political climate good						
25. Legislation favorable						

* *Rated* refers to rating of "very important" or "fairly important" given to items by interviewees. *Ranking* refers to rank of 1 to 11 assigned to items by interviewees.

Table C-1
IMPORTANCE GIVEN TO PRINCIPLES OR FACTORS
(by Greenville leaders)

Explanatory code: N—Number of interviewees (out of a total of twenty) (P)—Percent of interviewees (based on total of twenty interviewees)	Based on individual weightings* given to each item by all interviewees in Greenville					
	Rating given to items by individual interviewees					
	(A) Very important	(B) Fairly important	(A) + (B) = High rating	(C) Slightly important	(D) Not important	(C) + (D) = Low rating
Item no. DESCRIPTION	by: N(P)	by: N(P)	by: N(P)	by: N(P)	by: N(P)	by: N(P)
1. School board leadership	1(5%)	2(10%)	3(15%)	1(5%)	16(80%)	17(85%)
2. School superintendent leadership	2(10%)	2(10%)	4(20%)	2(10%)	14(70%)	16(80%)
3. Board policy clear	3(15%)	2(10%)	5(25%)	1(5%)	14(70%)	15(75%)
4. Police policy clear	5(25%)	9(45%)	14(70%)	1(5%)	5(25%)	6(30%)
5. Press support	2(10%)	2(10%)	4(20%)	2(10%)	14(70%)	16(80%)
6. Religious support	3(15%)	4(20%)	7(35%)	3(15%)	10(50%)	13(65%)
7. Business support	3(15%)	7(35%)	10(50%)	2(10%)	8(40%)	10(50%)
8. Power structure support	4(20%)	5(25%)	9(45%)	1(5%)	7(35%)	8(40%)
9. Political support	1(5%)	2(10%)	3(15%)	2(10%)	15(75%)	17(85%)
10. Negro leaders' support	9(45%)	7(35%)	16(80%)	3(15%)	1(5%)	4(20%)
11. Federal funds influence	1(5%)	2(10%)	3(15%)	2(10%)	15(75%)	17(85%)
12. Legal action threat	8(40%)	3(15%)	11(55%)	—	9(45%)	9(45%)
13. Federal court order	20(100%)	—	20(100%)	—	—	—
14. Federal agency pressure	2(10%)	—	2(10%)	2(10%)	16(80%)	18(90%)
15. Civil rights pressure	9(45%)	4(20%)	13(65%)	1(5%)	6(30%)	7(35%)
16. Human relations groups prepare community	2(10%)	5(25%)	7(35%)	8(40%)	5(25%)	13(65%)
17. Press prepares community	2(10%)	3(15%)	5(25%)	2(10%)	13(65%)	15(75%)
18. Other desegregation	7(35%)	7(35%)	14(70%)	4(20%)	2(10%)	6(30%)
19. White education high	2(10%)	3(15%)	5(25%)	2(10%)	13(65%)	15(75%)
20. Negro education high	—	—	—	6(30%)	14(70%)	20(100%)
21. Race communication good	3(15%)	7(35%)	10(50%)	6(30%)	4(20%)	10(50%)
22. Social climate moderate	3(15%)	4(20%)	7(35%)	7(35%)	6(30%)	13(65%)
23. Negro population low	9(45%)	6(30%)	15(75%)	1(5%)	4(20%)	5(25%)
24. Political climate good	3(15%)	2(10%)	5(25%)	4(20%)	11(55%)	15(75%)
25. Legislation favorable	—	2(10%)	2(10%)	1(5%)	17(85%)	18(90%)

* Each interviewee was asked to assign a weight of 1, 2, 3, or 4 to each item to indicate its importance, namely, 1—not important, 2—slightly important, 3—fairly important, 4—very important.

Table C-2
IMPORTANCE GIVEN TO PRINCIPLES OR FACTORS
(by groups in Greenville)

Interviewee groups:

A—All leaders
B—White leaders
C—Negro leaders
D—Religious leaders
E—School leaders
F—Business leaders

Based on group and subgroup averages of weightings given to each item by all of the interviewees in Greenville*

Item no. DESCRIPTION	Very important						Fairly important						Slightly important						Not important					
	A	B	C	D	E	F	A	B	C	D	E	F	A	B	C	D	E	F	A	B	C	D	E	F
1. School board leadership													X	X		X	X			X				X
2. School supt. leadership												X	X	X	X	X		X						
3. Board policy clear												X	X	X	X	X		X						
4. Police policy clear				X			X	X	X	X		X												
5. Press support													X	X		X	X		X	X				
6. Religious support								X		X			X		X	X		X						
7. Business support							X	X		X	X				X	X								
8. Power structure support								X		X	X		X		X	X								
9. Political support													X	X		X	X		X	X				
10. Negro leaders' support	X	X	X	X	X	X																		
11. Federal funds influence													X	X		X	X		X	X				
12. Legal action threat							X	X	X	X	X	X												
13. Federal court order	X	X	X	X	X	X																		
14. Federal agency pressure													X	X		X	X		X	X				
15. Civil rights pressure				X			X	X	X	X		X												
16. Human relations groups prepare community							X	X		X	X					X	X							
17. Press prepares community												X	X	X	X	X		X						
18. Other desegregation				X			X	X	X	X		X												
19. White education high												X	X	X	X	X		X						
20. Negro education high													X	X	X	X	X	X						
21. Race communication good							X	X	X	X	X	X												
22. Social climate moderate							X	X	X	X	X							X						
23. Negro population low		X		X			X	X		X		X												
24. Political climate good												X	X	X	X	X		X						
25. Legislation favorable													X	X		X	X				X	X		

* Each interviewee was asked to assign a weight of 1, 2, 3, or 4 to each item to indicate its importance, namely, 1—not important, 2—slightly important, 3—fairly important, and 4—very important.

Table C-3
PRINCIPLES OR FACTORS RATED HIGH
(by individuals in Greenville)

Explanatory code: N—Number of interviewees (out of total of twenty) (P)—Percent of interviewees (based on total of twenty interviewees)	Based on individual weightings* given to each item by all interviewees in Greenville			
	Rating given to items		Items rated high	
	Very important	Fairly important	by (P)	by 60 percent or more of interviewees
Item no. DESCRIPTION	by: N(P)	by: N(P)		
1. School board leadership	1(5%)	2(10%)	15%	
2. School superintendent leadership	2(10%)	2(10%)	20%	
3. Board policy clear	3(15%)	2(10%)	25%	
4. Police policy clear	5(25%)	9(45%)	70%	X
5. Press support	2(10%)	2(10%)	20%	
6. Religious support	3(15%)	4(20%)	35%	
7. Business support	3(15%)	7(35%)	50%	
8. Power structure support	4(20%)	5(25%)	45%	
9. Political support	1(5%)	2(10%)	15%	
10. Negro leaders' support	9(45%)	7(35%)	80%	X
11. Federal funds influence	1(5%)	2(10%)	15%	
12. Legal action threat	8(40%)	3(15%)	55%	
13. Federal court order	20(100%)	—	100%	X
14. Federal agency pressure	2(10%)	—	10%	
15. Civil rights pressure	9(45%)	4(20%)	65%	X
16. Human relations groups prepare community	2(10%)	5(25%)	35%	
17. Press prepares community	2(10%)	3(15%)	25%	
18. Other desegregation	7(35%)	7(35%)	70%	X
19. White education high	2(10%)	3(15%)	25%	
20. Negro education high	—	—	—	
21. Race communication good	3(15%)	7(35%)	50%	
22. Social climate moderate	3(15%)	4(20%)	35%	
23. Negro population low	9(45%)	6(30%)	75%	X
24. Political climate good	3(15%)	2(10%)	25%	
25. Legislation favorable	—	2(10%)	10%	

* Each interviewee was asked to assign a weight of 1, 2, 3, or 4 to each item to indicate its importance, namely, 1—not important, 2—slightly important, 3—fairly important, 4—very important.

Table C-4
PRINCIPLES OR FACTORS RATED HIGH
(by groups in Greenville)

Interviewee groups:
A—All leaders
B—White leaders
C—Negro leaders
D—Religious leaders
E—School leaders
F—Business leaders
B-F—60 percent or more of subgroups (three or more)

Based on averages of weightings* given to each item by total interviewee group and by the five interviewee subgroups in Greenville

Item no. DESCRIPTION	Very important						Fairly important						Items rated high by	
	A	B	C	D	E	F	A	B	C	D	E	F	A	B-F
1. School board leadership														
2. School superintendent leadership										X				
3. Board policy clear										X				
4. Police policy clear						X	X	X	X	X		X	X	X
5. Press support														
6. Religious support								X		X				
7. Business support	X	X								X	X		X	X
8. Power structure support								X		X	X			X
9. Political support														
10. Negro leaders' support	X	X	X	X	X	X							X	X
11. Federal funds influence														
12. Legal action threat							X	X	X	X	X	X	X	X
13. Federal court order	X	X	X	X	X	X							X	X
14. Federal agency pressure														
15. Civil rights pressure						X	X	X	X	X		X	X	X
16. Human relations groups prepare community							X	X		X	X		X	X
17. Press prepares community										X				
18. Other desegregation						X	X	X	X	X		X	X	X
19. White education high											X			
20. Negro education high														
21. Race communication good							X	X	X	X	X	X	X	X
20. Social climate moderate							X	X	X	X	X		X	X
23. Negro population low		X				X	X	X		X		X	X	X
24. Political climate good											X			
25. Legislation favorable														

* Each interviewee was asked to assign a weight of 1, 2, 3, or 4 to each item to indicate its importance, namely, 1—not important, 2—slightly important, 3—fairly important, 4—very important.

Table C-5
PRINCIPLES OR FACTORS RATED LOW
(by individuals in Greenville)

Explanatory code: N—Number of interviewees (out of total of twenty) (P)—Percent of interviewees (based on a total of twenty interviewees) Item no. DESCRIPTION	Based on individual weightings* given to each item by all interviewees in Greenville			
	Rating given to items		Items rated low	
	Slightly important by: N(P)	Not important by: N(P)	by (P)	by 60 percent or more of interviewees
1. School board leadership	1(5%)	16(80%)	85%	X
2. School superintendent leadership	2(10%)	14(70%)	80%	X
3. Board policy clear	1(5%)	14(70%)	75%	X
4. Police policy clear	1(5%)	5(25%)	30%	
5. Press support	2(10%)	14(70%)	80%	X
6. Religious support	3(15%)	10(50%)	65%	X
7. Business support	2(10%)	8(40%)	50%	
8. Power structure support	1(5%)	7(35%)	40%	
9. Political support	2(10%)	15(75%)	85%	X
10. Negro leaders' support	3(15%)	1(5%)	20%	
11. Federal funds influence	2(10%)	15(75%)	85%	X
12. Legal action threat	—	9(45%)	45%	
13. Federal court order	—	—	—	
14. Federal agency pressure	2(10%)	16(80%)	90%	X
15. Civil rights pressure	1(5%)	6(30%)	35%	
16. Human relations groups prepare community	8(40%)	5(25%)	65%	X
17. Press prepares community	2(10%)	13(65%)	75%	X
18. Other desegregation	4(20%)	2(10%)	30%	
19. White education high	2(10%)	13(65%)	75%	X
20. Negro education high	6(30%)	14(70%)	100%	X
21. Race communication good	6(30%)	4(20%)	50%	
22. Social climate moderate	7(35%)	6(30%)	65%	X
23. Negro population low	1(5%)	4(20%)	25%	
24. Political climate good	4(20%)	11(55%)	75%	X
25. Legislation favorable	1(5%)	17(85%)	90%	X

* Each interviewee was asked to assign a weight of 1, 2, 3, or 4 to each item to indicate its importance, namely, 1—not important, 2—slightly important, 3—fairly important, 4—very important.

Table C-6

PRINCIPLES OR FACTORS RATED LOW
(by groups in Greenville)

Interviewee Groups: A—All leaders B—White leaders C—Negro leaders D—Religious leaders E—School leaders F—Business leaders B-F—60 percent or more of subgroups (three or more)							Based on averages of weightings* given to each item by the total interviewee group and by the five interviewee subgroups in Greenville								
							Slightly important						Not important						Items rated low by	
Item no. DESCRIPTION	A	B	C	D	E	F	A	B	C	D	E	F	A	B-F
1. School board leadership	X	X		X	X				X			X	X	X
2. School superintendent leadership	X	X	X	X		X							X	X
3. Board policy clear	X	X	X	X		X							X	X
4. Police policy clear														
5. Press support	X	X			X	X			X	X			X	X
6. Religious support	X		X	X		X							X	X
7. Business support			X	X										
8. Power structure support	X		X	X									X	
9. Political support	X	X			X	X			X	X			X	X
10. Negro leaders' support														
11. Federal funds influence	X	X			X	X			X	X			X	X
12. Legal action threat														
13. Federal court order														
14. Federal agency pressure	X	X			X	X			X	X			X	X
15. Civil rights pressure														
16. Human relations groups prepare community			X	X										
17. Press prepares community	X	X	X	X		X							X	X
18. Other desegregation														
19. White education high	X	X	X	X		X							X	X
20. Negro education high	X	X	X	X	X	X							X	X
21. Race communication good														
22. Social climate moderate						X								
23. Negro population low														
24. Political climate good	X	X	X	X		X							X	X
25. Legislation favorable	X	X			X	X			X	X			X	X

*Each interviewee was asked to assign a weight of 1, 2, 3, or 4 to each item to indicate its importance, namely, 1—not important, 2—slightly important, 3—fairly important, 4—very important.

Table C-7
PRINCIPLES OR FACTORS
(as ranked by Greenville groups)

Interviewee Groups: A—All leaders B—White leaders C—Negro leaders D—Religious leaders E—School leaders F—Business leaders	Rankings given by total group of twenty interviewees, and by five subgroups of interviewees					
Item no. DESCRIPTION	Rank assigned to twenty-five items by each of the groups					
	A	B	C	D	E	F
1. School board leadership	22.	22.	22.5	23.	19.5	25.
2. School superintendent leadership	18.5	19.	14.5	20.	12.	23.5
3. Board policy clear	16.	19.	12.	23.	9.5	18.
4. Police policy clear	6.	6.5	6.	8.	4.5	4.
5. Press support	18.5	15.	22.5	16.	16.	23.5
6. Religious support	12.5	13.	17.5	10.5	14.	13.5
7. Business support	9.	6.5	14.5	9.	7.5	10.
8. Power structure support	12.5	9.	17.5	12.5	12.	10.
9. Political support	20.5	17.	22.5	16.	21.	18.
10. Negro leaders' support	2.	2.	2.	2.	3.	2.
11. Federal funds influence	20.5	19.	22.5	12.5	25.	21.
12. Legal action threat	7.	6.5	8.5	4.	18.	6.5
13. Federal court order	1.	1.	1.	1.	1.	1.
14. Federal agency pressure	25.	22.	22.5	16.	24.	15.5
15. Civil rights pressure	5.	6.5	4.5	4.	7.5	4.
16. Human relations groups prepare community	10.5	12.	10.	6.	19.5	10.
17. Press prepares community	16.	15.	17.5	16.	16.	12.
18. Other desegregation	4.	3.5	4.5	4.	6.	4.
19. White education high	16.	22.	11.	23.	16.	15.5
20. Negro education high	23.	25.	17.5	23.	22.	21.
21. Race communication good	8.	10.5	7.	16.	9.5	8.
22. Social climate moderate	10.5	10.5	8.5	10.5	4.5	13.5
23. Negro population low	3.	3.5	3.	7.	2.	6.5
24. Political climate good	14.	15.	13.	19.	12.	18.
25. Legislation favorable	24.	24.	22.5	23.	23.	21.

Table C-8
PRINCIPLES OR FACTORS RANKED HIGH
(by groups in Greenville)

Interviewee Groups: A—All leaders B—White leaders C—Negro leaders D—Religious leaders E—School leaders F—Business leaders B–F—60 percent or more of subgroups (three or more)	Principles or factors ranked from 1 to 11 by all interviewees and/or by one or more subgroups of interviewees in Greenville							
	Rank assigned by						Items ranked 1 to 11 by	
Item no. DESCRIPTION	A	B	C	D	E	F	A	B–F
1. School board leadership								
2. School superintendent leadership								
3. Board policy clear	—	—	—	—	9.5	—		
4. Police policy clear	6.	6.5	6.	8.	4.5	4.	X	X
5. Press support								
6. Religious support	—	—	—	10.5	—	—		
7. Business support	9.	6.5	—	9.	7.5	10.	X	X
8. Power structure support	—	9.	—	—	—	10.		
9. Political support								
10. Negro leaders' support	2.	2.	2.	2.	3.	2.	X	X
11. Federal funds influence								
12. Legal action threat	7.	6.5	8.5	4.	—	6.5	X	X
13. Federal court order	1.	1.	1.	1.	1.	1.	X	X
14. Federal agency pressure								
15. Civil rights pressure	5.	6.5	4.5	4.	7.5	4.	X	X
16. Human relations groups prepare community	10.5	—	10.	6.	—	10.	X	X
17. Press prepares community								
18. Other desegregation	4.	3.5	4.5	4.	6.	4.	X	X
19. White education high	—	—	11.	—	—	—		
20. Negro education high								
21. Race communication good	8.	10.5	7.	—	9.5	8.	X	X
22. Social climate moderate	10.5	10.5	8.5	10.5	4.5	—	X	X
23. Negro population low	3.	3.5	3.	7.	2.	6.5	X	X
24. Political climate good								
25. Legislation favorable								

Table C-9
PRINCIPLES OR FACTORS RANKED LOW
(by groups in Greenville)

Interviewee Groups: A—All leaders B—White leaders C—Negro leaders D—Religious leaders E—School leaders F—Business leaders B–F—60 percent or more of subgroups (three or more)	Principles or factors ranked from 20 to 25 by all interviewees and/or by one or more subgroups of interviewees in Greenville							
	Rank assigned by						Items ranked 20 to 25 by	
Item no. DESCRIPTION	A	B	C	D	E	F	A	B–F
1. School board leadership	22.	22.	22.5	23.	—	25.	X	X
2. School superintendent leadership	—	—	—	20.	—	23.5		
3. Board policy clear	—	—	—	23.	—	—		
4. Police policy clear								
5. Press support								
6. Religious support								
7. Business support								
8. Power structure support								
9. Political support	20.5	—	22.5	—	21.	—	X	
10. Negro leaders' support								
11. Federal funds influence	20.5	—	22.5	—	25.	21.	X	X
12. Legal action threat								
13. Federal court order								
14. Federal agency pressure	25.	22.	22.5	—	24.	—	X	X
15. Civil rights pressure								
16. Human relations groups prepare community								
17. Press prepares community								
18. Other desegregation								
19. White education high	—	22.	—	23.	—	—		
20. Negro education high	23.	25.	—	23.	22.	21.	X	X
21. Race communication good								
22. Social climate moderate								
23. Negro population low								
24. Political climate good								
25. Legislation favorable	24.	24.	22.5	23.	23.	21.	X	X

Table C-10
RANK ORDER CORRELATIONS*
(for groups in Greenville)

Read across and up		Based on rankings assigned to twenty-five principles or factors by total interviewee group and by five interviewee subgroups					
		GREENVILLE INTERVIEWEES					
		White leaders	Negro leaders	Religious leaders	School leaders	Business leaders	All other leaders
GREENVILLE INTERVIEWEES	White leaders	——	.791				.791
	Negro leaders	.791	——				.791
	Religious leaders			——	.566	.854	.641
	School leaders			.566	——	.692	.652
	Business leaders			.854	.692	——	.792
	All other leaders	.791	.791	.641	.652	.792	——

* Computed by formula for rank order correlation coefficient:

$$\text{Rho} = 1 - \frac{6\Sigma D^2}{n(n^2 - 1)}$$

Correlation significance:
.396 = 5 percent significance
.505 = 1 percent significance

∴ All of the correlations on the above chart are statistically significant beyond the 1 percent level.

The three major interviewee groupings are in agreement also in giving a rating of "very important" or "fairly important" to six items. On five other items there is agreement between the total interviewee group and most subgroups in giving a similar rating.[10]

Ratings of "not important" or only "slightly important" are given to fifteen factors by 65 percent or more of the individual leaders in Greenville. Of these items, as shown on Table C-5, twelve are rated by a majority of the leaders as having no importance in the local situation. Nine of these are rated as "not important" by 70 percent or more of the interviewees. None of the items is rated as "slightly important" by any sizeable number of the interviewees.

The Greenville interviewees as a total group, as shown on Table

[10] See Tables C-3 and C-4.

Table D
LEAST IMPORTANT PRINCIPLES OR FACTORS
(as rated and/or ranked by Greenville leaders)

Explanatory code: A. Total interviewee group B. 60 percent or more of subgroups (three or more out of five) C. 60 percent or more of individual interviewees (twelve or more from total of twenty) D. Most groups and individuals (60 percent or more)			As *rated* and/or *ranked** by total group of Greenville interviewees, by most individual interviewees, and by majority of interviewee subgroups			
	Rated low by			Ranked low by		Rated and/ or ranked low by: D
Item no. DESCRIPTION	A	B	C	A	B	
1. School board leadership	X	X	X	X	X	X
2. School superintendent leadership	X	X	X			X
3. Board policy clear	X	X	X			X
4. Police policy clear						
5. Press support	X	X	X			X
6. Religious support	X	X	X			X
7. Business support						
8. Power structure support	X					
9. Political support	X	X	X	X		X
10. Negro leaders' support						
11. Federal funds influence	X	X	X	X	X	X
12. Legal action threat						
13. Federal court order						
14. Federal agency pressure	X	X	X	X	X	X
15. Civil rights pressure						
16. Human relations groups prepare community			X			
17. Press prepares community	X	X	X			X
18. Other desegregation						
19. White education high	X	X	X			X
20. Negro education high	X	X	X	X	X	X
21. Race communication good						
22. Social climate moderate			X			
23. Negro population low						
24. Political climate good	X	X	X			X
25. Legislation favorable	X	X	X	X	X	X

* *Rated* refers to rating of "not important" or "slightly important" given to items by interviewees.
Ranking refers to rank of 20 to 25 assigned to items by interviewees.

Table E
MOST IMPORTANT PRINCIPLES OR FACTORS
(as rated and/or ranked by all leaders in both communities)

Explanatory code: A. Total interviewee group (in each community) B. 60 percent or more of subgroups C. 60 percent or more of individual interviewees D. Most groups and individuals (60 percent or more)						As rated and/or ranked* by total group of interviewees, by most individual interviewees, and by majority of interviewee subgroups in Greensboro and Greenville		
	Both communities					Rated and/or ranked high		
	Rated high by			Ranked high by		in Greensboro	in Greenville	Both
Item no. DESCRIPTION	A	B	C	A	B	D	D	D
1. School board leadership								
2. School superintendent leadership						X		
3. Board policy clear						X		
4. Police policy clear	X	X	X	X	X	X	X	X
5. Press support						X		
6. Religious support						X		
7. Business support							X	
8. Power structure support								
9. Political support								
10. Negro leaders' support	X	X	X	X	X	X	X	X
11. Federal funds influence								
12. Legal action threat	X	X		X	X	X	X	X
13. Federal court order							X	
14. Federal agency pressure								
15. Civil rights pressure	X	X	X	X	X	X	X	X
16. Human relations groups prepare community	X	X		X		X	X	X
17. Press prepares community								
18. Other desegregation		X					X	
19. White education high						X		
20. Negro education high						X		
21. Race communication good	X	X			X	X	X	X
22. Social climate moderate	X	X		X	X	X	X	X
23. Negro population low						X		
24. Political climate good								
25. Legislation favorable								

* *Rated* refers to rating of "very important" or "fairly important" given to items by interviewees. *Ranking* refers to rank of 1 to 11 assigned to items by interviews.

C-6, give only slight importance to fourteen principles or factors, an almost identical group to that rated "slightly important" or "not important" by individual interviews. The total interviewee group does not rate any item as "not important." Sixty percent or more of the interviewee subgroups agree with the total interviewee group in rating thirteen items as "slightly important."[11] No item is rated as "not important" by a majority of the subgroups. However, five of the above thirteen items are rated by both the black and religious leaders rate as having no importance, and one other item is rated "not important" by the black and business leaders.

There is no agreement among the three major interviewee groupings as to factors rated "not important." The twelve items given this rating by most individuals are rated as "slightly important" by the total interviewee group and by most subgroups. There is agreement, however, by all three groupings in rating thirteen items in the range from "slightly important" to "not important."

Some indication of the relative importance of each factor and how each relates to the others in order of importance in the Greenville school desegregation situation can be obtained from the rank order listings by several interviewee groups (Table C-7).[12]

Among the items ranked by various groups as "most important"[13] in Greenville (Table C-8), the top ranking one among the interviewees as a total group is federal court order. The five interviewee subgroups also rank this item in first place. The next four items, as ranked by the total interviewee group, are black leaders' support, a low black population, other desegregation, and civil rights pressure. Sixty percent or more of the leadership subgroups rank each of these five items within the range of 1.0 to 5.0.

Of all the principles or factors ranked by all groups within the "most important" range, there is agreement by the interviewee group and at least 60 percent of the subgroups on eleven items. On ten of these there is agreement by the total interviewee group and at least 80 percent of the subgroups as to ranking within the 1.0 to

---

[11] Table C-6. The one other item, power structure support, which is rated as "slightly important" by the total interview group, is given this rating by only two subgroups. The other three subgroups rate it as "fairly important."

[12] Table C-7 shows rankings given to all factors by Greenville interviewees as a total group and by five subgroups (white leaders, black leaders, religious leaders, school leaders, and business leaders).

[13] For the purpose of this study, items ranked from 1.0 to 11.0 have been designated as "most important" principles or factors. This includes the top 45 percent of the ranks.

11.0 range, and on six there is agreement by the total group and all subgroups.

Of the factors ranked as "least important"[14] by Greenville leaders (Table C-9) the lowest ranking item among the total group is federal agency pressure, the same item which ranks lowest among the total group in Greensboro. Other items within the "least important" range, according to the Greenville total interviewee group rankings include school board leadership, political support, influence of federal funds, a high level of education among blacks, and legislation favorable to desegregation. With the exception of political support, all these items are ranked also within this same range by 60 percent or more of the Greenville subgroups.

Rank order correlation coefficients help show something of the relationships or differences in how factors are viewed by various groups of leaders in Greenville. The coefficients (Table C-10) indicate that the relationships between various pairs of the five Greenville interviewee subgroups and between each subgroup and all other interviewees in the community are all very close.[15] Statistically, all of the correlations are highly significant (at the 1 percent level or beyond). Just as in Greensboro, this seems to indicate that Greenville leaders, regardless of race or vocation, tend to view the principles or factors in the local school desegregation situation quite similarly. Just as in the other community, there are also important differences and relationships between various groups of the local leaders.

Religious leaders and business leaders seem to be nearer to each other in their thinking on these matters (Rho = .854) than any other two subgroups. Their group rankings are identical or vary no more than 1.0 point on eight of the items, and no more than 4.0 points on twenty of the total items. There are no variations in rank of more than 8.5 points between the two subgroups.

On the other hand, religious leaders and school leaders in Greenville seem to be further apart in their thinking (Rho = .566) than any other two subgroups. Their rankings on the twenty-five factors

---

[14] Items ranked from 20.0 to 25.0 among the twenty-five factors have been designated as "least important." This includes the bottom 25 percent of the ranks.

[15] Correlation coefficients were computed between thirteen white and seven black leaders, between six religious and seven school leaders, between six religious and six business leaders, between seven school and six business leaders, and between each of these five subgroups and all other interviewees in this community.

are identical or vary no more than 1.0 point on seven items, and no more than 4.0 points on thirteen items.

However, there are four items on which there is a sharp difference (12.0 to 14.0 points) in rankings given by the two subgroups, including a clear school board policy, which is ranked much higher by school leaders than by religious leaders, and three items—influence of federal funds, threat of legal action, and human relations preparation—which are ranked much lower by the schoolmen than by religious leaders.

School leaders in Greenville seem to be somewhat closer to business leaders (Rho = .692) than to religious leaders (Rho = .566) in their thinking on the desegregation issue. On fifteen items the rankings given by the schoolmen and business leaders are identical or vary only slightly. A similar relationship exists between the schoolmen and religious leaders on thirteen items.

The school leaders differ rather sharply (8.5 to 14.0 points) with both of the other leadership groups in ranking three items, however. The threat of legal action and human relations preparation are ranked much lower by the schoolmen than by the other groups. In contrast, a clear board policy, is ranked much higher by school leaders than by others.

Religious leaders seem to deviate more in their thinking from all the other Greenville leaders combined (Rho = .641) than do any of the other subgroups. There are seven items on which their rankings are identical or vary no more than 1.0 point. On thirteen items the variation is no more than 4.0 points. At the same time sharp differences in rankings (9.0 to 11.0 points) occur on five items. Press support and good race communications are ranked much lower by religious leaders than by all others. The other three items—influence of federal funds, federal agency pressure, and human relations preparation—are ranked considerably higher by religious leaders than by all others.

Business leaders in Greenville seem to deviate less in their thinking from all other leaders combined (Rho = .792) than do any of the other subgroups. They coincide with or vary no more than 1.0 point in their rankings on nine items and no more than 4.0 points on seventeen items. There are only two items on which there is any considerable variation in ranking (9.5 to 10.0 points). Both of these items—a clear police policy and federal agency pressure—are ranked much higher by the businessmen than by the other leaders. The Greenville business leaders seem to be considerably closer to local religious leaders (Rho = .854) than to school leaders (Rho = .692) in their thinking on desegregation.

The school leaders, when compared to all other leaders combined (Rho = .652), seem to give similar rankings to most items. On eight of the items their rankings are identical or vary no more than 1.0 point. On eighteen items the deviation is no more than 4.0 points. However, there is a rather sharp contrast (9.0 to 13.0 points) between the rankings given by school leaders and those given by all other Greenville leaders on six items. Three are ranked much lower by the school leaders than by all others—influence of federal funds, threat of legal action, and human relations preparation. In contrast, school superintendent leadership, a clear board policy, and presence of a moderate social climate are ranked much higher by the schoolmen than by other leaders.

Black and white leaders, groupings which include all the interviewees, also tend to rank most items quite similarly. On seven items their rankings are identical or vary no more than 1.0 point. On sixteen items the variation in ranking is no more than 4.0 points. There is little sharp difference in rankings by the two groups. Only one item, a high level of education among whites, is ranked fairly high by black leaders, but very low by whites, resulting in a variation of more than 8.5 points.

BOTH COMMUNITIES—QUESTIONNAIRE DATA ANALYZED JOINTLY

By comparing and jointly analyzing the questionnaire data from the two communities, some indication can be obtained as to which of the twenty-five factors are operative in both places, what their importance is, if any, and whether there is any correlation between their presence and importance in the two places. The frequency distribution tables showing weightings assigned to each item by individual interviewees (Tables A-1 and C-1) and by various groupings of interviewees (Tables A-2 and C-2) are helpful in determining which principles or factors are operative in the two communities, how frequently each item is mentioned or emphasized, and what degree of importance, if any, is attached to each. From these findings, some determination can be made as to which item or items might be omitted or removed without affecting the desegregation process in either community.

A comparison of the weightings assigned by individual leaders in the two communities to "very important" and "fairly important" items is presented in Table E-1. Whereas 60 percent or more of the interviewees in Greensboro give considerable importance to thirteen principles or factors, only six items are given similar high ratings

Table E-1
PRINCIPLES OR FACTORS RATED HIGH
(by individuals in both communities)

		Based on individual weightings* given to each item by all interviewees in each community						Items rated high by most interviewees in		
Explanatory code: A—"Very important" B—"Fairly important"		Rating given to items by percentage of interviewees in								
		Greensboro			Greenville					
Item no. DESCRIPTION		A	B	A + B	A	B	A + B	Greensboro	Greenville	Both
1. School board leadership										
2. School superintendent leadership		55%	15%	70%				X		
3. Board policy clear		40%	20%	60%				X		
4. Police policy clear		40%	20%	60%	25%	45%	70%	X	X	X
5. Press support		35%	30%	65%				X		
6. Religious support		15%	55%	70%				X		
7. Business support										
8. Power structure support										
9. Political support										
10. Negro leaders' support		55%	15%	70%	45%	35%	80%	X	X	X
11. Federal funds influence										
12. Legal action threat		45%	25%	70%				X		
13. Federal court order					100%	—	100%		X	
14. Federal agency pressure										
15. Civil rights pressure		65%	10%	75%	45%	20%	65%	X	X	X
16. Human relations groups prepare community		30%	35%	65%				X		
17. Press prepares community										
18. Other desegregation					35%	35%	70%		X	
19. White education high		20%	70%	90%				X		
20. Negro education high		30%	55%	85%				X		
21. Race communication good		15%	45%	60%				X		
22. Social climate moderate		20%	45%	65%				X		
23. Negro population low					45%	30%	75%		X	
24. Political climate good										
25. Legislation favorable										

* Each interviewee was asked to assign a weight to each item to indicate its importance, namely, 1—not important, 2—slightly important, 3—fairly important, 4—very important.

Table E-2
PRINCIPLES OR FACTORS RATED HIGH
(by groups in both communities)

Interviewee groups:
A—All leaders
B—White leaders
C—Negro leaders
D—Religious leaders
E—School leaders
F—Business leaders

Based on group and subgroup averages of weightings given to each item by all of the leaders in both communities*

Item no. DESCRIPTION	Greensboro Very important						Greensboro Fairly important						Greenville Very important						Greenville Fairly important					
	A	B	C	D	E	F	A	B	C	D	E	F	A	B	C	D	E	F	A	B	C	D	E	F
1. School board leadership							X	X		X	X	X												
2. School superintendent leadership	X	X	X							X	X	X												X
3. Board policy clear							X	X	X	X	X	X												X
4. Police policy clear							X	X	X	X	X	X					X		X	X	X	X		X
5. Press support		X					X		X	X	X	X												
6. Religious support							X	X	X	X	X	X								X		X		
7. Business support								X					X	X									X	X
8. Power structure support												X		X									X	X
9. Political support																								
10. Negro leaders' support	X		X	X	X			X					X	X	X	X	X	X						
11. Federal funds influence																								
12. Legal action threat		X	X	X	X		X	X											X	X	X	X	X	X
13. Federal court order													X	X	X	X	X	X						
14. Federal agency pressure																								
15. Civil rights pressure	X		X	X				X				X					X		X	X	X	X		X
16. Human relations groups prepare community			X	X			X	X			X	X							X	X			X	X
17. Press prepares community							X	X	X	X	X	X											X	
18. Other desegregation									X	X	X						X		X	X	X	X		X
19. White education high	X		X		X		X		X	X														X
20. Negro education high	X		X		X		X		X	X														
21. Race communication good							X	X	X	X	X	X							X	X	X	X	X	X
22. Social climate moderate							X	X	X	X	X	X							X	X	X	X	X	
23. Negro population low								X							X		X		X	X		X		X
24. Political climate good							X	X	X	X	X												X	
25. Legislation favorable							X	X	X	X	X	X												

* Each interviewee was asked to assign a weight of 1, 2, 3, or 4 to each item to indicate its importance, namely, 1—not important, 2—slightly important, 3—fairly important, 4—very important.

Table E-3
PRINCIPLES OR FACTORS RATED LOW
(by individuals in both communities)

	Based on individual weightings* given to each item by all interviewees in each community						Items rated low by most interviewees in		
Explanatory code: A—"Slightly important" B—"Not important"	Rating given to items by percentage of interviewees in								
	Greensboro			Greenville					
Item no. DESCRIPTION	A	B	A+B	A	B	A+B	Greensboro	Greenville	Both Places
1. School board leadership				5%	80%	85%		X	
2. School superintendent leadership				10%	70%	80%		X	
3. Board policy clear				5%	70%	75%		X	
4. Police policy clear									
5. Press support				10%	70%	80%		X	
6. Religious support				15%	50%	65%		X	
7. Business support	25%	40%	65%				X		
8. Power structure support	15%	60%	75%				X		
9. Political support	10%	75%	85%	10%	75%	85%	X	X	X
10. Negro leaders' support									
11. Federal funds influence	10%	85%	95%	10%	75%	85%	X	X	X
12. Legal action threat									
13. Federal court order		90%	90%				X		
14. Federal agency pressure		90%	90%	10%	80%	90%	X	X	X
15. Civil rights pressure									
16. Human relations groups prepare community				40%	25%	65%		X	
17. Press prepares community				10%	65%	75%		X	
18. Other desegregation	20%	50%	70%				X		
19. White education high				10%	65%	75%		X	
20. Negro education high				30%	70%	100%		X	
21. Race communication good									
22. Social climate moderate				35%	30%	65%		X	
23. Negro population low	60%	20%	80%				X		
24. Political climate good	45%	20%	65%	20%	55%	75%	X	X	X
25. Legislation favorable	50%	10%	60%	5%	85%	90%	X	X	X

* Each interviewee was asked to assign a weight to each item to indicate its importance, namely, 1—not important, 2—slightly important, 3—fairly important, 4—very important.

Table E-4
PRINCIPLES OR FACTORS RATED LOW
(by groups in both communities)

Interviewee groups:
A—All leaders
B—White leaders
C—Negro leaders
D—Religious leaders
E—School leaders
F—Business leaders

Based on group and subgroup averages of weightings given to each item by all of the leaders in both communities*

Item no. DESCRIPTION	Greensboro												Greenville											
	Slightly important						Not important						Slightly important						Not important					
	A	B	C	D	E	F	A	B	C	D	E	F	A	B	C	D	E	F	A	B	C	D	E	F
1. School board leadership		X											X	X		X	X				X			X
2. School superintendent leadership													X	X	X	X		X						
3. Board policy clear													X	X	X	X		X						
4. Police policy clear																								
5. Press support													X	X		X	X				X	X		
6. Religious support													X		X	X		X						
7. Business support	X		X	X	X										X	X								
8. Power structure support	X	X	X	X	X								X		X	X								
9. Political support	X	X	X	X	X							X	X	X		X	X				X	X		
10. Negro leaders' support																								
11. Federal funds influence	X	X	X	X	X	X							X	X		X	X				X	X		
12. Legal action threat																								
13. Federal court order	X	X	X		X				X	X														
14. Federal agency pressure			X		X		X	X	X		X		X	X		X	X				X	X		
15. Civil rights pressure																								
16. Human relations groups prepare community															X	X								
17. Press prepares community													X	X	X	X		X						
18. Other desegregation	X	X			X																			
19. White education high													X	X	X	X		X						
20. Negro education high													X	X	X	X	X	X						
21. Race communication good																								
22. Social climate moderate																		X						
23. Negro population low	X		X	X	X																			
24. Political climate good					X								X	X	X	X		X						
25. Legislation favorable													X	X		X	X				X	X		

* Each interviewee was asked to assign a weight to each item to indicate its importance, namely, 1—not important, 2—slightly important, 3—fairly important, 4—very important.

Table E-5
PRINCIPLES OR FACTORS RANKED HIGH
(by groups in both communities)

Interviewee groups: A—All leaders B—White leaders C—Negro leaders D—Religious leaders E—School leaders F—Business leaders Item no. DESCRIPTION	Principles or factors ranked from 1 to 11 by all interviewees in one or both communities, and/or by one or more of the interviewee subgroups Rank assigned to items by various groups											
	Greensboro						Greenville					
	A	B	C	D	E	F	A	B	C	D	E	F
1. School board leadership	—	—	—	—	8.5	—						
2. School superintendent leadership	4.5	2.	7.	3.5	2.5	6.						
3. Board policy clear	—	4.5	—	8.	5.	10.5	—	—	—	—	9.5	—
4. Police policy clear	9.5	11.	9.	—	8.5	—	6.	6.5	6.	8.	4.5	4.
5. Press support	6.5	1.	—	3.5	1.	6.						
6. Religious support	11.	8.	—	5.	8.5	10.5	—	—	—	10.5	—	—
7. Business support							9.	6.5	—	9.	7.5	10.
8. Power structure support							—	9.	—	—	—	10.
9. Political support												
10. Negro leaders' support	2.	8.	2.	1.5	—	3.	2.	2.	2.	2.	3.	2.
11. Federal funds influence												
12. Legal action threat	6.5	—	3.	8.	—	3.	7	6.5	8.5	4.	—	6.5
13. Federal court order							1.	1.	1.	1.	1.	1.
14. Federal agency pressure												
15. Civil rights pressure	1.	8.	1.	1.5	—	6.	5.	6.5	4.5	4.	7.5	4.
16. Human relations groups prepare community	8.	—	4.5	—	—	8.	10.5	—	10.	6.	—	10.
17. Press prepares community	—	—	—	—	11.5	—						
18. Other desegregation							4.	3.5	4.5	4.	6.	4.
19. White education high	4.5	4.5	4.5	8.	5.	3.		11.		—	—	—
20. Negro education high	3.	3.	6.	8.	2.5	1.						
21. Race communication good	—	8.	10.	8.	5.	10.5	8.	10.5	7.	—	9.5	8.
22. Social climate moderate	9.5	—	8.	—	11.5	10.5	10.5	10.5	8.5	10.5	4.5	—
23. Negro population low							3.	3.5	3.	7.	2.	6.5
24. Political climate good												
25. Legislation favorable	—	8.	—	—	8.5	—						

Table E-6
PRINCIPLES OR FACTORS RANKED LOW
(by groups in both communities)

Interviewee groups:
A—All leaders
B—White leaders
C—Negro leaders
D—Religious leaders
E—School leaders
F—Business leaders

Principles or factors ranked from 20 to 25 by all interviewees in one or both communities, and/or by one or more interviewee subgroups

Rank assigned to items by groups in

Item no. DESCRIPTION	Greensboro						Greenville					
	A	B	C	D	E	F	A	B	C	D	E	F
1. School board leadership							22.	22.	22.5	23.	—	25.
2. School superintendent leadership							—	—	—	20.	—	23.5
3. Board policy clear							—	—	—	23.	—	—
4. Police policy clear												
5. Press support												
6. Religious support												
7. Business support												
8. Power structure support	21.	20.	23.5	20.	21.	—						
9. Political support	22.	22.	20.5	20.	21.	25.	20.5	—	22.5	—	21.	—
10. Negro leaders' support												
11. Federal funds influence	23.	24.	22.	23.5	24.5	24.	20.5	—	22.5	—	25.	21.
12. Legal action threat												
13. Federal court order	24.	23.	25.	23.5	24.5	22.5						
14. Federal agency pressure	25.	25.	23.5	25.	23.	22.5	25.	22.	22.5	—	24.	—
15. Civil rights pressure												
16. Human relations groups prepare community												
17. Press prepares community												
18. Other desegregation	20.	21.	—	22.	21.	21.						
19. White education high							—	22.	—	23.	—	—
20. Negro education high							23.	25.	—	23.	22.	21.
21. Race communication good												
22. Social climate moderate												
23. Negro population low	—	—	20.5	—	—	20.						
24. Political climate good	—	—	—	20.	—	—						
25. Legislation favorable							24.	24.	22.5	23.	23.	21.

Table E-7
RANK ORDER CORRELATIONS*
(for comparable groups in both communities)

Based on rankings assigned to the twenty-five principles or factors in Greensboro and Greenville by total interviewee groups and by five interviewee subgroups in each community

Read across and up

		GREENSBORO INTERVIEWEES					
		White leaders	Negro leaders	Religious leaders	School leaders	Business leaders	All leaders
GREENVILLE INTERVIEWEES	White leaders	−.276					
	Negro leaders		.367				
	Religious leaders			−.052			
	School leaders				−.059		
	Business leaders					−.041	
	All leaders						.121

* Computed by formula for rank order correlation coefficient:

$$\text{Rho} = 1 - \frac{6\Sigma D^2}{n(n^2 - 1)}$$

Correlation significance:
.396 = 5 percent significance
.505 = 1 percent significance
∴ None of the correlations on the above chart are statistically significant at the 5 percent level or beyond.

by most Greenville leaders. There is agreement between the two sets of ratings on a clear police policy, black leaders' support, and civil rights pressure. None of these are rated specifically as "very important" or as "fairly important" by most interviewees in both communities.

The averaged weightings given to items of importance by the total interviewee groups in both communities are compared on Table E-2. Greensboro leaders as a group rate seventeen factors as "very important" or "fairly important." The total interviewee group in Greenville gives similar high ratings to only eleven items. There is agreement between the two sets of total interviewee group ratings on a clear police policy, black leaders' support, threat of legal action, civil rights pressure, human relations preparation, good communication between the races, and a moderate social climate. Black leaders' support is rated as "very important" by the total groups in both communities. Civil rights pressure is rated as "very important" in Greensboro but only "fairly important" in Greenville. The other five items are rated "fairly important" in both places

Table E-8
PRINCIPLES OR FACTORS RANKED SIMILARLY
(by groups in both communities)

Explanatory code:
1—Greensboro
2—Greenville
A—Total interviewee group
B—White leaders
C—Negro leaders
D—Religious leaders
E—School leaders
F—Business leaders
B–F and A–F (see below)*

Based on rank order variations of 4.0 or less between total interviewee groups and between each of five sets of comparable interviewee subgroups in both communities

Item no. DESCRIPTION	A 1	A 2	B 1	B 2	C 1	C 2	D 1	D 2	E 1	E 2	F 1	F 2	Rank varies 4.0 or less for A	B–F	A–F
1. School board leadership															
2. School superintendent leadership															
3. Board policy clear	12.5	16.			15.	12.							X		
4. Police policy clear	9.5	6.			9.	6.			8.5	4.5			X		
5. Press support															
6. Religious support	11.	12.5									10.5	13.5	X		
7. Business support					12.	9.									
8. Power structure support															
9. Political support	22.	20.5			20.5	22.5	20.	16.	21.	21.			X	X	X
10. Negro leaders' support	2.	2.			2.	2.	1.5	2.			3.	2.	X	X	X
11. Federal funds influence	23.	20.5			22.	22.5			24.5	25.	24.	21.	X	X	X
12. Legal action threat	6.5	7.					8.	4.	14.5	18.	3.	6.5	X	X	X
13. Federal court order															
14. Federal agency pressure	25.	25.	25.	22.	23.5	22.5			23.	24.			X	X	X
15. Civil rights pressure	1.	5.	8.	6.5	1.	4.5	1.5	4.			6.	4.	X	X	X
16. Human relations groups prepare community	8.	10.5	16.	12.					16.5	19.5	8.	10.	X	X	X
17. Press prepares community	15.	16.	14.5	15.			14.5	16.			14.5	12.	X	X	X
18. Other desegregation															
19. White education high															
20. Negro education high															
21. Race communication good			8.	10.5	10.	7.					10.5	8.		X	
22. Social climate moderate	9.5	10.5	12.	10.5	8.	8.5					10.5	13.5	X	X	X
23. Negro population low															
24. Political climate good	17.	14.	18.	15.	14.	13.	20.	19.			18.5	18.	X	X	X
25. Legislation favorable															

* B–F = 60 percent or more of subgroups (three or more)
  A–F = 60 percent or more of all groups and subgroups

Table E-9
PRINCIPLES OR FACTORS RANKED VERY DIFFERENTLY
(by groups in both communities)

Explanatory code:
1—Greensboro
2—Greenville
A—Total interviewee group
B—White leaders
C—Negro leaders
D—Religious leaders
E—School leaders
F—Business leaders

Based on rank order variations of 10.0 or more between total interviewee groups and between each of five sets of interviewee subgroups in both communities

Item no. DESCRIPTION	A		B		C		D		E		F		Rank varies 10.0 or more for*		
	1	2	1	2	1	2	1	2	1	2	1	2	A	B–F	A–F
1. School board leadership									8.5	19.5	13.	25.			
2. School superintendent leadership	4.5	18.5	2.	19.			3.5	20.			6.	23.5	X	X	X
3. Board policy clear			4.5	19.			8.	23.							
4. Police policy clear											14.5	4.			
5. Press support	6.5	18.5	1.	15.	12.	22.5	3.5	16.	1.	16.	6.	23.5	X	X	X
6. Religious support															
7. Business support			18.	6.5					18.	7.5					
8. Power structure support			20.	9.											
9. Political support															
10. Negro leaders' support									13.	3.					
11. Federal funds influence							23.5	12.5							
12. Legal action threat															
13. Federal court order	24.	1.	23.	1.	25.	1.	23.5	1.	24.5	1.	22.5	1.	X	X	X
14. Federal agency pressure															
15. Civil rights pressure															
16. Human relations groups prepare community															
17. Press prepares community															
18. Other desegregation	20.	4.	21.	3.5	16.5	4.5	22.	4.	21.	6.	21.	4.	X	X	X
19. White education high	4.5	16.	4.5	22.			8.	23.	5.	16.	3.	15.5	X	X	X
20. Negro education high	3.	23.	3.	25.	6.	17.5	8.	23.	2.5	22.	1.	21.	X	X	X
21. Race communication good															
22. Social climate moderate															
23. Negro population low	18.5	3.	18.	3.5	20.5	3.	18.	7.	19.	2.	20.	6.5	X	X	X
24. Political climate good															
25. Legislation favorable	14.	24.	8.	24.			12.	23.	8.5	23.			X		X

* B–F = 60 percent or more of subgroups (three or more)
A–F = 60 percent or more of all groups and subgroups

Table F
LEAST IMPORTANT PRINCIPLES OR FACTORS
(as rated and/or ranked by all leaders in both communities)

Explanatory code:
- A. Total interviewee group (in each community)
- B. 60 percent or more of subgroups
- C. 60 percent or more of individual interviewees
- D. Most groups and individuals (60 percent or more)

As *rated* and/or *ranked** by total group of interviewees, by most individual interviewees, and by majority of interviewee subgroups in Greensboro and Greenville

Item no. DESCRIPTION	Both communities — Rated low by A	B	C	Ranked low by A	B	Rated and/or ranked low — in Greensboro D	in Greenville D	Both D
1. School board leadership						X		
2. School superintendent leadership						X		
3. Board policy clear						X		
4. Police policy clear								
5. Press support						X		
6. Religious support						X		
7. Business support						X		
8. Power structure support	X					X		
9. Political support	X	X	X	X		X	X	X
10. Negro leaders' support								
11. Federal funds influence	X	X	X	X	X	X	X	X
12. Legal action threat								
13. Federal court order						X		
14. Federal agency pressure	X	X	X	X	X	X	X	X
15. Civil rights pressure								
16. Human relations groups prepare community								
17. Press prepares community							X	
18. Other desegregation						X		
19. White education high							X	
20. Negro education high							X	
21. Race communication good								
22. Social climate moderate								
23. Negro population low						X		
24. Political climate good			X				X	
25. Legislation favorable			X				X	

* *Rated* refers to rating of "not important" or "slightly important" given to items by interviewees. *Ranking* refers to a rank of 20 to 25 assigned to items by interviewees.

by the total interviewee groups. Factors rated by the five interviewee subgroups in each community as being of considerable importance are shown on Table E-2 also. In Greensboro most of the subgroups rate eighteen items as being "very important" or "fairly important." The equivalent figure for Greenville is twelve items. There is agreement between 60 percent or more of the subgroups in both communities on the high ratings given to a clear police policy, black leaders' support, the threat of legal action, civil rights pressure, human relations preparation, other desegregation, good communication between the races, and a moderate social climate. Black leaders' support is rated as "very important" by 80 percent or more of the subgroups in both communities. The threat of legal action and civil rights pressure are rated "very important" by most Greensboro subgroups but only "fairly important" by most subgroups in Greenville. The other five items are rated "fairly important" by most subgroups in both places.

There is agreement among the three major interviewee groupings (most individuals, all leaders as a group, and most subgroups) in both communities in giving a rating of "very important" to "fairly important" to a clear police policy, black leaders' support, and civil rights pressure. Four other factors—the threat of legal action, human relations preparation, good communication between the races, a moderate social climate—are given this rating by all leaders as a group and by most subgroups in both places.

The comparisons of factors rated as having little or no importance in the two communities are shown on Tables E-3 and E-4.

Table E-3 shows that ten items are rated as "not important" or only "slightly important" by most Greensboro leaders. In Greenville most leaders give similar low ratings to fifteen items. There is agreement between the two sets of individual interviewee ratings on political support, the influence of federal funds, federal agency pressure, presence of a good political climate, and favorable legislation. Political support, the influence of federal funds, and federal agency pressure are rated as "not important" by 75 percent or more of the individual leaders in both places. The other two items are rated as "not important" by most Greenville leaders, but the Greensboro leaders are divided between "not important" and "slightly important" in their ratings on these items.

Table E-4 presents the averaged weightings given to items of little or no importance by the total interviewee groups in both communities. It shows that the Greensboro leaders as a total group rate eight principles or factors as "not important" or only "slightly important." The total group of Greenville leaders gives similar low ratings to fourteen items. There is agreement between the two sets of total interviewee group ratings only on power structure support, political support, the influence of federal funds, and federal agency pressure. Three of these items are rated as "slightly important" by the total groups in both communities, while the remaining item, federal agency pressure, is rated as "slightly important" by Greenville leaders and "not important" by Greensboro interviewees.

Factors rated as having little or no importance by the five interviewee subgroups in each community are shown on Table E-4 also. In Greensboro ratings of "not important" or "slightly important" are given to seven items by most of the subgroups. In Greenville thirteen items are given similar low ratings by most subgroups. There is agreement between 60 percent or more of the subgroups in both communities only on the low ratings given to political support, the influence of federal funds, and federal agency pressure. Two of these items are rated as "slightly important" by 60 percent or more of the subgroups in both communities, and the other item, federal agency pressure, is rated as "not important" by most Greensboro subgroups and as only "slightly important" by most Greenville subgroups.

The three major interviewee groupings in both communities give a rating of "not important" or "slightly important" to political support, influence of federal funds, and federal agency pressure.

A comparison of the rank order listings of the twenty-five factors by various interviewee groups in the two communities is helpful in determining the relative importance of each item in both communities. The principles or factors which are ranked by various interviewee groups as "most important" in both communities are shown on Table E-5. All interviewees as a group in Greensboro rank eleven items in the "most important" range. The total interviewee group in Greenville also ranks eleven items in this category. There is agreement between the two sets of total interviewee group rankings on six of these items—a clear police policy, black leaders' support, threat of legal action, civil rights pressure, human relations preparation, and a moderate social climate. There are twelve items ranked within the "the most important" range (1.0 to 11.0) by most Greensboro subgroups. Most Greenville subgroups rank eleven items in this category. There is agreement between 60 percent or more of the subgroups in both communities on the high rankings given to a clear police policy, black leaders' support, the threat of legal action, civil rights pressure, good communication between the races, and a moderate social climate. Of the principles or factors ranked within the "most important" range by all groups and subgroups in the two communities, there is agreement by the two total interviewee groups and by most of the ten subgroups on five items—a clear police policy, black leaders' support, the threat of legal action, civil rights pressure, and a moderate social climate.

The principles or factors ranked as "least important" by various groups in both communities are compared on Table E-6. Six items are assigned to this category by the total interviewee groups in Greensboro and Greenville. There is agreement between the two sets of total interviewee group rankings on political support, the influence of federal funds, and federal agency pressure. Both groups assign the bottom rank of 25.0 to federal agency pressure.

"Least important" factors as ranked by the five subgroups in each community can be found also in Table E-6. In Greensboro six items are assigned to this category by most subgroups, while only five items are so assigned by most Greenville subgroups. There is agreement on the low rankings given to the influence of federal funds and federal agency pressure. Of the principles or factors ranked within the "least important" range by all groups and subgroups in the two communities, there is agreement by the two total interviewee groups and by most of the ten subgroups on the influence of federal funds and federal agency pressure.

To show whether there is any significant relationship between the importance attached to the various factors by comparable or related interviewee groups and subgroups in the two communities, the computation of rank order correlation coefficients is shown on Table E-7. Even though none of the correlations are statistically significant, they show some relationships worth noting. The two highest correlations, one positive and one negative, are between black leaders in both places (Rho = .367) and between white leaders in both places (Rho = −.276).[16] The other correlations show little or no statistical relationship. Several deductions may be drawn from these correlations. First, there is no statistically significant relationship between how the comparable interviewee groups or subgroups in the two places view the school desegregation process.

At the same time, there are noteworthy similarities, as well as strong contrasts, in how the groups in the two places view the twenty-five factors. The rankings given by the total interviewee groups in the two communities are identical or vary no more than 4.0 points on thirteen of the items as shown on Table E-8. Of these, six are on the list of the items ranked "most important" and three

[16] A correlation of .367 is significant at about the 7 percent level, while −.276 correlation is significant at about the 15 percent level.

on the list of items ranked "least important" by the total interviewee groups in both communities.

There are strong differences (10.0 to 23.0 points) in how the two total groups rank eight of the items as shown on Table E-9. Five are ranked moderately high to very high in Greensboro but low in Greenville. The other three are ranked low in Greensboro but high in Greenville.

Black leaders in the two places (Rho = .367) seem to be nearer to each other in their views on these matters than any other two subgroups. Their rankings are identical or vary no more than 4.0 points on ten items. Of these, five are on the list of items ranked "most important" and three on the list of items ranked "least important" by most subgroups in both committees. Sharp differences (10.0 to 24.0 points) show up, however, on five items. Three of these rank high among Greenville blacks but low among Greensboro blacks. The other two rank moderately high in Greensboro but low in Greenville.

In contrast, white leaders in the two communities (Rho = −.276) seem to be further apart in their views on the desegregation process than any other two groups or subgroups. Their group rankings on the twenty-five factors are identical or vary no more than 4.0 points on only seven of the items. Of these, three are on the list of items ranked "most important" and one is on the list of items marked "least important" by most subgroups in both communities. Sharp differences (10.0 to 22.0 points) appear in the ranking of eleven of the items, however. Six of these rank moderately high to high among Greensboro whites, but low among Greenville whites. The other five rank low in Greensboro but high in Greenville.

Religious leaders in the two communities show little statistical correlation (Rho = −.052) in how they view the desegregation process. As groups they rank only seven of the items within 4.0 points of each other. Of these, three are on the list of items ranked "most important" and one is on the list of items ranked "least important" by most subgroups in both communities. Sharp differences appear in their rankings of ten items. Six of these rank moderately high to very high among Greensboro religious leaders, but very low among comparable leaders in Greenville. The other four rank very low in Greensboro but moderately high to very high in Greenville.

School leaders in the two places show little or no statistical correlation in their views on the desegregation process (Rho = −.059). Their group rankings on the principles or factors are identical or vary no more than 4.0 points on only six items. Of these, three are on the "most important" list and three on the "least important" list of items as ranked by most subgroups in both communities. Sharp differences appear in the rankings given by these two leadership groups to ten items. Five of these rank high among the Greensboro leaders, but fairly low to very low among the Greenville group. The other five rank fairly low to very low in Greensboro but quite high in Greenville.

Business leaders in the two communities likewise show little correlation in their views on the desegregation issue (Rho = −.041). As groups they rank ten of the items within 4.0 points of each other. Of these, six are on the "most important" list and one on the "least important" list of items as ranked by most subgroups in both communities. Sharp differences show up in rankings given by these two groups to nine items. Five rank fairly high to very high among the Greensboro business leaders, but low in Greenville. The other four rank fairly low to very low in Greensboro but very high in Greenville.

BIBLIOGRAPHICAL ESSAY

Despite the major significance and widespread incidence of school desegregation, comparatively little scientific research has been done concerning the social phenomenon itself. Much has been said and written by civil rights and anti-civil rights leaders, politicians, religious leaders and mass media personnel. Social scientists, however, have produced few important studies which help us to speak with authority about school desegregation as a social process, how it takes place and what determines its success or failure. At the same time, a considerable amount of social science research relating to the social and psychological needs for desegregation and the evils of segregation has appeared during the past two decades.

The scholarly and serious literature relating to school desegregation can be divided into three general categories, namely, (1) analyzing the background setting and interpreting the need for this social change, (2) setting forth the principles and factors which social scientists have advanced as being relevant and important in this and similar social changes, and (3) dealing with case studies of desegregation situations.

The literature analyzing the background setting and interpreting the need for desegregation includes a number of studies relating to racial factors in the South, community structure in this region, and the inequities and harmful effects of segregated schools and the need for desegregation.

In the first group are such classic studies of the South and race as those by Myrdal, Cash, Key, and Woodward. Gunnar

Myrdal's *An American Dilemma*, even though published a generation ago, still stands as probably the most comprehensive study of the nation's racial problem. A valuable condensation and interpretation of this study is found in Arnold M. Rose's *The Negro in America*. Wilbur J. Cash's *The Mind of the South*, written by this North Carolina newspaperman just prior to World War II, remains as one of the most perceptive analyses of regional thought and action available. *Southern Politics in State and Nation*, by V. O. Key, Jr., provides an excellent analysis, state by state, of the political scene. His chapters on North and South Carolina are especially helpful. C. Vann Woodward's *The Strange Career of Jim Crow* is a fast-paced yet scholarly presentation of the extremely transient history of racial segregation in the South from the 1860s to the 1950s. Other historical studies which provide valuable insights include Woodward's *Origins of the New South, 1877–1913*, Thomas D. Clark's *The Emerging South*, which analyzes the social scene from 1920 to 1960, and George B. Tindall's *The Emergence of the New South, 1913–1945.*

An economic view of the region, with a good analysis of the economic factors involved in segregation and desegregation, is offered by William H. Nicholls in *Southern Tradition and Regional Progress*.

A historian's analysis of the desperate political and social struggle by white leaders to maintain segregation in one southern state, South Carolina, from 1954 to 1958, is provided by Howard H. Quint's *Profile in Black and White*. A similar study of Mississippi as a microcosm of the South's politico-social struggle against racial change is offered by James H. Silver in *Mississippi: The Closed Society*.

Several studies of individual southern communities provide valuable analyses of leadership patterns and community decision-making processes. John Dollard's *Caste and Class in a Southern Town*, one of the earliest of such studies, presents a keen view of the racial structure in a southern community, with strong emphasis on the psychological factors involved.

Floyd Hunter's *Community Power Structure*, an analysis of leadership in Atlanta, has become a classic study of how community decisions are made. *Negro Political Leadership in the South*, by Everett Carll Ladd, Jr., is a valuable case study of leadership patterns in Greenville and Winston-Salem and the strong contrast offered by racial change in the two communities. Other important research dealing with community leadership patterns, with particular emphasis on black leadership, is described in Margaret E. Burgess' *Negro Leadership in a Southern City*, a sociological analysis of leadership and power in Durham, and in Daniel C. Thompson's *The Negro Leadership Class*, a sociological study of leadership development in New Orleans. A good sociological analysis of leadership patterns and community attitudes toward racial change among white urban Southerners is provided by Melvin M. Tumin's *Desegregation: Resistance and Readiness*, a study made in Greensboro just before the beginning of school desegregation. Another study which deals specifically with community attitudes during a racial crisis is Ernest Q. Campbell's survey in Norfolk, *When a City Closes Its Schools*.

The role of religious leadership in a southern community and its reaction to a desegregation crisis is analyzed by Ernest Campbell and Thomas Pettigrew in "Racial and Moral Crisis: The Role of Little Rock Ministers." Killian and Grigg, in a sociological work dealing with several Florida communities during the early 1960s, *Racial Crisis in America: Leadership in Conflict*, point to the conflict pattern between black and white leadership groups and how it becomes accentuated during a racial crisis.

For an analysis of the segregated public educational system which existed in the South up to 1954 and even afterward, studies by Ashmore, Pierce, Swanson, and Griffin are quite helpful. Harry Ashmore's report on *The Negro and the Schools*, published almost simultaneously with the Supreme Court's *Brown* decision, is an interpretative summary of the findings of forty or more scholars regarding biracial education nationally, but especially in the South. It provides an excellent background study, tracing the history of segregated education, explaining the litigation leading up to the 1954 Court ruling, and describing the efforts of various states to equalize educational facilities just prior to the Court decision. Truman M. Pierce's *White and Negro Schools in the South: An Analysis of Bi-Racial Education* and Ernest W. Swanson and John A. Griffin's *Public Education in the South: A Statistical Survey* provide detailed statistical data and interpretation concerning numerous aspects of the segregated school systems in each of the southern states.

Three of the best overall accounts of the progress and problems of school desegregation throughout the South from 1954 to 1964 are provided by studies which were sponsored by the Southern Educational Reporting Service. Included are Don C. Shoemaker's *With All Deliberate Speed: Segregation-Desegregation in Southern Schools,* Reed Sarratt's *Ordeal of Desegregation* and Patrick McCauley and Edward Ball's *Southern Schools: Progress and Problems.*

The harmful effects of segregation in the public schools and the need for desegregation are stated or implied in many research studies, including most of those already cited. Among the latter, the works of Myrdal, Rose, Woodward, Quint, Ladd, Burgess, Ashmore, Pierce, and Swanson and Griffin are especially noteworthy.

Three other research pieces which deal specifically with this problem should be mentioned also. Two of these were cited by the Supreme Court in the *Brown* v. *Board of Education of Topeka* decision, the first time the Court had ever admitted such social science data as legal evidence. One of the sources was a study co-ordinated by Kenneth B. Clark, social psychologist, signed by thirty-five nationally known social scientists, and entitled "The Effects of Segregation and the Consequences of Desegregation: A Social Science Statement." Later incorporated into *Prejudice and Your Child,* this study gives a clear and perceptive analysis of the harmful effects of

segregation and points to the positive results achieved in desegregation situations. The other study, also cited by the
Court, was M. Deutscher and Isidor Chein's "The Psychological Effects of Enforced Segregation," a compilation of evidence
against segregation from various social science sources. A third
study, *The Psychiatric Aspects of Desegregation* (1957) was
published by the Group for the Advancement of Psychiatry.
It provides a fairly comprehensive report on the psychological
factors related to desegregation and how groups and individuals react to the change. A number of valuable compen-
diums on the school desegregation issue have been provided
by special issues of professional journals. These usually have
attempted, through a collection of articles by various scholars,
to trace the history of the problem, analyze the factors involved, predict the future trends, and point to the need for
certain kinds of research. Among these are special issues of the
Journal of Negro Education (1954), *Journal of Social Issues*
(1953, 1959), *Annals of the American Academy of Political
and Social Science* (1956), *Current History* (1957), *Notre
Dame Lawyer* (1959), and the *Journal of Educational Sociology* (1954).

The literature seeking to identify and to explain the social
changes involved in the school desegregation process itself
includes numerous intergroup relations principles and factors,
some tested but many untested. A number of social scientists
have set forth specific lists of these principles or factors which
they believe to be most relevant to this social change. Some of
these scholars base their lists on particular case studies. The
fifteen "propositions and factors" found in Robert J. Dwyer's
"A Study of Desegregation and Integration in Selected School
Districts in Central Missouri" (unpublished doctoral thesis),
for example, result from his study of desegregation in several
school districts. Harold Turner, in "A Study of Public School
Integration in Two Illinois Communities" (unpublished doctoral thesis), sets forth fourteen "principles or factors" on
the basis of his study of two communities in Illinois. Robin M.

Williams, Jr. and Margaret Ryan's ten "factors," as listed in *Schools in Transition: Community Experience in Desegregation*, are drawn from their collected field reports on desegregation in twenty-four communities across the nation. Other social scientists have proposed lists of principles and factors formulated from their surveys of various field reports or other studies of desegregation or from their participant-observer experiences in desegregation situations. Clark lists ten groups of "factors" in his article, "Some Principles Related to the Problem of Desegregation." Dodson and Linders discuss "seven variables affecting the course of desegregation," and Dodson, in another article, "Toward Integration," lists twelve "principles of integration." Vander Zanden sets forth nineteen "generalizations or propositions." Reuter, from a survey of desegregation practices in more than one hundred southern school districts, has drawn up a list of ninety-nine "factors and action techniques." On the basis of a survey of desegregation in southern Illinois communities, Bonita Valien has developed a list of thirteen "principles and factors."

Various theories, principles, and factors relating to school desegregation as well as to other intergroup relations problems can be found in three valuable research and action manuals prepared by four social scientists, Dean, Rosen, Williams, and Suchman. John P. Dean and Alex Rosen's *Manual of Intergroup Relations* is an excellent general work, discussing principles and techniques which intergroup relations practitioners have found useful in dealing with racial and religious tensions and discrimination. A somewhat similar study, *The Reduction of Intergroup Tensions*, by Robin M. Williams, Jr., also deals with techniques and procedures used by various human relations agencies in dealing with group conflict and hostility. Beyond this, it suggests a number of needed research projects. Another analysis of research relating especially to desegregation was prepared jointly by Edward A. Suchman, John P. Dean, and Robin M. Williams, Jr., and entitled *Desegregation: Some Propositions and Research Sug-*

gestions. This summary and evaluation of social science knowledge relevant to desegregation as a social process also includes a number of hypotheses and suggested research projects.

Two other works which provide numerous examples of factors and techniques that have been successful in desegregation situations are Herbert Wey and John Corey's *Action Patterns in School Desegregation* and Harry Giles's *The Integrated Classroom.* Wey and Corey's survey of action techniques used by school officials in the desegregation of schools in seventy or more southern communities suggests or provides clues to a number of factors operative in the local situations. Giles's study deals with various kinds of intergroup relations problems in the classroom, cites examples of how such problems have been handled in various places, and points to some of the social and psychological factors in such situations. A pamphlet by Jean Grambs, also aimed at educators, discusses a number of factors and techniques which have been used successfully by community and school leaders in several school desegregation situations.

The literature dealing with case studies of school desegregation situations includes a few scholarly works, but most of it is aimed at a more general audience and is not designed to test or to validate research propositions. Among the earlier studies, aimed particularly at providing the general public with successful accounts of desegregation in southern or border states, are Bonita H. Valien's *The St. Louis Story,* Omer Carmichael and Weldon James's *The Louisville Story,* three studies of desegregation in Washington, D. C., by Hansen, Osborne, and Bennett, two reports on Baltimore's desegregation, and a brief report by Van Til on "The Nashville Story." These studies are valuable as descriptive accounts, and in varying degrees they point to or provide clues as to the forces operating locally in connection with desegregation. They are not cast in hypothesis-testing frames of reference, however.

Later studies which fall into this same general category, except that they deal with less than successful situations, are two accounts of the desegregation crisis in the Norfolk schools by Reif and Brewbaker, and a scholarly report by Gaston and Hammond on the long struggle to bring about desegregation in Charlottesville. A number of reports on individual communities have also been published by the U. S. Commission on Civil Rights or by its state advisory committees. Among these federal reports are several short but rather perceptive and carefully documented accounts of desegregation in some of the major communities in North Carolina (including Greensboro), Kentucky, and Texas, as well as special studies dealing specifically with St. Louis and New Orleans.

A series of community field reports on Clinton, Tennessee (1956), Dallas, Texas (1962), Mansfield, Texas (1957), and Sturgis, Kentucky (1957), published by the Anti-Defamation League from 1956 to 1962 was designed to provide a social science analysis of various types of school desegregation situations. The two most extensive community case studies of school desegregation which have been reported attempt to isolate and analyze the social forces operating in specific community desegregation situations. Both monographs, prepared as doctoral research studies, are quite helpful for their methodology, procedures, techniques, and bibliographies. Robert J. Dwyer's study of "Desegregation and Integration in Selected School Districts in Central Missouri" analyzes the varied patterns of desegregation in seven communities, making use of data collected from school administrators, black and white teachers, and black and white students, by use of individual and group interviews, observations and questionnaires. Harold E. Turner's study of "Public School Integration in Two Illinois Communities" examines the desegregation process in two similar communities, Alton and East St. Louis.

The great need for comprehensive research of the various social forces involved in the desegregation process has been expressed well by R. Nevitt Sanford in his "Foreword" to *The Role of the Social Sciences in Desegregation: A Symposium*

(New York: Anti-Defamation League of B'nai B'rith, August 1958):

The scientific significance of research on desegregation rests on two major considerations. First, when a community undertakes to desegregate its schools, it acts as a whole; such a basic change in the community structure brings transformation in all that community's processes, and in the correlated processes in its constituent individuals. This means that by observing group actions and individual behavior in respect to desegregation the researcher may gain insight into virtually any of the processes that ordinarily command the attention of social scientists; he is offered special opportunities to study a given process in its relations to diverse others.

The second consideration is closely related to the first; desegregation affords the scientist opportunities to observe communities in states of crisis. Pressure to desegregate its schools induces strains within the community, and its efforts to adapt itself exposes its dynamic structure in a way that nothing else does.

Martin Deutsch, in "Some Perspectives on Desegregation Research," from *The Role of the Social Sciences in Desegregation: A Symposium,* emphasizes this need for desegregation research which is not fragmented:

Too often in social science history, community studies have been horizontal and ahistorical, with the emphasis being determined by the particular discipline of the researchers. Sociologists have tended to emphasize caste, class, power structure, and the like, while social psychologists have all too frequently limited their interests to attitude surveys. A multi-disciplinary, multi-variate approach in the study of the desegregating community, however, could focus on the interrelationships among attitudinal, personality, behavioral and social factors.

BIBLIOGRAPHY

Aber, Elaine M. "A Reverse Pattern of Integration," *Journal of Educational Sociology*. 32:283–89, February 1959.

Adorno, T. W., et al. *The Authoritarian Personality*. New York: Harper, 1950.

Allport, Gordon. *The Nature of Prejudice*. Boston: Beacon Press, 1954.

American Friends Service Committee, Southeastern Regional Office (High Point, N. C.). *Staff Reports, Field Reports*, and *Staff Memos* (unpublished), 1956–65.

———— and Southern Regional Council. *Intimidation, Reprisal and Violence in the South's Racial Crisis*. Atlanta: A.F.S.C. and S.R.C., 1959.

Anderson, Arnold C. "Inequalities in Schooling in the South," *American Journal of Sociology*. 60:54–61, 1955.

Ashmore, Harry. *An Epitaph for Dixie*. New York: W. W. Norton Co., 1958.

————. *The Negro and the Schools*. Chapel Hill: University of North Carolina Press, 1954.

Backrach, A. J. and G. W. Blackwell (eds). "Human Problems in the Changing South," *Journal of Social Issues*. 10:1–44, 1954.

Bard, Harry. "Observations on Desegregation in Baltimore: Three Years Later," *Teachers College Record*. 59:1–14, No. 5, February 1958.

Bardolph, Richard. *The Negro Vanguard*. New York: Rinehart and Co., 1959.

Bennett, Lerone. *Before the Mayflower*. Chicago: Johnson Publishing Co., 1962.

Bidwell, James K., et al. "Desegregation in Washington Schools—

Two Years Later," *Journal of Educational Sociology*. 30:405–413, May 1957.

Bittle, William E. "The Desegregated All-White Institution . . . the University of Oklahoma," *Journal of Educational Sociology*. 32:275–82, February 1959.

Blaustein, Albert P. and Clarence C. Ferguson, Jr. *Desegregation and the Law: The Meaning and Effect of the School Segregation Cases*. New Brunswick, N. J.: Rutgers University Press, 1957.

Blossom, Virgil T. *It Happened Here*. New York: Harper, 1959.

Blumer, Herbert. "Research on Racial Relations: United States of America," *International Social Science Bulletin*. 10:87–133; No. 3, 1958.

―――. "Social Science and the Desegregation Process," *The Annals of the American Academy of Political and Social Science*. 304:137–43, March, 1956.

Bower, R. T. and N. Walker. *Early Impacts of Desegregation in D. C.* Washington, D. C.: American University Bureau of Social Science Research, August 1955.

Brewbaker, John J. *Desegregation in the Norfolk Public Schools*. Atlanta: Southern Regional Council, 1960.

Burgess, Margaret Elaine. *Negro Leadership in a Southern City*. Chapel Hill: University of North Carolina Press, 1962.

Caliver, Ambrose. "Segregation in American Education: An Overview," *The Annals of the American Academy of Political and Social Science*. 304:17–25, March 1956.

Campbell, Ernest Q. *When a City Closes Its Schools*. Chapel Hill: University of North Carolina, Institute for Research in Social Science, 1960.

――― and Thomas Pettigrew. *Christians in Racial Crisis: A Study of Little Rock Ministry; including statements on desegregation and race relations by the leading religious denominations of the United States*. Washington, D. C.: Public Affairs Press, 1959.

―――. "Racial and Moral Crisis: The Role of Little Rock Ministers," *American Journal of Sociology*. 64:509–516, March 1959.

Carmack, William R. and Theodore Freedman. *Dallas, Texas: Factors Affecting School Desegregation*. Field Reports on Desegregation in the South, No. 7. New York: Anti-Defamation League of B'nai B'rith, 1962.

Carmichael, Omer and Weldon James. *The Louisville Story*. New York: Simon and Schuster, 1957.

Cash, Wilbur J. *The Mind of the South*. New York: Alfred A. Knopf, 1941.

Chapin, F. Stuart, Jr. (ed.). *Urban Growth Dynamics*. New York: John Wiley & Sons, 1962.

Chatto, Clarence I. and Alice L. Halligan. *The Story of the Springfield Plan*. New York: Barnes & Noble, 1945.

Chein, Isidor. "What Are the Psychological Effects of Segregation Under Conditions of Equal Facilities," *International Journal of Opinion and Attitude Response*. 2:229–34; 1949.

Clark, Kenneth B. "Desegregation, An Appraisal of the Evidence," *Journal of Social Issues*. 9:1–80; No. 4, 1953.

————. *Prejudice and Your Child* (Second Edition). Boston: Beacon Press, 1963.

————. *Social and Economic Implications of Integration in the Public Schools* (Report on Seminar on Manpower, Automation and Training, November 1965, sponsored by United States Department of Labor). Washington, D. C.; United States Government Printing Office, 1965.

————. "Some Principles Related to the Problem of Desegregation," *Journal of Negro Education*. 23:339–47; No. 3, 1954.

Clark, Thomas D. *The Emerging South*. New York: Oxford University Press, 1961.

Coates, Albert and James C. W. Paul. *The School Segregation Decision*. Chapel Hill: University of North Carolina, Institute of Government, 1954. (Law and Government Series).

Coles, Robert. *The Desegregation of Southern Schools: A Psychiatric Study*. Atlanta, Ga.: Southern Regional Council, July 1963.

Cook, Stuart. "Desegregation: A Psychological Analysis," *American Psychologist*. 12:1–13; January 1957.

Coombe, Philip H. "The Search for Facts," *The Annals of the American Academy of Political and Social Science*. 304:26–34; March 1956.

Dean, John R. and Alex Rosen. *A Manual of Intergroup Relations*. Chicago: University of Chicago Press, 1955.

Desegregation in the Baltimore City Schools. Baltimore: Maryland Commission on Interracial Problems and Relations and Baltimore Commission on Human Relations, 1955.

"Desegregation Research in the North and South," *Journal of Social Issues.* 15:1–76, No. 4, 1959.

Deutsch, Martin. "Some Perspectives on Desegregation Research," from *The Role of the Social Sciences in Desegregation: A Symposium.* New York: Anti-Defamation League of B'nai B'rith, August 1958, p. 4.

Deutscher, M. and Isidor Chein. "The Psychological Effects of Enforced Segregation: A Survey of Social Science Opinion," *Journal of Psychology.* 26:259–87; 1948.

Doddy, Hurley H. and G. Franklin Edwards. "Apprehensions of Negro Teachers Concerning Desegregation in South Carolina," *Journal of Negro Education.* 24:26–43; Winter 1955.

Dodson, Dan W. "The Creative Role of Conflict in Intergroup Relations," *Merrill-Palmer Quarterly.* 4:189–95; Summer 1958.

―――. *Power Conflict and Community Organizations.* New York: Council for American Unity, 1967.

―――. "Social Change as a New Frontier in Education," from *New Frontiers in Education.* New York: Grune and Stratton, Inc., 1966, Ch. 18, pp. 289–302.

―――. "Toward Integration," *Journal of Educational Sociology.* 28:49–58, October 1954.

――― and Margaret E. Linders. "School Desegregation and Action Programs in Intergroup Relations," *Review of Educational Research.* 29:378–87, October 1957.

――― et al. *Racial Imbalance in Public Education in New Rochelle, New York.* New York: New York University Center for Human Relations and Community Studies, 1957.

Dohlstrom, Arthur H. "A Study to Determine How the Emotional Attitude of Dade County, (Miami) Florida Teachers May Aid or Hinder Desegregation in Public School Classes." Unpublished doctoral thesis, New York University, 1955.

Dollard, John. *Caste and Class in a Southern Town.* Garden City, N. Y.: Doubleday (Third Edition), 1957.

Dwyer, Robert J. "Administrative Role in Desegregation," *Sociology and Social Research.* 43:183–88; January 1959.

―――. "A Study of Desegregation and Integration in Selected School Districts of Central Missouri." Unpublished doctoral thesis, University of Missouri, 1957.

Fleming, Harold C. "Resistance Movements and Racial Desegregation," *The Annals of the American Academy of Political and Social Science.* 304:44–52, March 1956.

————— and John Constable. *What's Happening in School Integration?* Washington, D. C.: Public Affairs Committee, 1956. (Public Affairs Pamphlet No. 244).

Foster, Charles R. "Phi Delta Kappans Tackle Desegration," *Phi Delta Kappan.* 38:96–100; December 1956.

Frank, Lawrence K. "Research for What?" *Journal of Social Issues.* Supplement Series: No. 10, 1957, pp. 1–24.

Franklin, Laline O. "A Study of Problems Relative to Desegregation Encountered by Selected Teachers During the First Year of Desegregation in Washington, D. C. Public Schools." Unpublished doctoral thesis, New York University, 1956.

Frazier, E. Franklin. *The Negro in the United States.* New York: MacMillan, 1957.

Galtung, Johann. "A Model for Studying Images of Participants in a Conflict: Southville," *Journal of Social Issues.* 15:38–43; No. 4, 1959.

Gaston, Paul M. and Thomas T. Hammond. Public School Desegregation: Charlottesville, Virginia, 1955–62 (A report presented to the Nashville Conference on "The South: The Ethical Demands of Integration," a consultation sponsored by the Southern Regional Council and the Fellowship of Southern Churchmen, December 28, 1962).

Giffin, Roscoe. *Sturgis, Kentucky: A Tentative Description and Analysis of the School Desegregation Crisis.* Field Reports of Desegregation in the South, No. 1. New York: Anti-Defamation League of B'nai B'rith, 1957.

Giles, H. Harry. *The Integrated Classroom.* New York: Basic Books, Inc., 1959.

Gilman, Glenn. *Human Relations in the Industrial Southeast.* Chapel Hill: University of North Carolina Press, 1956.

Ginsberg, Eli. *The Negro Potential.* New York: Columbia University Press, 1956.

Grambs, Jean. *Education in a Transition Community* (An Intergroup Education Pamphlet). New York: National Conference of Christians and Jews, 1954.

Greenberg, Jack. *Race Relations and American Law.* New York: Columbia University Press, 1959.

Greensboro Board of Education. *Minutes,* 1954–65.

Greensboro Daily News, 1954–64.

Greensboro Record, 1954–64.

Greensboro Interracial Commission. *Minutes,* 1950–60.

Greenville Board of Education. *Minutes,* 1954–65.

Greenville Council on Human Relations. *Newsletter,* 1957–64.

Greenville News, 1954–65.

Greenville Piedmont, 1954–65.

Griffin, J. Howard and Theodore Freedman. *Mansfield, Texas: A Report on the Crisis Situation Resulting from Efforts to Desegregate the School System,* Field Reports on Desegregation in the South, No. 4. New York: Anti-Defamation League of B'nai B'rith, 1957.

Group for the Advancement of Psychiatry. *Psychiatric Aspects of School Desegregation.* (Report No. 37) New York, 1957.

Hansen, Carl F. *Addendum: A Five Year Report on Desegregation in Washington, D. C.* New York: Anti-Defamation League of B'nai B'rith, 1960.

———. *Miracle of Social Adjustment: Desegregation in the Washington, D. C. Schools.* New York: Anti-Defamation League of B'nai B'rith, 1957.

Hayes, Brooks. *A Southern Moderate Speaks.* Chapel Hill: University of North Carolina Press, 1959.

Henderson, Vivian. "Economic Dimensions in Race Relations," in Marsouka, Jitsuichi and Preston Valein (eds.), *Race Relations: Problems and Theory.* Chapel Hill: University of North Carolina Press, 1964.

———. *The Economic Status of Negroes: In the Nation and in the South.* Atlanta: Southern Regional Council, 1964.

Herskovits, Melville J. *The Myth of the Negro Past.* Boston: Beacon Press, 1958.

Hill, Herbert and Jack Greenberg. *Citizen's Guide to Desegregation: A Study of Social and Legal Change in American Life.* Boston: Beacon Press, 1955.

Himes, Joseph S., Jr. "Changing Social Roles in the New South," *Southwestern Social Science Quarterly.* 37:234–42, December 1956.

Hindman, Baker M. "The Emotional Problems of Negro High School

Youth Which are Related to Segregation and Discrimination in a Southern Urban Community," *Journal of Educational Sociology.* 27:115–27; November 1953.

Holden, Anna, Bonita Valien, and Preston Valien. *Clinton, Tennessee: A Tentative Description and Analysis of the School Desegregation Crisis.* Field Reports on Desegregation in the South. New York: Anti-Defamation League of B'nai B'rith, December 1956.

Howard, Perry H. and Joseph L. Brent III. "Social Change, Urbanization, and Types of Society," *Journal of Social Issues.* 22:73–84, January 1966.

Hughes, Langston. *Fight for Freedom: The Story of the NAACP.* New York: W. W. Norton Co., 1962.

Human Relations Programming in South Carolina. Frogmore, S. C.: Penn Community Services, October 1960 (mimeographed report, circulated privately).

Hunter, Floyd. *Community Power Structure: A Study of Decision Makers.* Chapel Hill: University of North Carolina Press, 1953.

Hyman, Herbert H. and Paul B. Sheatsley. "Attitudes Toward Desegregation," *Scientific American.* 195:35–39; December 1956.

"Integration: The South's Historic Problem," *Current History.* 32: 257–320, May 1957 (Special Issue).

Intimidation, Reprisal and Violence in the South's Racial Crisis. Atlanta: Southern Regional Council and American Friends Service Committee, 1959.

Johnson, Guy B. "Progress in the Desegregation of Higher Education," *Journal of Educational Sociology.* 32:254–59; February 1959.

Key, V. O. *Southern Politics in State and Nation.* New York: Alfred A. Knopf, 1949.

Killian, Lewis and Charles Grigg. "Race Relations in an Urbanized South," *Journal of Social Issues.* 22:20–29; January 1966.

————. *Racial Crisis in America.* Englewood Cliffs, N. J.: Prentice-Hall, Inc., 1964.

Ladd, Everett Carll, Jr. *Negro Political Leadership in the South.* Ithaca, N. Y.: Cornell University Press, 1966.

Larkins, John R. *Patterns of Leadership Among Negroes in North Carolina.* Raleigh: Irving-Swain Press, 1959.

Lefler, Hugh T. and Albert R. Newsome. *North Carolina: The History of a Southern State.* Chapel Hill: University of North Carolina Press, 1954.

Lewin, Kurt. *Resolving Social Conflicts*. New York: Harper, 1948.

Logan, Rayford W. "The United States Supreme Court and the Segregation Issue," *The Annals of the American Academy of Political and Social Science*. 304:10–16; March 1956.

Lomax, Louis E. *The Negro Revolt*. New York: Harper & Row, 1962.

Lundberg, George A. *Social Research, A Study in Methods of Gathering Data*. New York: Longmans, Green, 1942.

Lynd, Robert S. and Helen M. *Middletown in Transition*. New York: Harcourt, Brace & Co., 1937.

McCauley, Patrick and Edward Bell (eds.). *Southern Schools: Progress and Problems*. Nashville: Southern Education Reporting Service, 1959.

McNeil, Elaine O. "Policy-Makers and the Public," *Southwest Social Science Quarterly*. 39:95–99; September 1958.

Maddox, George L. and Joseph H. Fichter. "Religious and Social Change in the South," *Journal of Social Issues*. 22:44–58; January 1966.

Margolis, Joseph. "The Role of the Segregationist," *New South*. 13: 7–11; January 1958.

Merton, Robert K. *Social Theory and Social Structure*. Glencoe, Illinois: Free Press, 1949.

Miller, Dalbert. "Decision-Making Cliques in Community Power Structures: A Comparative Study of an American and an English City," *American Journal of Sociology*. 64:299–310; November 1958.

Morland, J. Kenneth. *Token Desegregation and Beyond*. Atlanta: Southern Regional Council, June 1963.

Muse, Benjamin. *Virginia's Massive Resistance*. Bloomington, Indiana: Indiana University Press, 1961.

Myrdal, Gunnar. *An American Dilemma: The Negro Problem and Modern Democracy*. New York: Harper, 1944.

Nabrit, James M., Jr. "Legal Inventions and the Desegregation Process," *The Annals of the American Academy of Political and Social Science*. 304:35–43; March 1956.

New South. Atlanta: Southern Regional Council. Vol. 9–20 (January 1954–December 1965).

"Next Steps in Racial Desegregation in Education," *Journal of Negro Education*. 23:201–399; Summer 1954.

Nicholls, William H. *Southern Tradition and Regional Progress.* Chapel Hill: University of North Carolina Press. 1960.

Nichols, Lee. *Breakthrough on the Color Front.* New York: Random House, 1954.

North Carolina, State Advisory Committee on Education. *Reports to the Governor, the General Assembly, the State Board of Education, and the County and Local School Boards of North Carolina.* Raleigh: State of North Carolina, 1956–60.

Odum, Howard W. *Southern Regions of the United States.* Chapel Hill: University of North Carolina Press, 1936.

Osborne, Irene and Richard Bennett. "Eliminating Educational Segregation in the Nation's Capital, 1951–1956," *The Annals of the American Academy of Political and Social Science.* 304:98–108; March 1956.

Patterson, Barbara, et al. *The Price We Pay for Discrimination.* Atlanta: Southern Regional Council, 1964.

Peltason, Jack W. *Fifty-eight Lonely Men: Southern Federal Judges and School Desegregation.* New York: Harcourt, Brace and World, Inc., 1961.

Peters, William. *The Southern Temper.* Garden City, N. Y.: Doubleday and Co., 1959.

Pettigrew, Thomas F. "Desegregation and its Chances for Success: Northern and Southern Views," *Social Forces.* 35:339–44; 1957.

———— (ed.). "Desegregation Research in the North and South," *Journal of Social Issues.* 15:1–76; No. 4, 1959.

———— and M. Richard Cramer. "The Demography of Desegregation," *Journal of Social Issues.* 15:61–71; No. 4, 1959.

Phylon. The Atlanta University Review of Race and Culture (January 1958–January 1965).

Pierce, Truman M., et al. *White and Negro Schools in the South: An Analysis of Bi-Racial Education.* Englewood Cliffs, N. J.: Prentice-Hall, 1955.

Pollitt, Daniel H. "Equal Protection in Public Education: 1954–61," *American Association of University Professors' Bulletin.* 47:197–205; Autumn 1961.

Price, Margaret. *The Negro and the Ballot.* Atlanta: Southern Regional Council, 1959.

"Problems and Responsibilities of Desegregation: A Symposium," *Notre Dame Lawyer.* 34:607–779: 1959.

Quint, Howard H. *Profile in Black and White: A Frank Portrait of South Carolina.* Washington, D. C.: Public Affairs Press, 1958.

Race Relations Law Reporter. Nashville: Vanderbilt University School of Law, Vol. 1–10 (1956–65).

"Racial Integration: Some Principles and Procedures." *Journal of Educational Sociology.* 28:49–96; 1954.

Reid, Ira DeA. "Desegregation and Social Change at the Community Level," *Social Problems.* 2:199; April 1955.

——— (ed.). "Racial Desegregation and Integration," *The Annals of the American Academy of Political and Social Science.* 304: 1–143; March 1956.

Reif, Jane. *Crisis in Norfolk.* Richmond, Va.: Virginia Council on Human Relations, 1960.

Reissman, Leonard. "Social Development and the American South," *Journal of Social Issues.* 22:101–116; January 1966.

——— and Thomas Ktsanes (eds.). "Urbanization and Social Change in the South," *Journal of Social Issues.* 22:1–119; January 1966.

Report on Charlotte, Greensboro and Winston-Salem, North Carolina. Atlanta: Southern Regional Council, September 1957 ("Special Report" series).

Report on Summary of Recent Segregation Laws Enacted in Southern States. Atlanta: Southern Regional Council, June 21, 1957. ("Special Report" series).

Reuter, Fred B. "An Administrator's Guide to Successful Desegregation of the Public Schools." Unpublished doctoral thesis, New York University, 1961.

Roberts, Harry W. "Responsibilities and Obligations," *Phi Delta Kappan.* 38:344; May 1956.

Rose, Arnold M. "Intergroup Relations vs. Prejudice: Pertinent Theory for the Study of Social Change," *Social Problems.* 4:173–76; October 1956.

———. *The Negro in America.* Boston: Beacon Press, 1956.

Sarratt, Reed. *Ordeal of Desegregation.* New York: Harper and Row, 1966.

School Desegregation: The First Six Years. Atlanta: Southern Regional Council, May 1960.

Selltiz, Claire, Marie Jahoda, Morton Deutsch, and Stuart W. Cook.

Research Methods in Social Relations. (Revised edition). New York: Henry Holt & Co., 1959.

Shoemaker, Don C. (ed.). *With All Deliberate Speed: Segregation-Desegregation in Southern Schools.* New York: Harper and Brothers, 1957.

Silver, James W. *Mississippi: The Closed Society.* New York: Harcourt, Brace and World, 1963.

Simpson, George E. and J. Milton Yinger. *Racial and Cultural Minorities.* New York: Harper, 1953.

Sindler, Allen P. (ed.). *Change in the Contemporary South.* Durham, N. C.: Duke University Press, 1963.

Society for the Psychological Study of Social Issues. *The Role of the Social Sciences in Desegregation: A Symposium.* New York: Anti-Defamation League of B'nai B'rith, August 1958.

South Carolina, State School Committee. *Interim Reports to His Excellency the Governor and the Honorable Presiding Officers and Members of the General Assembly.* Columbia: State of South Carolina, July 28, 1954–May 20, 1966.

Southern Education Reporting Service. *Southern School News.* Nashville: S.E.R.S., Vol. 1–11 (September 1954–June 1965).

———. *Statistical Summary of School Segregation-Desegregation in the Southern and Border States.* 1957–66.

Southern Regional Council. *New South.* Atlanta: SRC., vols. 9–20. (January 1954–December 1965).

———. *Report on Charlotte, Greensboro and Winston-Salem, North Carolina.* September 1957 ("Special Report" series).

———. *Report on Student Protest Movement. A Recapitulation.* September 1961 ("Special Report" series).

———. *Report on Summary of Recent Segregation Laws Enacted in Southern States.* June 21, 1957 ("Special Report" series).

———. *School Desegregation: The First Six Years.* May 1960.

——— and American Friends Service Committee. *Intimidation, Reprisal and Violence in the South's Racial Crisis.* 1959.

Southern School News. Nashville: Southern Education Reporting Service, vols. 1–11 (September 1954–June 1965).

Sskwor, Frank. "St. Louis Three Years Later." *American Unity,* 13:10–14; No. 5, 1958.

Statistical Summary of School Segregation-Desegregation in the

Southern and Border States. Nashville: Southern Education Reporting Service, 1957–66.

Suchman, Edward A., John P. Dean, and Robin M. Williams, Jr. *Desegregation: Some Propositions and Research Suggestions.* New York: Anti-Defamation League of B'nai B'rith, 1958.

Swanson, Ernst W. and John A. Griffin (eds.). *Public Education in the South, a Statistical Survey.* Chapel Hill: University of North Carolina Press, 1955.

Thompson, Daniel C. *The Negro Leadership Class.* Englewood Cliffs, N. J.: Prentice-Hall, 1963.

———. "The New South," *Journal of Social Forces.* 22:7–19; January 1966.

Tindall, George Brown. *The Emergence of the New South, 1913–1945.* Baton Rouge: Louisiana State University Press, 1967.

———. *South Carolina Negroes, 1877–1900.* Columbia: University of South Carolina Press, 1952.

Tipton, James H. *Community in Crisis: The Elimination of Segregation from a Public School System.* New York: Teachers College, Columbia University, 1953.

Tumin, Melvin M. (ed.). *Desegregation: Resistance and Readiness.* Princeton: Princeton University Press, 1958.

———. *Segregation and Desegregation: A Digest of Recent Research.* New York: Anti-Defamation League of B'nai B'rith, 1957.

———. *Segregation and Desegregation: A Digest of Recent Research. 1956–59* (Supplement). New York: Anti-Defamation League of B'nai B'rith, 1960.

——— et al. "Education, Prejudice and Discrimination: A Study in Readiness for Desegregation," *American Sociological Review.* 23:41–49; February 1958.

Turner, Harold E. "A Study of Public School Integration in Two Illinois Communities." Unpublished doctoral thesis. George Peabody College, 1956.

United Nations Educational, Scientific and Cultural Organization. *Research on Racial Relations.* Paris: UNESCO, 1966.

United States Bureau of Census. *Seventeenth Census of the United States, 1950.* Washington, D. C.: United States Government Printing Office, 1952.

———. *United States Census of Housing, 1960.* Washington, D. C.: United States Government Printing Office, 1961.

———. *United States Census of Population, 1960.* Washington, D. C.: United States Government Printing Office, 1962.

United States Commission on Civil Rights. *Civil Rights U. S. A.: Public Schools Southern States, 1962.* Washington, D. C.: United States Government Printing Office, 1962.

———. *Civil Rights U. S. A.: Public Schools Southern States, 1963 (Texas).* Washington, D. C.: United States Government Printing Office, 1963.

———. *Civil Rights U. S. A.: Public Schools North and West, 1962.* Washington, D. C.: United States Government Printing Office, 1962.

———. *Conference on Education (Nashville, Tennessee, March, 1959).* Washington, D. C.: United States Government Printing Office, 1959.

———. *Conference on Education (Gatlinburg, Tennessee, March, 1960).* Washington, D. C.: United States Government Printing Office, 1960.

———. *Conference on Education (Williamsburg, Virginia, February, 1961).* Washington, D. C.: United States Government Printing Office, 1961.

———. *Conference on Education (Washington, D. C., May, 1962).* Washington, D. C.: United States Government Printing Office, 1962.

———. *Equal Protection of the Laws in Public Higher Education, 1960.* Washington, D. C.: United States Government Printing Office, 1960.

———. *Survey of School Desegregation in the Southern and Border States, 1965–66.* Washington, D. C.: United States Government Printing Office, 1966.

———. *1959 Report of the United States Commission on Civil Rights.* Washington, D. C.: United States Government Printing Office, 1959.

———. *1961 United States Commission on Civil Rights Report, Education.* Washington, D. C.: United States Government Printing Office, 1961.

———. *1963 Report of the United States Commission on Civil Rights.* Washington, D. C.: United States Government Printing Office, 1963.

———. *1963 Staff Report: Public Education.* Washington, D. C.: United States Government Printing Office, 1963.

————. *1964 Staff Report: Public Education.* Washington, D. C.: United States Government Printing Office, 1964.

————. Louisiana State Advisory Committee. *The New Orleans School Crisis.* Washington, D. C.: United States Government Printing Office, 1961.

————. North Carolina State Advisory Committee. *Equal Protection of the Laws in North Carolina, 1959–62.* Washington, D. C.: United States Government Printing Office, 1962.

————. South Carolina State Advisory Committee. "South Carolina Cities Meet the Challenge." (Mimeographed "Confidential Report," dated August 1, 1963.)

Valein, Bonita H. "Racial Desegregation of the Public Schools in Southern Illinois," *Journal of Negro Education.* 23:303–309; No. 3, 1954.

————. *The St. Louis Story: A Study of Desegregation.* New York: Anti-Defamation League of B'nai B'rith, 1956.

Van Til, William A. (ed.). "Integrating Minority Groups into the Public Schools," *Educational Leadership.* 13:69–140; November 1955.

————. "Intercultural Education," *Encyclopedia of Educational Research.* Third Edition, Chester Harris, ed. New York: Macmillan, 1960.

————. "The Nashville Story," *Educational Leadership.* 15:481–85, 502; May 1958.

————. "Now It's 'How' and 'When'—Not 'Whether,' " *Educational Leadership.* 13:70–73; November 1955.

Vander Zanden, James W. *American Minority Relations.* New York: Ronald Press, 1963.

————. "Desegregation and Social Strains in the South," *Journal of Social Issues.* 15:53–60; No. 4, 1959.

————. *Race Relations in Transition.* New York: Random House, 1965.

————. "The Southern White Resistance Movement to Integration." Unpublished doctoral thesis, University of North Carolina, 1958.

————. "Turbulence Accompanying School Desegregation," *Journal of Educational Sociology.* 32:68–75; October, 1958.

Waynick, Capus (ed.). *North Carolina and the Negro.* Raleigh, N. C.: North Carolina Mayors' Cooperating Committee, 1964.

Wertham, Frederic. "Psychiatric Observations on Abolition of School Segregation," *Journal of Educational Sociology.* 26:333–36; March 1953.

———. "Psychological Effects of School Segregation," *American Journal of Psychotherapy.* 61:94–103; No. 1, 1952.

Wey, Herbert. "The South Calls for Research," *Phi Delta Kappan.* 38: 19; October 1956.

——— and John Corey. *Action Patterns in School Desegregation, A Guide Book.* Bloomington, Indiana: Phi Delta Kappa, 1959.

Williams, Robin M., Jr. *The Reduction of Intergroup Tensions: A Study of Research on Problems of Ethnic, Racial, and Religious Group Relations.* New York: Social Science Research Council, 1947.

———. Barton R. Fischer, and Irving Janis. "Educational Desegregation as a Context for Basic Social Research," *American Sociological Review.* 21:577–83; October 1956.

——— and Margaret Ryan (ed.). *Schools in Transition: Community Experiences in Desegregation.* Chapel Hill: University of North Carolina Press, 1954.

Williamson, Joel. *After Slavery: The Negro in South Carolina During Reconstruction, 1861–1877.* Chapel Hill: University of North Carolina Press, 1965.

Woodward, C. Vann. *The Burden of Southern History.* (Revised Edition) Baton Rouge: Louisiana State University Press, 1968.

———. *Origins of the New South, 1877–1913.* Baton Rouge: Louisiana State University Press, 1951.

———. *The Strange Career of Jim Crow.* New York: Oxford University Press, 1957.

Wormer, M. H. and C. Selltiz. *How to Conduct a Community Self-Survey of Civil Rights.* New York: Association Press, 1951.

Yinger, J. Milton. "Desegregation in American Society: The Record of a Generation of Change," *Sociology and Social Research.* 48: 428–45; July 1963.

INDEX

School Desegregation in the Carolinas

Composed in linotype Century Expanded by
Kingsport Press with tables in monotype Century
Expanded. Printed letterpress by Kingsport Press
on Warren's University Text, an acid-free paper
noted for its longevity. The paper was expressly
watermarked for the University of South Carolina
Press with the Press colophon. Binding by Kingsport Press in GSB natural finish fabric over .080
boards.